Road Maps

for the

Pauline Epistles

Detailed Expositional Outlines to Help Rightly Divide the Word of Truth

Road Maps for the Pauline Epistles

Detailed Expositional Outlines to Help Rightly Divide the Word of Truth

Published by
Kress Biblical Resources
www.kressbiblical.com

ISBN: 978-1-934952-74-0

This is now a second offering[1] in the New Testament of these metaphorical "Road Maps" to help guide the student and Bible expositor in his or her journey of studying, understanding, living, and proclaiming the glorious truth of God's Word.

May the grace of our Lord Jesus Christ, the love of God, and the fellowship of the Holy Spirit be with you all.

---

[1] The first book of detailed expositional outlines in the New Testament was titled, *Road Maps for the Non-Pauline Epistles and Revelation* published in 2016 by Kress Biblical Resources.

Contents

ROMANS

Kress Biblical Resources

Romans—The Big Picture

The Gospel of Salvation by Faith Unites All Believers—Jew and Greek

I. The Prologue, Prayer Report, and Primary Theme of the Epistle (1:1-17)

II. The Proclamation of the Gospel (1:18-4:25)

III. The Promises, Provisions, and Privileges of the Gospel (5:1-8:39)

IV. The Problem of Israel and the Gospel (9:1-11:36)

V. The Practice of the Gospel (12:1-15:13)

VI. The Plans and Partnership of the Gospel (15:14-16:24)

VII. The Purpose of the Gospel—Praise to God Forever! (16:25-27)

Overview Outline of Romans

The Gospel of Salvation by Faith Unites All Believers—Jew and Greek

The Prologue, Prayer Report, and Primary Theme of the Epistle (1:1-17)

I. Paul's Introduction (1:1-7)

A. The author (1:1-5)

B. The audience (v. 6-7a)

C. The aim (see detailed outline)

D. The Apostolic greeting (1:7bc)

II. Paul's prayer report (1:8-13)

A. His prayers for the Roman church (1:8-10)

B. His passion for the Roman church (1:11-13)

III. Paul's passion and primary theme in the epistle (1:14-17)

A. His duty in regard to the gospel and all men (1:14)

B. His desire in regard to the gospel and those in Rome (1:15)

C. His delight in regard to the gospel itself (1:16-17)

The Proclamation of the Gospel (1:18-4:25)

I. The gospel proclaims the guilt of all men—condemnation before the righteous Judge (1:18-3:20)

A. God's wrath against unrighteousness [sin characteristic of Gentiles] (1:18-32)

B. God's judgment against self-righteousness [sin characteristic of Jews] (2:1-3:8)

C. God's verdict against all humanity (3:9-20)

II. The gospel proclaims the gift of God—justification by grace through faith in the righteous Savior (3:21-4:24)

A. Justification by faith proclaimed [The revelation of the righteousness of God, received by faith] (3:21-31)

B. Justification by faith pictured in the Old Testament [The reception of the righteousness of God by faith, illustrated] (4:1-25)

The Promises, Provisions, and Privileges of the Gospel (5:1-8:39)

I. Salvation—freedom from the wrath of God, and the joyous hope of glory (5:1-21)

A. The results of being justified by faith (5:1-11)

B. The results of Adam's sin—sin and death (5:12-14)

C. The reversal of the results of Adam's sin—grace and life in Christ (5:15-21)

II. Sanctification—freedom from the captivity of sin, the condemnation of the Law, and freedom to conduct ourselves in view of the certain hope of glory (6:1-8:30)

A. The gospel sets us free from captivity to sin (6:1-23)

B. The gospel sets us free from the condemnation of the law (7:1-25)

C. The gospel sets us free to conduct our lives according to the Spirit, as sons of God rather than slaves to the flesh (8:1-17)

D. The gospel seals us for glory in God's sovereign plan and power (8:18-30)

III. Security—freedom to live victoriously no matter the circumstances we may face, because of God's indestructible love in Christ (8:31-39)

A. The indestructible love of God extolled in poetic form (8:31-37)

B. The indestructible love of God apprehended by faith (8:38-39)

The Problem of Israel and the Gospel (9:1-11:36)

I. God's sovereign plan and Israel's election (9:1-29)

A. The sorrow concerning Israel confessed (9:1-5)

B. The sovereign freedom of God in election introduced (9:6-13)

C. The sovereign freedom of God in election defended (9:14-29)

II. God's sovereign plan and Israel's rejection (9:30-10:21)

A. They stumbled over faith in Christ (9:30-33)

B. They stumbled in self-righteousness (10:1-13)

C. They stumbled in willful unbelief (10:14-21)

III. God's sovereign plan and Israel's salvation (11:1-29)

A. There remains a remnant—the present rejection of Israel is not total (11:1-10)

B. There remains an opportunity for repentance—the present rejection of Israel is not final [but it should warn us against arrogance and unbelief] (11:11-24)

C. There remains the predetermined plan and promise of God—the promised redemption of Israel is irrevocable (11:25-29)

IV. God's sovereign plan and irrepressible exultation (11:30-36)

A. The undeserved mercy of God's sovereign plan (v. 30-32)

B. The unfathomable majesty of God's sovereign plan (v. 33-36)

The Practice of the Gospel (12:1-15:13)

I. Worship God and humbly serve others in love (12:1-21)

A. The gospel calls believers to a life of worship (12:1-2)

B. The gospel calls believers to a life of humility and ministry within in the body of Christ (12:3-8)

C. The gospel calls believers to a life of love (12:9-21)

II. Walk in submission to civil authorities and walk in love (13:1-14)

A. Walking in submission to civil authorities (13:1-7)

B. Walking in love (13:8-14)

III. Willingly accept one another and walk in love—in spite of divergent personal convictions on how to apply biblical principles to culture (14:1-15:13)

A. Refuse to condemn other believers' opinions/personal convictions on how to personally apply the faith (14:1-13a)

B. Refrain from allowing your personal opinions/convictions on how to apply the faith to become a stumbling block to others (14:13b-23)

C. Reflect the same perspective and purpose as Christ (15:1-13)

The Plans and Partnership of the Gospel (15:14-16:24)

I. The plans explained [to Paul's ministry partners in Rome] (15:14-33)

A. The encouragement and explanation as to why Paul had not yet visited them (15:14-22)

B. The expectations in regard to Paul's desired future visit (15:23-29)

C. The exhortation to intercessory prayer concerning Paul's future visit (15:30-33)

II. The partners encouraged (16:1-24)

A. A call to help a partner in the ministry (16:1-2)

B. A concern to honor and encourage gospel partners (16:3-16)

C. A caution and encouragement in hope (16:17-20)

D. A continued concern for the encouragement of gospel partners (16:21-24)

The Purpose of the Gospel—Praise Be to God Forever! (16:25-27)

I. Praise God for His power (16:25-26)

A. The recognition of God's power (16:25a)

B. The revelation of God's power (16:25bc-26)

C. The results of God's power (16:25a, 26c)

II. Praise God for His wisdom (16:27ab)

A. His wisdom is unique (16:27a)

B. His wisdom is mediated through Jesus Christ (16:27b)

III. Praise God forever (16:27c)

A. He possesses eternal glory

B. Amen

Introductory Matters

I. The author

A. The human author (1:1-5)

1. The man Paul (v. 1a; cf. Acts 7:58; 8:1; 9:1-30; 11:25-30; 12:25-28:31; 1 Cor. 15:30-32; 2 Cor. 6:4-5; 11:23-30; Gal. 1:13-2:16; Phil. 3:4-14; 2 Thes. 3:8)
2. The ministry that Paul was given (v. 1b-d)
   a. *Christ's slave (v. 1b)*
   b. *Called as an Apostle (v. 1c)*
   c. *Commissioned for the Gospel of God (v. 1d)*
3. The message Paul preached (v. 2-4)
   a. *The promise of the Gospel in the Old Testament (v. 2)*
   b. *The Person of the Gospel—God's Son, Jesus Christ our Lord (v. 3-4)*
      i. God's Son became a man (v. 3)
      ii. God's Son is the promised Messiah-King, born of the seed of David (v. 3)
      iii. God's Son is identified as the powerful Savior through His resurrection from the dead (v. 4a; cf. 1:16)
      iv. God's Son is Jesus Christ our Lord (v. 4b)
4. The mission that Paul was on (v. 5)
   a. *The power for his mission (v. 5a)*
   b. *The purpose for his mission (v. 5b,c)*
      ii. For the salvation of the Gentiles through the obedience of faith (v. 5b)
      iii. For the sake of Christ's name—i.e., the praise of Christ's Person (v. 5c)

B. The divine Author (2 Tim. 3:16-17; 2 Pet. 1:12-21, 3:15-16; cf. Col. 4:16; 1 Thes. 2:13; 5:27; 2 Thes. 3:1-4; 1 Tim. 5:18 [in which Paul quotes Luke alongside Deut. 25:4 and calls them "Scripture"])

II. The audience (1:6-7a)

A. The original recipients (1:6-7a)

1. A largely Gentile church—commingled with a growing number of Jewish background believers (v. 6a; cf. 2:17ff; 4:1ff; 9-11; 14-15:13; etc.)
2. A living church—called of Jesus Christ (v. 6b)
3. A loved church— in Rome—called as saints (v. 7a)

B. The current recipients (2 Tim. 3:16; cf. 2 Pet. 3:15-16)

III. The aim

A. To establish an Apostolic connection with the church at Rome, based upon the Gospel (1:11-15; 15:15-22; 16:1, 17-19, 25)

B. To reveal Paul's future missionary plans, and seek support from the church at Rome, for the sake of the Gospel that united them (15:22-32)

C. To foster biblical harmony between Jewish and Gentile believers in the church at Rome, based upon the Gospel and its practical implications (1:16; 2:17ff; 4:1ff; 9-11; 14-15:13).

D. Summary theme: The Gospel, which brings salvation to both Jew and Greek, reveals God's righteousness, and is received and lived out by faith (1:16-17)

1. The primacy of the gospel, salvation, righteousness, and faith

   a. *The gospel or preach the gospel (1:1, 9, 15, 16; 2:16; 10:15; 11:28; 15:16, 19, 20; 16:25)*

   b. *Salvation, saved, etc. (1:16; 5:9, 10; 8:24; 9:27; 10:1, 9, 10, 13; 11:11, 14, 26; 13:11)*

   c. *Righteousness, justified, etc. (1:17; 3:5, 21, 22, 25, 26; 2:13; 3:10, 26; 4:3, 5, 6, 9, 11, 13, 22; 5:17, 19, 21; 6:13, 16, 18, 19, 20; 7:12; 8:10; 9:30, 31; 10:3, 4, 5, 6, 10; 14:17)*

   d. *Faith, believes, etc. (1:5, 8, 12, 16, 17; 3:3, 22, 25, 26, 27, 28, 30, 31; 4:3, 5, 11, 12, 13, 14, 16, 17, 18, 19, 20, 24; 5:1, 2; 6:8; 9:30, 32, 33; 10:4, 6, 8, 9, 10, 11, 14, 16, 17; 11:20, 12:3, 6; 13:11; 14:1, 2, 22, 25; 15:13; 16:26)*

2. The parts of Paul's gospel letter

   The prologue, prayer, and primary theme (1:1-17)

   The proclamation of the gospel (1:18-4:25)

   The promises, provisions, and privileges of the gospel (5:1-8:39)

   The problem of Israel and the gospel (9:1-11:36)

   The practice of the gospel (12:1-15:13)

   The plans and partnership of the gospel (15:14-16:24)

   The Purpose of the Gospel—Praise Be to God Forever! (16:25-27)

Detailed Outline of Romans

The Gospel of Salvation by Faith Unites All Believers—Jew and Greek

The Prologue, Prayer Report, and Primary Theme of the Epistle (1:1-17)

I. Paul's Introduction (1:1-7)

A. The author

1. The human author (1:1-5)
   - *a. The man Paul (v. 1a; cf. Acts 7:58; 8:1; 9:1-30; 11:25-30; 12:25-28:31; 1 Cor. 15:30-32; 2 Cor. 6:4-5; 11:23-30; Gal. 1:13-2:16; Phil. 3:4-14; 2 Thes. 3:8)*
   - *b. The ministry that Paul was given (v. 1b-d)*
     - i. Christ's slave (v. 1b)
     - ii. Called as an Apostle (v. 1c)
     - iii. Commissioned for the Gospel of God (v. 1d)
   - *c. The message Paul preached (v. 2-4)*
     - i. The promise of the Gospel in the Old Testament (v. 2)
     - ii. The Person of the Gospel—God's Son, Jesus Christ our Lord (v. 3-4)
       - aa. God's Son became a man (v. 3)
       - bb. God's Son is the promised Messiah-King, born of the seed of David (v. 3)
       - cc. God's Son is identified as the powerful Savior through His resurrection from the dead (v. 4a; cf. 1:16)
       - dd. God's Son is Jesus Christ our Lord (v. 4b)
   - *d. The mission that Paul was on (v. 5)*
     - i. The power for his mission (v. 5a)
     - ii. The purpose for his mission (v. 5b,c)
       - aa. For the salvation of the Gentiles through the obedience of faith (v. 5b)
       - bb. For the sake of Christ's name—i.e., the praise of Christ's Person (v. 5c)
2. The divine Author (2 Tim. 3:16-17; 2 Pet. 1:12-21, 3:15-16; cf. Col. 4:16; 1 Thes. 2:13; 5:27; 2 Thes. 3:1-4; 1 Tim. 5:18 [in which Paul quotes Luke alongside Deut. 25:4 and calls them "Scripture"])

B. The audience (v. 6-7a)

1. The original recipients (1:6-7a)
   - *a. A largely Gentile church—commingled with a growing number of Jewish background believers (v. 6a; cf. 2:17ff; 4:1ff; 9-11; 14-15:13; etc.)*
   - *b. A living church—called of Jesus Christ (v. 6b)*
   - *c. A loved church— in Rome—called as saints (v. 7a)*
2. The current recipients (2 Tim. 3:16; cf. 2 Pet. 3:15-16)

B. The Apostolic greeting (1:7bc)

1. The greeting/prayer of grace to you and peace (1:7b)
2. The Giver of grace and peace (1:7c)

II. Paul's prayer report (1:8-13)

A. His prayers for the Roman church (1:8-10)

1. Paul consistently rendered thanks to God for them (1:8)
   - *a. The priority of prayer and thanksgiving (v. 8a)*
   - *b. The Person he thanked and the people he was thankful for (v. 8b)*
   - *c. The proclamation that inspired his prayers of thanksgiving (v. 8c)*
2. Paul consistently remembered them in prayer, and consistently requested success in coming to them (1:9-10)
   - *a. He was speaking sincerely about his prayer life on their behalf (v. 9ab)*
   - *b. He was seeking God consistently on their behalf (v. 9c)*
   - *c. He was seeking God consistently, yet submissively for success in coming to them (v. 10)*

B. His passion for the Roman church (1:11-13)

1. Edification: Paul desired that they be strengthened and encouraged (1:11-12)
   - *a. The ministry of an Apostle, which would strengthen the church (v. 11)*
   - *b. The mutual fellowship of believers, which would encourage both Paul and the believers in Rome (v. 12)*
2. Communication: Paul desired that they be informed of his previous plans to come to them (1:13a)
3. Sanctification and multiplication: Paul desired that they grow and be added to, through his gospel ministry in Rome (1:13b)

III. Paul's passion and primary theme in the epistle (1:14-17)

A. His duty in regard to the gospel and all men (1:14)

B. His desire in regard to the gospel and those in Rome (1:15)

C. His delight in regard to the gospel itself (1:16-17)

1. Paul embraced the preeminence of the gospel (1:16a)
2. Paul understood the power of the gospel (1:16b)

3. Paul apprehended the particulars of the gospel (1:16c-17)
    a. *It results in salvation for everyone who believes (v. 16c)*
    b. *It reveals the righteousness that comes from God on the basis of faith (v. 17)*
        i. The summary statement that encapsulates justification by faith (v. 17a)
        ii. The Scripture that encapsulates justification by faith (v. 17b)

The Proclamation of the Gospel (1:18-4:25)

I. The gospel proclaims the guilt of all men—condemnation before the righteous Judge (1:18-3:20)

A. God's wrath against unrighteousness [sin characteristic of Gentiles] (1:18-32)

1. The reality of the wrath of God (1:18)
    a. *God's wrath is recognized as essential to His holy nature*
    b. *God's wrath is revealed from heaven even now*
2. The reasons for the wrath of God (1:18-23)
    a. *Men have repressed the truth in unrighteousness (v. 18)*
    b. *Men have rejected the witness of creation concerning God's glory and authority (v. 19-20)*
        i. All men know that God exists and they are accountable to Him (v. 19)
        ii. All men are without excuse concerning God's transcendent glory and authority (v. 20)
    c. *Men have refused to honor God as He deserves and give thanks (v. 21)*
    d. *Men have replaced true worship with idolatry (v. 22-23)*
        i. They professed to be wise apart from God's revelation, and thus became fools (v. 22)
        ii. They perverted genuine worship, and turned to idolatry (v. 23)
3. The results of the wrath of God (1:24-32)
    a. *God gave men over to their defiled desires (v. 24-25)*
        i. The lusts that result in impurity [God gave them over] (v. 24)
        ii. The lie that results in idolatry [because they exchanged the truth for the lie] (v. 25)
    b. *God gave men over to their degrading passions (v. 26-27)*
        i. The passions that result in degradation [God gave them over] (v. 26)
        ii. The perversion that results in devastation [because they exchanged the natural for the unnatural] (v. 27)
    c. *God gave men over to their depraved minds (v. 28-32)*
        i. The decision that results in a depraved mind [God gave them over] (v. 28ab)

ii. The description that illustrates the results of a depraved mind (v. 28c-31)

aa. The summary—things which are not proper (v. 28c)

bb. Having been filled with four sins that reveal a lack of love for God (v. 29a)

cc. Full of five sins that reveal a lack of love for one's neighbor (v. 29b)

dd. Twelve sins listed in a separate grammatical unit—the last for all beginning with the alpha prefix (v. 29c-31)

iii The delight that results in the destruction of others (v. 32)

B. God's judgment against self-righteousness [sin characteristic of Jews] (2:1-3:8)

1. The impartiality of God's judgment—falls upon the self-righteous as well as the unrighteous (2:1-16)

a. God's judgment will come upon the impenitent [unrepentant] (v. 1-5)

i. Self-righteousness is inexcusable in light of God's righteous judgment (v. 1-3)

aa. Self-righteous judgment leads to self-condemnation (v. 1-2)

The judgment of the self-righteous is ridiculous (v. 1)

The judgment of God against sinners is right (v. 2)

bb. Self-righteous judgment leads to self-deception (v. 3)

ii. Self-righteousness is indicative of spiritual ignorance and an unrepentant heart (2:4-5)

aa. The self-righteous spurn the riches of God's kindness and patience (v. 4)

bb. The self-righteous store up for themselves the wrath of God (v. 5)

b. God's judgment will be consistent with His impartiality (v. 6-11)

i. God's righteous judgment will reward each man according to his deeds—whether Jew or Greek (v. 6-10)

aa. The reality of God's impartial judgment revealed in the Scriptures—each man will be judged according to his deeds (v. 6)

bb. The rewards of those who remain steadfast in good work, and the rewards of those who are selfishly ambitious (v. 7-10)

The steadfast workers of good seeking glory, honor, and incorruptibility—eternal life (v. 7)

The selfishly ambitious—wrath and indignation (v. 8)

The soul who does evil—tribulation and distress (v. 9)

The satisfaction of the one who is constantly working the good—glory, honor, and peace (v. 10)

ii. God's righteous judgment will reveal that He doesn't play favorites (v. 11)

c. God's judgment will be consistent with His impeccability (v. 12-16)

i. Judgment will fall upon all sinners in a manner appropriate to the revelation of God afforded to them (v. 12)

aa. Those who sin without the written Law, will be destroyed apart from the written Law (v. 12a)

bb. Those who sin in reference to the written Law, will be condemned by the written Law (v. 12b)

ii. Just being a hearer of the law is inadequate for righteousness, one must be a constant doer of the Law (v. 13)

iii. Judgment will be rendered toward the Gentiles without the Law, based upon the witness of their conscience (v. 14-15)

aa. The code by which Gentiles live is a kind of law to themselves (v. 14)

bb. The conscience of the Gentiles bears witness to the work of the Law written in their hearts (v. 15)

iv. Judgment will include the secrets of men, on the day when God judges through Jesus Christ (v. 16)

2. The inconsistency of an orthodox religion without the reality of faith—reveals an uncircumcised heart (2:17-29)

a. The boast of orthodox religion—the issue of spiritual privilege and Jewish perspective (v. 17-20)

i. The privilege of the Jew (v. 17-18)

aa. Recognized as one of God's covenant people and chosen nation (v. 17a)

bb. Resting upon the Law (v. 17b)

cc. Rejoicing in the true God (v. 17c)

dd. Recognizing the will of God (v. 18)

ii. The perspective of the Jew (v. 19-20)

aa. Confident of being a guide and a light to those who cannot see (v. 19)

bb. Correcting the foolish and teaching the immature (v. 20)

b. The blasphemy of religion without the reality of faith—the issue of spiritual blindness and Jewish hypocrisy (v. 21-24)

i. Their blindness questioned (v. 21-22)

aa. Do you not teach yourself (v. 21a)

bb. Do you steal (v. 21b)

cc. Do you commit adultery (v. 22a)

dd. Do you rob temples (v. 22b)

ii. Their blasphemy confirmed (v. 23-24)

aa. The breaking of the law and reproach of God (v. 23)

bb. The blasphemy of the Jews and the affirmation of the OT (v. 24)

c. *The bottom-line concerning the privilege of the Jew—the issue of spiritual circumcision and Jewish externalism (v. 25-29)*

i. Semitic circumcision (being a Jew physically) is of no value if you are a transgressor of the Law (v. 25)

ii. Specifically consider the scenario of a Gentile keeping the Law (v. 26-27)

aa. Will he not be regarded as one of God's people (v. 26)

bb. Will he not judge the Jew who has transgressed God's Law (v. 27)

iii. Spiritual circumcision is a matter of the heart, rather than an external rite (v. 28-29)

aa. A Jew is not a true Jew just because he is circumcised (v. 28)

bb. A Jew is a true Jew only if his heart is circumcised by the Spirit (v. 29)

3. The inferable objections to Paul's teaching, and his answers [anticipated objections to Paul's argument answered]—the Jews are privileged; God is faithful; God is just; and God calls for holy living (3:1-8)

a. *Objection #1 answered—Paul's gospel rejects God's covenant with Israel (v. 1-2)*

i. The anticipated question (v. 1)

ii. The answer (v. 2)

b. *Objection #2 answered—Paul's gospel rejects God's faithfulness (v. 3-4)*

i. The anticipated question (v. 3)

ii. The answer (v. 4)

c. *Objection #3 answered—Paul's gospel rejects God's justice (v. 5-6)*

i. The anticipated question (v. 5)

ii. The answer (v. 6)

d. *Objection #4 answered—Paul's gospel rejects holy living (v. 7-8)*

i. The anticipated question (v. 7-8ab)

ii. The answer (v. 8c)

C. God's verdict against all humanity (3:9-20)

1. The charge against both Jew and Greek restated (3:9)

a. *The final question concerning self-righteousness (v. 9a)*

b. *The final confirmation that both Jews and Greeks are all under sin (v. 9b)*

2. The confirmation of the Jewish Scriptures recounted (3:10-18)

a. *Man's depravity is universal (v. 10-12; cf. Ps. 14:1c, 2b-3; 53:1c, 2b-3)*

i. There is none who is righteous (v. 10)

ii. There is none who has faith (v. 11)

iii. There is none who does good (v. 12)

b. *Man's depravity is undeniable (v. 13-18; cf. Ps. 10:7; Is. 59:7-8; Ps. 36:1)*
   i. Men's words reveal their depravity (v. 13-14)
      aa. Death and deception (v. 13)
      bb. Damnation and displeasure (v. 14)
   ii. Men's works reveal their depravity (v. 15-17)
      aa. Injury (v. 15)
      bb. Misery (v. 16)
      cc. Hostility (v. 17)
   iii. Men's want [lack] of genuine faith reveals his depravity (v. 18)

3. The culpability of the Jew re-emphasized (3:19-20)
   a. *The Law renders all men accountable to God—even Jews (v. 19)*
   b. *The Law reveals the knowledge of sin—but by the works of the Law no flesh will be justified before God (v. 20)*

II. The gospel proclaims the gift of God—justification by grace through faith in the righteous Savior (3:21-4:24)

A. Justification by faith proclaimed [The revelation of the righteousness of God, received by faith] (3:21-31)

1. The righteousness of God [a right standing before God] is received apart from works of the Law—through the faith of Jesus Christ—for all who trust Him (3:21-22a)
   a. *The righteousness of God is revealed as apart from the Law (3:21a)*
   b. *The righteousness of God is reported by the Law and the Prophets (3:21b)*
   c. *The righteousness of God is received through the faith of Jesus Christ for all who believe (3:22a)*
2. The reckoning of sinners as righteous [a right standing before God] is a gift of God's grace, through faith in the redemption that is in Christ Jesus (3:22b-26)
   a. *The reckoning of a sinner as righteous is a gift of God's grace (v. 22b-24a)*
      i. The universal need for God's righteousness (v. 22b-23)
      ii. The unmerited favor that imputes God's righteousness to those who believe (v. 24a)
   b. *The reckoning of a sinner as righteous is obtained through faith in the redemption that Christ accomplished by His sacrifice (v. 24b-25a)*
      i. The redemption which is in Christ Jesus (v. 24b)
      ii. The Redeemer who was presented as the satisfactory sacrifice through faith (v. 25a)
   c. *The redemptive work of Christ is proof that God is both a righteous Judge and gracious Savior (v. 25b-26)*
      i. In Christ's sacrifice, God's justice is demonstrated in regard to not punishing sin long ago (v. 25b)

ii. In Christ's sacrifice, God's justice is demonstrated in regard to His justification of sinners who trust in Jesus (v. 26)

B. Justification by faith pictured in the Old Testament [The reception of the righteousness of God by faith, illustrated] (4:1-25)

1. The Scriptures testify that God justifies the ungodly by means of faith, apart from works (4:1-8)

a. The case of Abraham's justification (v. 1-5)

i. An inquiry into Abraham's right standing before God (v. 1-2)

aa. Abraham's pre-eminence in Jewish-Gentile justification (v. 1)

bb. Abraham's proud confidence before God—in works or God's promise? (v. 2)

ii. An inspired testimony concerning Abraham's right standing before God (v. 3)

iii. An incompatibility between works and grace (v. 4-5)

aa. Works depend on wages due (v. 4)

bb. Faith depends on Him who justifies the ungodly (v. 5)

b. The confirmation of David's psalm (v. 6-8)

i. The blessing of justification by faith, apart from works, introduced (v. 6)

ii. The blessing of lawless deeds forgiven (v. 7a)

iii. The blessing of sins covered (v. 7b)

iv. The blessing of sin not taken into account (v. 8)

2. The setting of Abraham's justification confirms that God justifies a man by means of faith, apart from an external rite like circumcision (4:9-12)

a. Who receives the divine favor of justification—the circumcised only or the uncircumcised also? (v. 9)

i. The question (v. 9a)

ii. The quotation (v. 9b)

b. When was Abraham justified—before or after his circumcision? (v. 10)

i. The question (v. 10a)

ii. The chronology (v. 10b)

c. Why then was Abraham circumcised after he had already been declared righteous before God? (v. 11-12)

i. Abraham was circumcised as a visible mark of the faith that he had while uncircumcised (v. 11a)

ii. Abraham was justified before he was circumcised, so that he might be the father of all who are justified by faith without being circumcised (v. 11b)

iii. Abraham was justified before he was circumcised, so that he might be the father of all who are circumcised, yet are justified by faith as he was (v. 12)

3. The sure promise of righteousness is not obtained by means of the law, but by means of faith (4:13-25)

a. The promise of God is obtained by faith rather than law (v. 13-17a)

i. The promise of God to Abraham and his seed is through the righteousness of faith rather than through Law keeping (v. 13)

ii. The promise of God is nullified if it must be earned through Law keeping (v. 14)

iii. The produce of Law keeping in order to obtain God's promise, is wrath and transgression (v. 15)

iv. The promise of God is guaranteed to those who are of faith, in accordance with grace (v. 16-17a)

aa. The principle of faith in accordance with grace (v. 16a)

bb. The people who are guaranteed the promise (v. 16b-17a)

b. The perspective of faith is one of trust in God and His Word (v. 17b-22)

i. Abraham trusted in God's Person as the object of his faith (v. 17b)

ii. Abraham trusted in God's power to keep His promise (v. 17c)

ii. Abraham trusted in God's promise as revealed in His Word (v. 18-21)

aa. Faith trusts specifically in God's revealed Word (v. 18)

bb. Faith trusts in God's Word even when circumstances would deny the possibility of it coming to pass (v. 19)

cc. Faith does not dispute with God's Word, but rather gives glory to God (v. 20)

dd. Faith leads to the conviction that what God has promised, He is able to do (v. 21)

iii. Abraham's trust was also credited to him as righteousness (v. 22)

c. The promise of imputed righteousness by faith, applies to New Testament believers as well (v. 23-25)

i. The principle of imputed righteousness through faith, applies not only to Abraham, but to New Testament believers as well (v. 23-24)

ii. The passion and resurrection of Christ is the ultimate basis for the believer's righteous standing before God (v. 25)

The Promises, Provisions, and Privileges of the Gospel (5:1-8:39)

I. Salvation—freedom from the wrath of God, and the joyous hope of glory (5:1-21)

A. The results of being justified by faith (5:1-11)

1. We have peace with God (5:1)
   a. *The prerequisite to peace with God (v. 1a)*
   b. *The peace explained (v. 1b)*
   c. *The Person through whom we have this peace with God (v. 1c)*
2. We have favor before God (5:2ab)
   a. *The Person who gives us favor before God (v. 2a)*
   b. *The privilege of standing in grace before God (v. 2b)*
3. We have joy in our hope in God (5:2c-5)
   a. *We rejoice in hope of the glory of God (v. 2c)*
   b. *We rejoice in our tribulations (v. 3-5)*
      i. The reality of our joy (v. 3a)
      ii. The reasons for our joy (v. 3b-5)
         aa. The process of divinely wrought hope (v. 3b-4)
         bb. The pouring out of the love of God within our hearts (v. 5)
4. We have love from God (5:5b-8)
   a. *The Person through whom we personally experience the love of God (v. 5b)*
   b. *The proof of the love of God (v. 6-8)*
      i. While we were still helpless, at the right time Christ died for the ungodly (v. 6)
      ii. While we were yet sinners, Christ died for us (v. 7-8)
5. We have salvation and reconciliation with God (5:9-11)
   a. *We <u>are</u> saved from the wrath of God through Christ (v. 9)*
   b. *We <u>have been</u> reconciled to God and <u>will be</u> saved by Christ's life (v. 10)*
   c. *We <u>are</u> rejoicing in God through our Lord Jesus Christ (v. 11)*

B. The results of Adam's sin—sin and death (5:12-14)

1. Because of Adam, sin entered the world, and all sinned (5:12)
2. Because of Adam, death entered the world, and all died (5:12-14)
   a. *Death entered the world through Adam's sin (v. 12b)*
   b. *Death spread to all men, because all sinned (v. 12c)*
   c. *Death came upon all sinners, even though many did not have special revelation from God that they violated (v. 13-14)*

C. The reversal of the results of Adam's sin—grace and life in Christ (5:15-21)

1. The reversal of death through the grace of Christ (v. 15)
2. The reversal of condemnation through justification in Christ (v. 16)
3. The reversal of death through the grace of Christ (v. 17)
4. The reversal of condemnation through justification in Christ (v. 18)
5. The reversal of disobedience through the obedience of Christ (v. 19)
6. The reason for the Law, and the response of grace (v. 20)
7. The reversal of death through the grace of Christ (v. 21)

II. Sanctification—freedom from the captivity of sin, the condemnation of the Law, and freedom to conduct ourselves in view of the certain hope of glory (6:1-8:30)

A. The gospel sets us free from captivity to sin (6:1-23)

1. Your position in Christ, under the rule of grace—you have died to sin and are alive to God (6:1-14)
   - *a. The possible objection to the rule of grace, and Paul's inspired answer (v. 1-2)*
     - i. The anticipated objection to the reign of abounding grace (v. 1)
     - ii. The answer (v. 2)
   - *b. The positional facts of our union with Christ (v. 3-10)*
     - i. The reminder of our position as having been submersed into Christ (v. 3-4)
       - aa. Baptized into Christ, baptized into His death (v. 3)
       - bb. Buried with Christ, raised so we too might walk in newness of life (v. 4)
     - ii. The results of being united with Christ in His death and resurrection (v. 5-7)
       - aa. The facts restated—if we have been united with Him in the likeness of His death, we shall also be in the likeness of His resurrection (v. 5)
       - bb. The freedom recognized—our old man was crucified with Christ, so that we would no longer be slaves to sin (v. 6-7)
     - iii. The recognition of our glorious hope—eternal life, living for God (v. 8-10)
       - aa. We believe that our union with Christ guarantees our eternal life (v. 8)
       - bb. We believe Christ's resurrection guarantees victory over death (v. 9)

cc. We believe Christ died to sin once for all, but lives eternally unto the glory of God (v. 10)

c. *The personal responsibility of living the resurrected life (v. 11-14)*

i. The principle stated: As Christ died to sin and was raised to eternally glorify God, so you must consider yourselves to be dead to sin, but alive to God in Christ (v. 11)

ii. The practice explained (v. 11-12)

aa. Do not let sin rule in your mortal body (v. 12-13a)

bb. Determine to live as someone who is alive from the dead, to the glory of God (v. 13b)

iii. The promise and privilege affirmed (v. 14)

2. Your privileges under the rule of grace—you have been freed from sin's mastery and are willing slaves of righteousness (6:15-23)

a. *The slightly modified objection to the rule of grace restated [and answered again] (v. 15)*

b. *The slave-master principle explained—you are slaves of the one whom you obey (v. 16)*

c. *The sovereign conversion extolled—you were slaves of sin, but through the gospel you became slaves of righteousness (v. 17-18)*

i. The Person responsible for your conversion (v. 17a)

ii. The position you were in before conversion (v. 17b)

iii. The personal repentance that attended your conversion (v. 17c)

iv. The positional change that took place at your conversion (v. 18)

d. *The simple application made—present your body a slave of righteousness (v. 19)*

e. *The sharp contrast developed—death to those who are slaves of sin and eternal life for those enslaved to God in Christ Jesus our Lord (v. 20-23)*

i. When you were slaves of sin, righteousness did not control you (v. 20)

ii. When you were slaves of sin, what fruit did you really get? Things of which you are now ashamed—whose outcome is death! (v. 21)

iii. As slaves of God, the fruit is sanctification—and the outcome is eternal life (v. 22)

iv. The summary statement that calls us to live as willing slaves of God (v. 23)

B. The gospel sets us free from the condemnation of the law (7:1-25)

1. The proclamation that believers are released from the Law's lordship (7:1-6)

a. *The law has lordship over a person as long as he lives (v. 1-3)*

i. The proposition stated (v. 1)

ii. The picture of marriage offered [as an illustration] (v. 2-3)

aa. The death of a husband releases the wife from the law of the husband (v.2)

bb. The death of a husband releases the wife to be joined to another man (v. 3)

b. The law no longer has lordship over those who have died and are joined to Him who was raised from the dead (v. 4-6)

i. Our death to the law and its purpose (v. 4)

ii. Our deplorable condition under the lordship of the law (v. 5)

iii. Our delightful freedom that results in submissive service in newness of the Spirit, and not the oldness of the letter (v. 6)

2. The proclamation of the Law's purity and its purpose in relation to sin [and its powerlessness to deliver from sin's bondage] (7:7-25)

a. The purity and purpose of the Law [in regard to sin] defended (v. 7)

i. The Law is not sin (v. 7a)

ii. The Law reveals sin (v. 7b)

b. The principle of sin and its use of the Law detailed (v. 8-11)

i. Sin uses the law to excite in me all kinds lusts (v. 8a)

ii. Sin uses the law to condemn me to death (v. 8b-9)

iii. Sin uses the law to deceive me and kill me (v. 10-11)

c. The purity and purpose of the Law [in relation to sin] declared and defended again (v. 12-13)

i. The Law is holy, and the commandment is holy and righteous and good (v. 12)

ii. The Law is the medium through which sin is exposed as utterly sinful (v. 13)

d. The portrayal of how the Law exposes the utter sinfulness of sin—and the powerlessness of the Law to subdue the flesh described (v. 14-25)[1]

i. The presupposition and prospectus statement [what Paul was going to cover] (v. 14)

aa. The Law is spiritual (v. 14a)

bb. I am of flesh, sold under sin (v. 14b)

ii. The principle of sin, and its utter sinfulness exposed by the Law (v. 15-23)

aa. As I assess my actions, I see my own inconsistencies, inner-conflict, and impotence—and the Law's beauty (v. 15-16)

- The Law reveals my inconsistencies and inner turmoil (v. 15)

---

[1] *[Alternate Outline for 7:14-25]* 3. The picture of trying to pursue sanctification under the Law [or the problem of trying to pursue sanctification under the Law; or the problem of trying to serve God by the letter of the law rather than the Spirit] (7:14-25)

- The Law reveals my impotence—and I agree that it is good (v. 16)

bb. As I assess my own inconsistencies and impotence—and the Law's beauty—I conclude that indwelling sin is the source of evil within me (v. 17-20)

- Sin is greater than I imagined—it is an enemy that lives in me (v. 17)
- I know the truth, and I want to do good—but I do not do it (v. 18)
- I actually practice the very evil that I do not want (v. 19)
- In light of this, I see that sin is greater than I imagined—it is an enemy that lives in me (v. 20)

cc. As I assess indwelling sin in light of my conflicting desires and actions, I see my captivity to the law of sin (v. 21-23)

- I see the law of evil present in me—though I want to do good (v. 21)
- I delight in the law of God in the inner man (v. 22)
- I see a war between the law of my body parts and the law of my mind—making me a prisoner of the law of sin in my body (v. 23)

iii. The proclamation that reveals the sinfulness of sin, and the problem of what the Law cannot do (v. 24; cf. 8:3)

iv. The praise for God's redemption in Jesus Christ our Lord (v. 25a)

v. The powerlessness of the Law to subdue the flesh (v. 25b; cf. 8:3)

C. The gospel sets us free to conduct our lives according to the Spirit, as sons of God rather than slaves to the flesh (8:1-17)

1. Freedom from condemnation, and the law of sin and death* (8:1-4)

a. The reality of our freedom—no condemnation (v. 1)

b. The reason for our freedom—justification (v. 2)

c. The route to our freedom—substitution (v. 3)

d. The result of our freedom—sanctification (v. 4)

2. Freedom to conduct our lives as sons of God, rather than slaves of the flesh (8:5-17)

a. The Spirit gives us a new orientation and new perspective (v. 5-11)

i. There are only two ways of life—and they are mutually exclusive (v. 5-6)

aa. The two ways of life introduced (v. 5)

- Those according to the flesh, who set their minds on the things of the flesh

* The following four sub-points of this outline are adapted from Kevin McAteer's sermon notes on Romans 8:1-4.

- Those according to the Spirit, who set their minds on the things of the Spirit

bb. The two ways of life assessed (v. 6)

- The mind set on the flesh is death
- The mind set on the Spirit is life and peace

ii. There are those who are in the flesh—unbelievers [those who are dead] (v. 7-8)

aa. They are unwilling and unable to submit to God's rule (v. 7)

bb. They are unable to please God (v. 8)

iii. There are those who are in the Spirit—believers [those who have life and peace] (v. 9-11)

aa. You have the Spirit of God/Christ and belong to Him (v. 9)

bb. You have a body that is subject to death, but are alive spiritually because of the righteousness of God (v. 10)

cc. You have the glorious promise/hope of resurrection (v. 11)

b. The Spirit gives us a new obligation and new position (v. 12-17)

i. Our new obligation—to live by the Spirit, putting to death the deeds of the body (v. 12-13)

aa. The reality—believers have no obligation to the flesh (v. 12-13a)

bb. The responsibility—believers are responsible to be putting to death—by the Spirit—the deeds of the body (v. 13b)

ii. Our new position—sons of God and fellow heirs with Christ (v. 14-17)

aa. We are sons of God: we are led by the Spirit of God (v. 14)

bb. We have intimacy with God: we are crying out Abba! Father!—rather than cringing in fear like slaves (v. 15)

cc. We have assurance from God: we are confident that we are children of God—because of the Spirit's witness with our spirit (v. 16)

dd. We have hope in God: we are heirs of God and fellow heirs with Christ—suffering with Him so that we may also be glorified with Him (v. 17)

D. The gospel seals us for glory in God's sovereign plan and power (8:18-30)

1. We have the promise/hope of glory, which incomparably outweighs our present suffering (8:18-25)

a. The Apostle's inspired reckoning—we will experience glory that is incomparably greater than any temporal sufferings now known (v. 18)

b. The anxious longing of creation—it waits eagerly for our glorification (v. 19-22)

i. Creation waits for the revealing of the sons of God (v. 19)

ii. Creation was subjected to futility—in hope (v. 20)

iii. Creation will be set free from its slavery to corruption (v. 21)

iv. Creation groans and suffers the pains of childbirth (v. 22)

c. *The anxious longing of believers—we wait eagerly for our glorification (v. 23-25)*

i. Believers [those who have the first fruits of the Spirit] wait for the future aspect of our adoption as sons, the redemption of our body (v. 23)

ii. Believers [those who have the first fruits of the Spirit] wait in hope for that which they do not currently see (v. 24-25)

aa. Hope is faith that looks forward to promises yet fulfilled (v. 24)

bb. Hope is evidenced by perseverance in waiting eagerly for God's promises to come to pass (v. 25)

2. We have the provision and prayers of the Spirit, who intercedes for us according to the will of God (8:26-27)

a. *We have the Spirit's provision in our weakness (v. 26a)*

b. *We have the Spirit's prayers of intercession on our behalf (v. 26b-27)*

i. He intercedes for us in our ignorance (v. 26b)

ii. He intercedes for us according to the will of God (v. 27)

3. We have the predetermined plan of God, which invariably leads to conformity to Christ's image, and eternal glory (8:28-30)

a. *God's predetermined plan providentially orders all things to ultimately work out for the good of those He has called (v. 28)*

b. *God's predetermined plan has foreordained our conformity to Christ's image (v. 29)*

c. *God's predetermined plan includes our effectual call, our justification, and our glorification (v. 30)*

III. Security—freedom to live victoriously no matter the circumstances we may face, because of God's indestructible love in Christ (8:31-39)

A. The indestructible love of God extolled in poetic form (8:31-37)

1. If God is for us—who can be against us? (8:31)

2. If God did not spare His own Son—what good thing will He withhold from us? (8:32)

3. If God justifies—who will bring a charge against His elect? (v. 33)

4. If Christ died, rose, and intercedes for us at the right hand of God—who is the one who condemns us? (v. 34)

5. If Christ loves us—who or what will separate us from His love (v. 35-37)
    a. *The rhetorical question (v. 35a)*
    b. *The realities of what believers may face (v. 35b-36)*
        i. A summary list (v. 35b)
            aa. Trouble
            bb. Pressure
            cc. Persecution
            dd. Hunger
            ee. Nakedness
            ff. Danger
            gg. Death
        ii. A scriptural reference—Psalm 44:22 (v. 36)
    c. *The recognition of believers' overwhelming victory through Christ (v. 37)*
        i. We will triumph spiritually
        ii. Our triumph is because of Christ and His love for us

B. The indestructible love of God apprehended by faith (8:38-39)

1. The comprehensive list of potential threats to our eternal security (v. 38b-39a)
    a. *Death can't separate us from the love of God in Christ*
    b. *Life [circumstances] can't separate us from the love of God in Christ*
    c. *Angelic beings can't separate us from the love of God in Christ*
    d. *Rulers can't separate us from the love of God in Christ*
    e. *Current events can't separate us from the love of God in Christ*
    f. *Future events can't separate us from the love of God in Christ*
    g. *Miraculous powers can't separate us from the love of God in Christ*
    h. *The highest height in the universe can't separate us from the love of God in Christ*
    i. *The deepest depths in the universe can't separate from the love of God in Christ*
2. The conviction of faith concerning the love of God in Christ Jesus our Lord (v. 38a, 39b)
    a. *A Spirit-inspired conviction and confirmation (v. 38a)*
    b. *A sovereign guarantee and Guarantor (v. 39b)*

The "Problem" of Israel and the Gospel (9:1-11:36)

I. God's sovereign plan and Israel's election (9:1-29)

A. The sorrow concerning Israel confessed (9:1-5)

1. The pain of the Apostle confessed (9:1-3)
   - *a. His pledge (v. 1)*
   - *b. His pain (v. 2)*
   - *c. His passion (v. 3)*
2. The privileges of the Jews confirmed (9:4-5)
   - *a. Their glorious gifts as a chosen nation (v. 4-5a)*
   - *b. Their glorious God and Messiah (v. 5b)*

B. The sovereign freedom of God in election introduced (9:6-13)

1. The Word of God has not failed (9:6a)
2. The Word of God has revealed sovereign election (9:6b-13)
   - *a. Not all physical descendants of Abraham are children of promise, chosen by God (v. 6b-9)*
     - i. The pithy statement recorded and clarified (v. 6b-7a)
     - ii. The promise stated (v. 7b)
     - iii. The promise further explained (v. 8-9)
   - *b. Nothing but God's purpose according to His choice determines sovereign election (v. 10-13)*
     - i. The twins born of Rebekah and Isaac (v. 10-11)
     - ii. The texts that confirm God's sovereign freedom to choose (v. 12-13)

C. The sovereign freedom of God in election defended (9:14-29)

1. Sovereign election extols the riches of God's mercy—yet in no way impugns His justice (9:14-24a)
   - *a. The charge against God's justice anticipated and answered (v. 14)*
   - *b. The confirmation of God's sovereign mercy (v. 15-18)*
     - i. Sovereign election reveals God's mercy and compassion—not injustice (v. 15-16)
       - aa. The quotation from Exodus 33:19 (v. 15)
       - bb. The confirmation of sovereign mercy (v. 16)
     - ii. Sovereign election reveals God's power and glory—not injustice (v. 17-18)
       - aa. The quotation from Exodus 9:16 (v. 17)
       - bb. The confirmation of sovereign mercy (v. 18)
   - *c. The charge against God's justice anticipated and answered again (v. 19-21)*
     - i. The repeated charge against God's justice (v. 19)
     - ii. The reality that man is incapable of rightly critiquing God (v. 20)

iii. The right of the potter over the clay—an illustration of both authority and mercy (v. 21)

d. The confirmation of God's sovereign mercy (v. 22-24a)

i. God is extremely patient—not unjust (v. 22)

ii. God is gloriously merciful—not unjust (v. 23-24a)

2. Sovereign election extends the riches of God's mercy to both Jew and Gentile (9:24b-29)

a. God's mercy upon both Jew and Gentile expressly stated (v. 24a)

b. God's mercy illustrated in Hosea—hope in God's character for the called among the Gentiles and the called among the Jews (v. 24b-26)

i. Hosea 2:23 (v. 25)

ii. Hosea 1:10 (v. 26)

c. God's mercy confirmed explicitly in Isaiah—hope in God's character for the remnant of Israel (v. 27-29)

i. Isaiah 10:22-23 (v. 27-28)

ii. Isaiah 1:9 (v. 29)

II. God's sovereign plan and Israel's rejection (9:30-10:21)

A. They stumbled over faith in Christ (9:30-33)

1. The reality of Israel's failure to attain a right standing before God (9:30-31)

a. The surprising reality concerning the Gentiles and the righteousness that comes through faith (v. 30)

b. The sad reality concerning Israel's pursuit of righteousness through law (v. 31)

2. The reason Israel failed to attain a right standing before God (9:32-33)

a. They sought righteousness by works (v. 32a)

b. They stumbled over faith in Christ as their only hope of righteousness (v. 32b-33)

B. They stumbled in self-righteousness (10:1-13)

1. The problem of self-righteousness (10:1-4)

a. The proper response to Israel's rejection (v. 1)

i. Intense longing for their salvation (v. 1a)

ii. Intercessory prayer for their salvation (v. 1b)

b. The problem of self-righteous zeal for God, which refuses to submit to God's way of righteousness (v. 2-3)

i. They wanted to jealously protect God's name, without truly knowing who He is (v. 2)

ii. They willfully ignored God's righteousness, sought to establish their own, and would not submit to God's righteousness (v. 3)

c. The Person who ends the futility of seeking to establish one's own righteousness before God—for everyone who believes (v. 4)

2. The proclamation of the righteousness that is based on faith (10:5-13)
    - *a. An exemplification of the life of law and the life of faith from Moses (v. 5-8ab)*
        - i. The righteousness based on law says that life depends on your practice—Leviticus 18:5 (v. 5)
        - ii. The righteousness based on faith says life depends on God's gracious promises—Deuteronomy 9:4-5; 30:12-14 (v. 6-8ab)
            - aa. The righteousness of faith speaks to the inner man—that God gives life because of His gracious promises, not because of your own righteousness (v. 6a; cf. Deut. 9:4-5)
            - bb. The righteousness of faith does not require that which is too difficult or out of reach to obtain life (v. 6b-7)
            - cc. The righteousness of faith says that life is found in trusting God (v. 8ab)
    - *b. An explanation of how faith in God's Word relates to salvation in Christ (v. 8c-10)*
        - i. The connection between Moses' call to faith and the gospel of faith (v. 8c)
        - ii. The confession of Jesus as Lord (v. 9a)
        - iii. The conviction that God raised Him from the dead (9b)
        - iv. The consequences of faith (v. 9c-10)
    - *c. An example of Isaiah's call to salvation by faith in Christ (v. 11)*
    - *d. An explanation of how salvation by faith is available to both Jew and Gentile (v. 12-13)*
        - i. The proclamation of God's salvation is for "all who call upon Him" (v. 12)
        - ii. The prophetic testimony of Joel 2:32 (v. 13)

C. They stumbled in willful unbelief (10:14-21)

1. Israel and the nations need the good news (10:14-15)
    - *a. The sequence of faith analyzed in reverse order (v. 14-15a)*
        - i. Calling on Him unto salvation requires faith (v. 14a)
        - ii. Coming to Him in faith requires hearing the message (v. 14b)
        - iii. Hearing the message requires someone proclaiming that message (v. 14c)
        - iv. Someone proclaiming that message requires being sent (v. 15a)
    - *b. The Scripture that explains that the good news would be announced and thus messengers sent (v. 15b)*
2. Israel and the nations need the good news, but not all have heeded the good news (10:16-17)
    - *a. The reality that not everyone has believed the good news (v. 16)*
    - *b. The reaffirmation that faith comes from hearing the Word concerning Christ (v. 17)*

3. Israel and the nations have heard the good news, but Israel has stubbornly refused to believe the Word of God (10:18-21)
    a. *Potential objection #1 anticipated and answered—surely they have never heard, have they? (v. 18)*
    b. *Potential objection #2 anticipated and answered—surely Israel did not know, did they? (v. 19-21)*
        i. The question (v. 19a)
        ii. The quotation from Moses concerning grace to the nations and the unbelief of Israel (v. 19b)
        iii. The quotation from Isaiah concerning grace (v. 20)
        iv. The quotation from Isaiah concerning faithlessness of Israel, in the face of God's persistent compassion (v. 21)

III. God's sovereign plan and Israel's salvation (11:1-29)

A. There remains a remnant—the present rejection of Israel is not total (11:1-10)

1. The Pauline testimony of God's faithfulness in preserving a remnant in Israel—remember, I too am an Israelite (11:1)
    a. *The anticipated question and the emphatic answer (v. 1a)*
    b. *The Apostle Paul's own testimony offered as evidence (v. 1b)*
2. The prophetic testimony of God's faithfulness in preserving a remnant in Israel—remember God's response to Elijah (11:2-4)
    a. *The sovereignty of God reintroduced (v. 2a)*
    b. *The Scripture that illustrates God's faithfulness to those He has foreknown (v. 2b-4)*
        i. The reference to 1 Kings 19 (v. 2b)
        ii. The response of Elijah to Israel's hardhearted unbelief (v. 3)
        iii. The response of God to Elijah's complaint (v. 4)
3. The pre-eminent issue concerning God's faithfulness in preserving a remnant in Israel—remember sovereign grace (11:5-6)
    a. *The reality of a present remnant (v. 5a)*
    b. *The reason for the present remnant (v. 5b)*
    c. *The recognition of what grace really means (v. 6)*
4. The prophetic testimony of God's faithfulness in blinding those who insist on establishing their own righteousness—remember the Scripture said this would happen (11:7-10)
    a. *The summary—the chosen within Israel have obtained a right standing before Him, but the rest were blinded (v. 7)*
    b. *The Scriptures that confirm judicial blindness for those who ignore and reject sovereign grace (v. 8-10)*
        i. Isaiah 29:10 and Deuteronomy 29:4 (v. 8)

ii. Psalm 69:22-23 (v. 9-10)

B. There remains an opportunity for repentance—the present rejection of Israel is not final [but it should warn us against arrogance and unbelief] (11:11-24)

1. The anticipated question and emphatic answer (11:11a)
2. The astounding ramifications of Israel's present rejection and future restoration (11:11b-15)
   a. *Salvation for the Gentiles through Israel's current unbelief (v. 11b)*
   b. *Super-abundant riches when the promise of Israel's salvation is fulfilled (v. 12)*
   c. *Salvation of Israelites now is of great apostolic importance (v. 13-14)*
   d. *Supernatural resurrection will be pictured in Israel's future salvation (v. 15)*
3. The Abrahamic promises and nation of Israel (11:16)
4. The admonition against Gentile arrogance, and the ability of God to restore Israel if they do not continue in their unbelief (11:17-24)
   a. *The analogy of Gentiles being grafted into the people of God, and unbelieving Jews being broken off (v. 17)*
   b. *The admonition against Gentile arrogance (v. 18-22)*
      i. Remember that it is God's promise to Abraham that has brought your salvation (v. 18)
      ii. Resist the temptation to think that you are more important than Israel—but rather live in humble fear (v. 19-21)
         aa. The conclusion stated (v. 19)
         bb. The caution against conceit given (v. 20-21)
      iii. Recognize the consequences of either trusting in God's kindness, or trusting in one's own righteousness (v. 22)
   c. *The ability of God to restore Israel if they do not continue in their unbelief (11:23-24)*
      i. The possibility of Israel's restoration (v. 23ab)
      ii. The power of God to accomplish Israel's restoration (v. 23c-24)

C. There remains the predetermined plan and promise of God—the promised redemption of Israel is irrevocable (11:25-29)

1. The fullness of the Gentiles and the future of Israel—God's predetermined plan is now revealed (11:25-26a)
   a. *The purpose of this mystery revealed (v. 25a)*
   b. *The partial hardening of Israel has happened until the fullness of the Gentiles has come in (v. 25b)*
   c. *The promise that all Israel will be saved (v. 26a)*

2. The fulfillment of the Scriptures concerning Israel—God's promise of the New Covenant will be fulfilled in regard to Israel (11:26b-27)
    a. *The Redeemer of Israel will come (v. 26b)*
    b. *The removal of ungodliness from Jacob will come (v. 26c)*
    c. *The reality of the New Covenant for Israel will come (v. 27)*
3. The faithfulness of God—God's predetermined plan is irrevocable (11:28-29)
    a. *Israel's current rejection is for the sake of the Gentiles (v. 28a)*
    b. *Israel's election is for the sake of the fathers—and thus an irrevocable gift (v. 28b-29)*
        i. Sovereign election guarantees Gentiles salvation now, and Israel's place in God's future program (v. 28b)
        ii. Sovereign grace is irrevocable (v. 29)

IV. God's sovereign plan and irrepressible exultation (11:30-36)

A. The undeserved mercy of God's sovereign plan (v. 30-32)

1. Mercy to the Gentile (11:30)
2. Mercy to the Jew (11:31)
3. Mercy manifest to all (11:32)

B. The unfathomable majesty of God's sovereign plan (v. 33-36)

1. His wisdom is unequalled—trust and rejoice in His wisdom (11:33-34)
    a. *God's wisdom is gloriously unfathomable (v. 33)*
    b. *God's wisdom is gloriously unique (v. 34)*
2. His sovereignty is unrivaled—trust and rejoice in His sovereignty (11:35-36a)
    a. *God's sovereignty is gloriously unfettered (v. 35)*
    b. *God's sovereignty is gloriously focused (v. 36a)*
3. His glory is unending—trust and rejoice in His glory (11:36b)

The Practice of the Gospel (12:1-15:13)

I. Worship God and humbly serve others in love (12:1-21)

A. The gospel calls believers to a life of worship (12:1-2)

1. Worship calls for the presentation of our bodies to God for His service (12:1)
    a. *The reason for a life abandoned to God for worship (v. 1a)*
    b. *The requirements of a life abandoned to God for worship (v. 1b)*
        i. Present yourself to God as alive to Him and at His disposal—"a living … sacrifice"

ii. Present yourself to God as set apart to Him and dead to self—"a … holy sacrifice"

iii. Present yourself to God as existing solely for His pleasure—"a sacrifice, acceptable to God"

c. *The reasonableness of a life abandoned to God for worship (v. 1c)*

2. Worship calls for the transformation of our thinking unto the will of God (12:2)

a. *Stop allowing this world shape who you are (v. 2a)*

b. *Start allowing the Word of God to transform who you are (v. 2b)*

i. The responsibility we have—constantly be transformed

ii. The route to transformation—by the renewing of your mind

iii. The result of ongoing transformation—recognizing the will of God as good pleasing and perfect

aa. God's will is discernable

bb. God's will is good and pleasing and lacks nothing

B. The gospel calls believers to a life of humility and ministry within in the body of Christ (12:3-8)

1. A life of worship and transformed thinking should lead to humility within the body (12:3-5)

a. *The proper perspective of the Apostle (v. 3a)*

b. *The proper perspective of self and others in Christ (v. 3b-5)*

i. The proper thinking (v. 3bcd)

aa. The call to humility (v. 3b)

bb. The call to controlled thinking (v. 3c)

cc. The content of controlled thinking—God has allotted to each a measure of faith (v. 3d)

ii. The picture of our need for one another as a unified body, yet distinct in our various functions (v. 4-5)

aa. The diversity and yet unity of the human anatomy (v. 4)

bb. The diversity and yet unity of the spiritual reality (v. 5)

2. A life of worship and transformed thinking should lead to ministry within the body (12:6-8)

a. *The source of our diverse ministries within the body (v. 6a)*

b. *The sample list of our diverse ministries within the body (v. 6b-8)*

i. Prophecy—proclaiming the truth to others in accordance with the faith (v. 6b)

ii. Service—supporting others (v. 7a)

iii. Teaching—instructing others in the doctrine (v. 7b)

iv. Exhortation—coming alongside others with encouragement and admonishment (v. 8a)

v. Giving—sharing of one's own resources with others (v. 8b)

vi. Leadership—standing before or over others (v. 8c)

vii. Mercy—acting in compassion toward others (8d)

C. The gospel calls believers to a life of love (12:9-21)

1. Characteristics of the life of love—manifest most often within the church (12:9-13)

   a. The life of love is marked by sincerity (v. 9a)

   b. The life of love is marked by hatred of evil and devotion to what is good (v. 9b)

   c. The life of love is marked by affection, loyalty, and respect for one another (v. 10)

   d. The life of love is marked by eagerness to serve (v. 11)

   e. The life of love is marked by joy, perseverance, and prayer (v. 12)

   f. The life of love is marked by generosity and hospitality (v. 13)

2. Characteristics of the life of love—manifest most often outside the church (12:14-21)

   a. The life of love is marked by blessing, rather than bitterness (v. 14)

   b. The life of love is marked by sympathy, rather than apathy (v. 15)

   c. The life of love is marked by humility, rather than haughtiness (v. 16)

   d. The life of love is marked by the pursuit of peace and trust in God's wisdom, rather than personal vengeance and taking matters into one's own hands (v. 17-21)

      i. Do not retaliate—but seek to live honorably among all men (v. 17)

      ii. Seek peace with all men—if possible, and as far as it depends on you (v. 18)

      iii. Never take your own revenge—but trust in God's righteous retribution, as promised in His Word (v. 19)

      iv. Seek the welfare of your enemy—for in doing so he may repent (v. 20)

      v. Do not be conquered by evil—but conquer evil with good (v. 21)

II. Walk in submission to civil authorities and walk in love (13:1-14)

A. Walking in submission to civil authorities (13:1-7)

1. The command and cause for submission to civil authorities (13:1)

   a. The command: Let every person be in subjection to the governing authorities (v. 1a)

   b. The core reason: For there is no authority except from God (v. 1b)

2. The consequences of resisting authority (13:2)

   a. Standing against the ordinance of God (v. 2a)

   b. Standing in the place of condemnation (v. 2b)

3. The commentary on the role of government in society (13:3-4)

   a. The general purpose of civil authorities (v. 3)

   b. The God-ordained ministry of civil authorities (v. 4)

4. The constraint of conscience in submission to God (13:5)
5. The connection between paying taxes and honoring God (13:6)
6. The charge of every believer in regard to all in positions of authority (13:7)

B. Walking in love (13:8-14)

1. Owe nothing to anyone except love (13:8-10)
   a. *The gospel perspective on debt (v. 8a)*
   b. *The gospel perspective on fulfilling law (v. 8b-10)*
2. Order your life in light of Christ and the glory to come (13:11-14)
   a. *Walking in love demands the proper perspective—shaking off spiritual slumber and focusing on the approaching glory (v. 11-12a)*
      i. Understand your need to wake up spiritually (v. 11a)
      ii. Understand that salvation is actually nearer than when we believed (v. 11b)
      iii. Understand that the day of the Lord is near (v. 12)
   b. *Walking in love demands the proper practice—laying aside sin and purposely pursuing Christ (v. 12b-14)*
      i. Put off the deeds of darkness (v. 12b)
      ii. Put on the armor of light (v. 12c)
      iii. Proper behavior described by simile (v. 13a)
      iv. Proper behavior described by what it is not (v. 13b)
      v. Purposely pursue Christ (v. 14a)
      vi. Purposely refuse to mentally coddle the desires of the flesh (v. 14b)

III. Willingly accept one another and walk in love—in spite of divergent personal convictions on how to apply biblical principles to culture (14:1-15:13)

A. Refuse to condemn other believers' opinions/personal convictions on how to personally apply the faith (14:1-13a)

1. The exhortation introduced: Receive the one who is weak in faith—without passing judgment on his opinions/personal convictions (14:1)
   a. *Welcome those who are not strong in the faith (v. 1a)*
   b. *Without passing judgment on his reasonings (1b)*
2. The example regarding food—and the appropriate response (14:2-4)
   a. *The person who believes that he may all things (v. 2a)*
   b. *The person who is weak eats vegetables only (v. 2b)*

c. *The proper perspective for both (v. 3-4)*
   i. The one who eats is not to regard with contempt the one who does not eat (v. 3a)
   ii. The one who does not eat is not to judge the one who eats (v. 3b)
   iii. The One to whom each is ultimately accountable is his own Master, the Lord (v. 4)

3. The example regarding special days—and the appropriate response (14:5-9)
   a. *The possible conflict concerning special days (v. 5a)*
   b. *The proper perspective (v. 5b-9)*
      i. Each person must be fully convinced in his own mind (v. 5b)
      ii. Each person is accountable to the Lord for his personal conviction on the matter (v. 6-9)
         aa. Can you genuinely give thanks to God for how you live out the faith in this matter (v. 6)
         bb. Do you understand that you belong to the Lord and He is sovereign over your entire life (v. 7-9)

4. The explanation of who is Judge (14:10-12)
   a. *The questions that rebuke (v. 10ab)*
   b. *The truth that should correct us all (v. 10c-12)*
      i. All will stand before the judgment seat of God (v. 10c)
      ii. Every knee will bow and every tongue confess to God (v. 11)
      iii. Each one will give an account of himself to God (v. 12)

5. The exhortation summarized: Stop passing judgment on one another (14:13a)

B. Refrain from allowing your personal opinions/convictions on how to apply the faith to become a stumbling block to others (14:13b-23)

1. Be careful to consider your brother's well being as more important than your liberty [Don't let your freedom cause your brother to stumble] (14:13b-15)
   a. *The Apostle's inspired command concerning the use of our liberty (v. 13b)*
   b. *The Apostle's inspired conviction concerning food and conscience (v. 14)*
   c. *The Apostle's inspired commentary concerning food/liberty and love (v. 15a)*
   d. *The Apostle's inspired command concerning liberty and love (v. 15b)*

2. Be careful to <u>consider your witness</u> to others about what is really important [Don't let your freedom obscure your witness] (14:16-18)
   a. *The command against bringing reproach upon God's kingdom (v. 16-17)*
      i. The care we ought to have about our testimony (v. 16)
      ii. The characteristics that reveal the reality of the kingdom of God (v. 17)
   b. *The concern for our testimony will bring pleasure to God and be revealed as genuine to men (v. 18)*
3. Be careful to <u>constantly edify one another</u> rather than tear down the work of God for the sake of your liberty [Don't let your freedom tear down the work of God—rather build up one another in the Lord] (14:19-21)
   a. *Keep pursuing the things that make for peace and the building up of one another (v. 19)*
   b. *Keep from tearing down the work of God for the sake of your liberty (v. 20-21)*
4. Be completely <u>convinced about your freedom</u> rather than violate your conscience and partake, but not in faith [Don't let your freedom violate your conscience] (14:22-23)
   a. *A clear conscience before God issues in contentment (v. 22)*
   b. *A conflicted conscience is a source of condemnation (v. 23)*

C. Reflect the same perspective and purpose as Christ (15:1-13)

1. Christ assisted others in their weakness, and came to glorify God the Father—not to please Himself (15:1-6)
   a. *The exhortation (v. 1-2)*
      i. Bear the weaknesses of the weak (v. 1)
      ii. Fit together with and build up one another (v. 2)
   b. *The example of Christ and the encouragement of the Scriptures (v. 3-4)*
      i. The example: Christ did not please Himself—but suffered for the good of others and the glory of God (v. 3)
      ii. The encouragement: The Scriptures offer instruction and hope in following Christ (v. 4)
   c. *The entreaty to God for Christ's perspective and purpose among His people (v. 5-6)*
      i. The Person of God [the God of steadfastness and encouragement] (v. 5a)
      ii. The petition [for like-mindedness according to Christ in regard to one another] (v. 5b)
      iii. The purpose of this Christ-like unity [the glory of the One true God] (v. 6)

2. Christ accepted us, unto the glory of God among both the Jews and the Gentiles (15:7-13)
   a. *The exhortation (v. 7)*
      i. The mandate (v. 7a)
      ii. The Model (v. 7b)
      iii. The motive (v. 7c)
   b. *The example of Christ and the encouragement of the Scriptures (v. 8-12)*
      i. Christ became a servant to the Jews as promised in the Scriptures—to the glory of God's truth and faithfulness (v. 8)
      ii. Christ became a servant to the Gentiles as promised in the Scriptures—to the glory of God's mercy (v. 9-12)
         aa. For the Gentiles to glorify God for His mercy (v. 9a)
         bb. Psalm 18:49; cf. 2 Samuel 22:50 (v. 9b)
         cc. Deuteronomy 32:43 (v. 10)
         dd. Psalm 17:1 (v. 11)
         ee. Isaiah 11:10 (v. 12)
   c. *The entreaty to God for joy and peace in the faith, and abounding hope (v. 13)*
      i. The Person of God [the God of hope] (v. 13a)
      ii. The petition [fill you with all joy and peace in the faith] (v. 13b)
      iii. The purpose/result [so that you will abound in hope by the power of the Holy Spirit] (v. 13c)

The Plans and Partnership of the Gospel (15:14-16:24)

I. The plans explained [to Paul's ministry partners in Rome] (15:14-33)

A. The encouragement and explanation as to why Paul had not yet visited them (15:14-22)

1. Paul was convinced that they were able to counsel one another (15:14)
   a. *Apostolic encouragement (v. 14a)*
   b. *Abundant provision (v. 14b)*
   c. *Actual ministry of counseling one another (v. 14c)*
2. Paul was continuing his God-given ministry (15:15-21)
   a. *A writing ministry to the Romans (v. 15)*
   b. *A worship ministry in offering the nations to God (v. 15b-16)*
   c. *A widespread ministry among the nations who had never before heard the name of Christ (v. 17-21)*
      i. A reason to rejoice (v. 17)

ii. A recognition of Who was accomplishing the ministry through him (v. 18-19)

iii. A righteous ambition (v. 20-21)

3. Paul was kept from coming to them due to ministry God had given him (v. 22)

B. The expectations in regard to Paul's desired future visit (15:23-29)

1. Fellowship and support for his future ministry of preaching Christ in Spain (15:23-24)
   - *a. The dependence on divine providence (v. 23a; cf. v. 22)*
   - *b. The desire to visit the church in Rome (v. 23b)*
   - *c. The determination to go to Spain (v. 24a)*
   - *d. The desire for ministry support and fellowship (v. 24b)*

2. Forbearance and a similar mindset in light of his current ministry of proving the bond of unity between Gentile and Jewish believers (15:25-29)
   - *a. The current ministry serving the saints (v. 25)*
   - *b. The contribution for the poor among the saints in Jerusalem (v. 26-27)*
     - i. The delight of Gentile believers in Macedonia and Achaia (v. 26)
     - ii. The debt of Gentile believers to their Jewish brethren (v. 27)
   - *c. The commitment to finish his current mission and then move on to Rome and Spain (v. 28)*
   - *d. The coming will ultimately be in the fullness of the blessing of Christ (v. 29)*

C. The exhortation to intercessory prayer concerning Paul's future visit (15:30-33)

1. Paul's petition for prayer on his behalf (15:30-32)
2. Paul's prayer on behalf of the Romans (15:33)

II. The partners encouraged (16:1-24)

A. A call to help a partner in the ministry (16:1-2)

1. The recommendation (16:1)
   - *a. Our sister*
   - *b. A servant of the church*
2. The responsibility (16:2a)
   - *a. Receive her in a worthy manner*
   - *b. Help her in whatever she may need of you*
3. The reason (16:2b)
   - *a. She has helped many*
   - *b. She has helped me*

B. A concern to honor and encourage gospel partners (16:3-16)

1. Greet Prisca and Aquila—and the church that is in their house (16:3-5a)
    a. *Labor (v. 3)*
    b. *Sacrifice (v. 4)*
    c. *Hospitality and fellowship (v. 5a)*
2. Greet Epaenetus—special to Paul as a first convert from Asia (16:5b)
3. Greet Mary—a hard worker for the church in Rome (16:6)
4. Greet Andronicus and Junias—Jewish believers before Paul's conversion, who also had experienced imprisonment for Christ, well-known among the Apostles (16:7)
5. Greet Ampliatus—loved by Paul in the Lord (16:8)
6. Greet Urbanus—our fellow worker—and Stachys loved by Paul (16:9)
7. Greet Apelles—approved in Christ (16:10a)
8. Greet those of the household of Aristobulus (16:10b)
9. Greet Herodion—a Jewish believer (16:11a)
10. Greet those of the household of Narcissus who are in the Lord (16:11b)
11. Greet Tryphaena and Tryphosa—workers in the Lord (16:12a)
12. Greet Persis—the beloved, who has worked hard in the Lord (16:12b)
13. Greet Rufus—a choice man in the Lord—and his mother (16:13)
14. Greet Asyncritus, Phlegon, Hermes, Patrobas, Hermas and the brethren with them (16:14)
15. Greet Philogus and Julia, Nereus and his sister, and Olympas, and all the saints who are with them (16:15)
16. Greet one another with a holy kiss (16:16a)
17. Greetings from all the churches of Christ (16:16b)

C. A caution and encouragement in hope (16:17-20)

1. A word of caution concerning the divisive (16:17-19)
    a. *Keep your eye on them (v. 17a)*
    b. *Keep away from them (v. 17b)*
    c. *Keep alert to the reality of their motives and methods (v. 18)*
    d. *Keep growing in your obedience and discernment (v. 19)*
2. A word of encouragement concerning our hope (16:20)

a. *The Person of God is the source of our peace (v. 20a)*
b. *The promise of God is the surety of our victory over Satan (v. 20b)*
c. *The prayer for grace is the reminder of God's favor until all evil is destroyed (v. 20c)*

D. A continued concern for the encouragement of gospel partners (16:21-24)

1. Greetings from Timothy, Lucius, Jason, and Sosipater (16:21)
2. Greetings from Tertius (16:22)
3. Greetings from Gaius, Erastus, and Quartus (16:23)
4. Grace be with you all (16:24)

The Purpose of the Gospel—Praise Be to God Forever! (16:25-27)

I. Praise God for His power (16:25-26)

A. The recognition of God's power (16:25a)

B. The revelation of God's power (16:25bc-26)

1. The Pauline gospel and the preaching of Jesus Christ (16:25b)
2. The past mystery now made clear, and made known to all the nations (16:25c-26)

a. *The mystery kept secret for long ages past (v. 25c)*
b. *The mystery now made known to all the nations (v. 26)*

C. The results of God's power (16:25a, 26c)

1. God's power in the gospel results in the strength to stand firm (16:25a)
2. God's power in the gospel results in salvation—the obedience of faith (16:26c)

II. Praise God for His wisdom (16:27ab)

A. His wisdom is unique (16:27a)

B. His wisdom is mediated through Jesus Christ (16:27b)

III. Praise God forever (16:27c)

A. He possesses eternal glory

B. Amen

1 Corinthians

Kress Biblical Resources

Overview Outline of 1 Corinthians

The Wisdom of the Cross Purifies and Unites Believers, the Wisdom of the World Pollutes and Divides

I. The wisdom of the cross and a charitable introduction (1:1-9)

A. The writer (1:1)

B. The recipients (1:2)

C. The reasons

D. The requisite greeting (1:3)

E. The remarkable thanksgiving [for a troubled church] (1:4-9)

II. The wisdom of the cross and Christian ministers (1:10-4:31)

A. The report of divisions over Christian ministers (1:10-17)

B. The rebuke of divisions over Christian ministers (1:18-4:5)

C. The remedy for divisions over Christian ministers (4:6-21)

III. The wisdom of the cross and Christian morality (5:1-6:20)

A. The church must deal with unrepentant sin (5:1-13)

B. The church must deal with disputes among its members (6:1-8)

C. The church must discern that liberty does not lead to lawlessness—freedom does not lead to fornication (6:9-20)

IV. The wisdom of the cross and Christian marriage (7:1-40)

A. Serve one another sexually within marriage (7:1-7)

B. Stay as you were called in Christ, whether married or single (7:8-24)

C. Stay focused on serving Christ whether married or single (7:25-40)

V. The wisdom of the cross and Christian liberty (8:1-11:1)

A. The instruction concerning our freedom in Christ (8:1-13)

B. The illustration concerning our freedom in Christ—the life of Paul (9:1-27)

C. The idolatry to avoid that corrupts our freedom in Christ (10:1-33)

VI. The wisdom of the cross and Christian gender roles (11:2-16)

A. The proper order for worship explained (11:2-10)

B. The proper perspective on male/female equality asserted (11:11-12)

C. The proper order for worship reaffirmed (11:13-16)

VII. The wisdom of the cross and communion/the Lord's Supper (11:17-34)

A. The rebuke of selfishness in regard to the Lord's Supper (11:17-22)

B. The right practice and purpose of the Lord's Supper [commemoration, proclamation, anticipation] (11:23-26)

C. The requirement of self-examination in regard to the Lord's Supper [self-examination] (11:27-32)

D. The requirement of selflessness in the practice of the Lord's Supper [unification] (11:33-34)

VIII. The wisdom of the cross and *charismata*/spiritual gifts (12:1-14:40)

A. Spiritual gifts should unify and build up the church—not divide and puff up (12:1-31)

B. Spiritual gifts should manifest faith, hope, and love—not self-exaltation (13:1-13)

C. Spiritual gifts should prioritize the proclamation of truth to others in an orderly manner—not pacification of self (14:1-40)

IX. The wisdom of the cross and the Christian's resurrection (15:1-58)

A. The resurrection is certain (15:1-34)

B. The resurrection is supernatural (15:35-49)

C. The resurrection is our sure hope and motivation (15:50-58)

X. The wisdom of the cross and the collection for the saints (16:1-4)

A. The Pauline directive on the collection (16:1)

B. The particular directions for the collection (16:2)

C. The painstaking discretion for the administration and distribution of the collection (16:2e-4)

XI. The wisdom of the cross and the concluding remarks (16:5-24)

A. Plans and their communication are important for an effective gospel ministry (16:5-12)

B. Personal relationships and their communication are important for an effective gospel ministry (16:13-24)

Introductory Matters

I. The author (1:1)

A. The human author[1]

1. His name
2. His office
3. His authority
4. His amanuensis/secretary (cf. Acts 18:17)

B. The divine Author (2 Tim. 3:16; 2 Pet. 1:21; 3:15-16)

II. The audience (1:2)

A. The original recipients (cf. Acts 18:1-18; 19:1)

1. The church and their city
2. Their holy position and calling
3. The wider audience

B. The current recipients (2 Tim. 3:16; cf. 2 Pet. 3:15-16)

III. The aim

A. To confront and address church factions (1:10-11; 11:18-19; 12:25; cf. 3:3-4; 6:1-7)

B. To confront and address immorality and improper conduct in the church (5:1ff; 6:1-20; 11:2ff)

C. To correct erroneous doctrine about the resurrection (15:1ff)

D. To comment on questions the Corinthians had raised (7:1ff; 8:1-11:1; 12:1-14:40; 16:1ff)

1. Questions concerning marriage, singleness, divorce and remarriage (7:1ff)
2. Questions concerning things sacrificed to idols and Christian liberty (8:1-11:1)
3. Questions concerning spiritual gifts (12:1-14:40)
4. Questions concerning the offering for the saints in Jerusalem (16:1ff)

E. Summary reason: To reveal that the gospel, properly understood and applied, is the answer to all the questions, problems, and issues the church faces. [**The wisdom of the cross purifies and unites believers—the wisdom of the world pollutes and divides**]

---

[1]For a biblical biography of the Apostle Paul see Acts 7:58; 8:1; 9:1-30; 11:25-30; 12:25-28:31; 1 Cor. 15:30-32; 2 Cor. 6:4-5; 11:23-30; Gal. 1:13-2:16; Phil. 3:4-14; 2 Thes. 3:8

Detailed Outline of 1 Corinthians

The Wisdom of the Cross Purifies and Unites Believers, the Wisdom of the World Pollutes and Divides

I. The wisdom of the cross and a charitable introduction (1:1-9)

A. The writer (1:1)

1. The human author[1]
   - a. *His name*
   - b. *His office*
   - c. *His authority*
   - d. *His amanuensis/secretary (cf. Acts 18:17)*
2. The divine Author (2 Tim. 3:16; 2 Pet. 1:21; 3:15-16)

B. The recipients (1:2)

1. The original recipients (cf. Acts 18:1-18; 19:1)
   - a. *The church and their city*
   - b. *Their holy position and calling*
   - c. *The wider audience*
2. The current recipients (2 Tim. 3:16; cf. 2 Pet. 3:15-16)

C. The requisite greeting (1:3)

1. The salutation of grace and peace
2. The Source of grace and peace

E. The remarkable thanksgiving [for a troubled church] (1:4-9)

1. For the grace given to the church (v. 4)
   - a. *Grateful always (v. 4a)*
   - b. *Grateful to God (v. 4b)*
   - c. *Grateful for the grace given to the church in Christ Jesus (4c)*
2. For the gifts given to the church (v. 5-9)
   - a. *Enriched spiritually in everything (v. 5)*
   - b. *Evidence of conversion (v. 6)*
   - c. *Every spiritual gift (v. 7a)*
   - d. *Eagerly awaiting the revelation of Christ (v. 7b)*
   - e. *Enduring to the end because of God's faithfulness (v. 8-9)*
     - i. Guaranteed blameless because of Christ (v. 8)
     - ii. Guaranteed fellowship with Christ, because of God (v. 9)

---

[1] For a biblical biography of the Apostle Paul see Acts 7:58; 8:1; 9:1-30; 11:25-30; 12:25-28:31; 1 Cor. 15:30-32; 2 Cor. 6:4-5; 11:23-30; Gal. 1:13-2:16; Phil. 3:4-14; 2 Thes. 3:8

II. The wisdom of the cross and Christian ministers (1:10-4:31)

A. The report of divisions over Christian ministers (1:10-17)

1. The call to unity is vital in the wake of divisions (1:10-12)
    a. *The call for unity (v. 10)*
        i. The authority and basis of the call for unity (v. 10a)
        ii. The agreement necessary for Christian unity (v. 10b)
    b. *The communique from Chloe's people (v. 11-12)*
        i. The source (v. 11a)
        ii. The strife (v. 11b)
        iii. The separation (v. 12)
            aa. Introduced (v. 12a)
            bb. Illustrated (v. 12b)
                - I am of Paul
                - I of Apollos
                - I of Cephas
                - I of Christ
2. The cross of Christ saves and unifies—cleaving to men separates and undermines the gospel (1:13-17)
    a. *The probing questions (v. 13)*
        i. Has Christ been divided?
        ii. Was Paul crucified for you?
        iii. Were you baptized in the name of Paul?
    b. *The priority of the cross of Christ (v. 14-17)*
        i. The symbol of baptism cannot save (v. 14-17a)
            aa. Paul's relief at not having baptized many (v. 14-15)
                - The relief expressed in praise (v. 14a)
                - The recall of the exceptions (v. 14b)
                - The reason—no one can say they were identifying with Paul (v. 15)
            bb. Paul's remembrance that reveals the symbolic nature of baptism (v. 16-17a)
                - A further recollection (v. 16a)
                - A final rejoinder (v. 16b)
                - A fundamental calling to preach the gospel (v. 17a)
        ii. The proclamation of the gospel is God's means of unleashing the saving power of the cross (v. 17b)
            aa. The priority of preaching the gospel
            bb. The power is in the message not the messenger or the delivery

B. The rebuke of divisions over Christian ministers (1:18-4:5)

1. Divisions reveal a misunderstanding of the message of the gospel (1:18-3:4)

   a. *The message of the gospel destroys the wisdom of the world (1:18-2:5)*

      i. The power of the cross contradicts the pride and wisdom of the world (v. 18-25)

         aa. The word of the cross is a matter of life and death (v.18-21)

         - It reveals your spiritual condition (v. 18 19)

           Folly or faith—dying or being delivered (v. 18)

           Judicially blinded or joyously believing (v. 19)

         - It requires faith and reveals the foolishness of human wisdom (v. 20-21)

           The wisdom of the world is inadequate for salvation (v. 20)

           The Word of the cross *is* salvation for those who believe (v. 21)

         bb. The weakness of God is stronger than the wisdom of men (v. 22-25)

         - The wisdom of men (v. 22)

           Seeking for signs

           Searching for wisdom

         - The weakness of God (v. 23-25)

           Christ crucified—a stumbling block or silly to the unbelieving (v. 23)

           Christ crucified—salvation to the called (v. 24)

           Christ crucified—wiser than men, stronger than men (v. 25)

      ii. The people God has chosen condemns the pride and wisdom of the world (v. 26-31)

         aa. Examine the sinners called of God in Corinth (v. 26)

         - Not many wise according to the flesh
         - Not many mighty
         - Not many noble

         bb. Examine the sovereign choice of God in summary (v. 27-29)

         - God chooses the foolish
         - God chooses the weak
         - God chooses the nobodies (v. 28)
         - God chooses so that no one may boast before Him (v. 29)

         cc. Examine the sufficiency of God's provision in Christ (v. 30)

         - God's doing

- God's wisdom
- God's righteousness
- God's sanctification
- God's redemption

dd. Exalt the supremacy of God and God's wisdom in the cross of Christ (v. 31)

iii. The preaching of the cross converts people by the power of God rather than the wisdom of men (v. 1-5)

aa. The message that converts sinners (v. 1-2)

- The testimony of God rather than human eloquence (v. 1)
- The teaching of Jesus Christ's Person and work (v. 2)

bb. The manner that commends God's saving power rather than men's wisdom (v. 3-5)

- Reverence and humility (v. 3)
- Revealing the Spirit-inspired Word (v. 4)
- Recognizing sovereignty elicits faith, not the wisdom of men (v. 5)

b. The message of the gospel declares the wisdom of God (2:6-3:4)

i. God's wisdom is *not* revealed through natural means (v. 6-9)

aa. God's wisdom is recognized only by those who are mature (v. 6a)

bb. God's wisdom does not rise from the natural realm (v. 6b)

cc. God's wisdom is referenced as an eternal plan (v. 7)

dd. God's wisdom was not recognized by the rulers of this age (v. 8)

ee. God's wisdom is revealed as a gift to those who love Him (v. 9)

ii. God's wisdom *is* revealed through God's Spirit (v. 10-13)

aa. God's Spirit alone makes known God's wisdom (v. 10a)

bb. God's Spirit alone knows God's wisdom (v. 10b-11)

cc. God's Spirit makes known God's Word to God's people (v. 12)

dd. God's Spirit makes known God's Word to God's people through the Apostles (v. 13)

iii. God's wisdom is received only by those who are receptive to God's Spirit (2:14-3:4)

aa. God's wisdom is rejected by the natural man/unbeliever (v. 14)

- Because it is foolishness to him
- Because he cannot understand it
- Because it is spiritually appraised, and he has not been born of the Spirit

bb. God's wisdom is received by the spiritual man/Spirit-filled believer (v. 15-16)

- Because a Spirit-indwelled person can discern truth, though the world does not recognize it (v. 15)
- Because he is illumined by the Spirit of God (v. 16)

cc. God's wisdom is not received well by the carnal/immature believer (v. 1-4)

- The brethren at Corinth were babies in Christ (v. 1)
- The babe in Christ/spiritually immature cannot digest the truth of God's Word well (v. 2)
- The barometer of immaturity is the presence of jealousy, strife, and divisions (v. 3-4)

  The world is driven by jealousy and strife (v. 3)

  The world is driven by divisions (v. 4)

2. Divisions reveal a misunderstanding of the role of ministers of the gospel (3:5-4:5)

a. Ministers of the gospel serve as workers in God's field (v. 5-9)

i. Ministers are servants of salvation—the Lord is sovereign over salvation (v. 5-6)

aa. The servants—Apollos, Paul (v. 5a)

bb. The Sovereign—the Lord (v. 5b)

cc. The servants—Apollos, Paul (v. 6a)

dd. The Sovereign—God (v. 6b)

ii. Ministers are powerless in and of themselves—God is Potentate alone over His people (v. 7-9)

aa. The servants compared to the Sovereign (v. 7)

bb. The unity of the servants and the uniqueness of their reward (v. 8)

cc. The fellow workers and the field explained (v. 9)

b. Ministers of the gospel serve as workers on God's building (v. 10-23)

i. God will evaluate each minister's work (v. 10-15)

aa. The wise master builder and the foundation of true ministry (v. 10-11)

- The start of the work by the master builder (v. 10a)
- The sub-contractors' work in ministry (v. 10b)
- The scrupulous care needed in ministry (v. 10c)
- The sole foundation for ministry (v. 11)

bb. The work of the ministry and the test of true ministry (v. 12-15)

- The illustration of imperishable vs. perishable materials (v. 12)
- The inspection of each man's ministry (v. 13)

- The inheritance of the faithful ministry (v. 14)
- The inglorious but merciful result of a perishable ministry (v. 15)

ii. God will execute vengeance on those who vandalize God's building (v. 16-17)

aa. Recognize that the church is God's dwelling (v. 16)

bb. Recognize that vengeance will come on those who vandalize God's dwelling (v. 17)

iii. God will exalt the humble and humble the proud—so that He alone is exalted (v. 18-23)

aa. God exalts the humble and humbles the proud (v. 18-20)

- The warning—don't be deceived by pride (v. 18)
- The Word of God that confirms this (v. 19-20)

  Job 5:13 (v. 19)

  Psalm 94:11 (v. 20)

bb. God alone is worthy of our boasting (v. 21-23)

- Let no one boast in men (v. 21a)
- Let us examine the magnitude of our blessing in Christ (v. 21a-22)
- Let God alone through Christ be our boast (v. 23)

c. Ministers of the gospel serve as waiters of God's wisdom (4:1-5)

i. The proper view of Christian ministers (v. 1)

ii. The personal responsibility of Christian ministers (v. 2)

iii. The proper judgment of Christian ministers (v. 3-5)

aa. The examination of men is partial at best (v. 3-4a)

bb. The examination of the Lord is preeminent and perfect (v. 4b-5)

C. The remedy for divisions over Christian ministers (4:6-21)

1. Learn that extra-biblical judgements lead to pride rather than humility (4:6-13)

a. The purpose of the preceding comparison between Paul and Apollos (v. 6)

b. The perspective of self-grandeur rather than gratefulness and future glory (v. 7-8)

i. God's gifts should lead to gratefulness not self-grandeur (v. 7)

ii. God's coming Kingdom should lead to hope for future glory not haughtiness in the church (v. 8-13)

aa. The condescending self-grandeur of the Corinthian church (v. 8a)

bb. The contrasting selflessness of the apostles (v. 8b-13)

- The exaltation of the Kingdom is still future (v. 8b)

- The example of the apostles reveals the glory of humility to men and angels (v. 9)
- The example of the apostles should humble the Corinthians church (v. 10)
- The example of the apostles' hope should be evident by what they endure now (v. 11-13)

  Poverty (v. 11)

  Persecution (v. 12ab)

  Perseverance in hope (v. 12c-13)

2. Learn to imitate Paul's apostolic example (4:14-17)
   - *a. His example—love (v. 14-16)*
     - i. Paul wrote not to shame or embarrass (v. 14a)
     - ii. Paul wrote to exhort and encourage in love (v. 14b)
     - iii. Paul was not just a tutor but a father in the faith (v. 15)
   - *b. His emissary—Timothy (v. 17)*
     - i. Timothy was a faithful and beloved example of Paul's ministry (v. 17a)
     - ii. Timothy was a faithful teacher of Paul's doctrine (v. 17b)
3. Learn to humble yourself before God rather than be humbled by His discipline (4:18-21)
   - *a. God will surely reveal the truth about our pride (v 18-20)*
     - i. Pride thinks it will never be humbled (v. 18)
     - ii. Power is revealed in humility not proud talk (v. 19-20)
       - aa. God will expose the empty words of the proud (v. 19)
       - bb. God's kingdom will not be filled with haughty talkers, but rather the humble who walk in His power (v. 20)
   - *b. God will surely humble His erring people (v. 21)*
     - i. The type of training/discipline is dependent on the response of His people (v. 21a)
     - ii. Tough training is for those who will not humble themselves upon hearing the Word of God (v. 21b)
     - iii. Tenderness and love await those who humble themselves upon hearing the Word of God (v. 21c)

III. The wisdom of the cross and Christian morality (5:1-6:20)

A. The church must deal with unrepentant sin (5:1-13)

1. The particular case of church discipline detailed (5:1-8)
   - *a. The appalling report—incestuous immorality of a church member (v. 1)*
   - *b. The arrogant response of the Corinthians Church—insensitivity to sin and inactivity (v. 2)*
   - *c. The apostolic response—intense interest in the purity of the church and well-being of the offender (v. 3-8)*
     - i. Such sin must be dealt with immediately (v. 3)

ii. Such sin must be dealt with authoritatively (v. 4-5)
    aa. In the name and power of our Lord Jesus (v. 4)
    bb. With the motive of love and the ultimate restoration of the offender (v. 5)
        - No more spiritual safety within the body of Christ
        - Not wanting him to perish but to be saved

iii. Such sin must be viewed as affecting the whole church (v. 6-7)
    aa. Tolerance of such sin is toxic (v. 6)
    bb. Taking action is true to the gospel (v. 7)

iv. Such sin must be dealt with appropriately (v. 8)
    aa. Deal with sin (v. 8a)
    bb. Not in wickedness in malice (v. 8b)
    cc. But with sincerity and truth (v. 8c)

2. The proper realm of church discipline clarified (5:9-13)

a. The clarification (v. 9-13a)

i. The prior instruction—separate from immoral people (v. 9)

ii. The particular clarification about separation (v. 10-13a)
    aa. This is not about separation from non-believers (v. 10)
    bb. This is about separation from a so-called brother living in sin (v. 11)

iii. The proper perspective on dealing with immoral people (v. 12-13a)
    aa. Those within the church are subject to the judgement of the church (v. 12)
    bb. Those outside the church God will judge (v. 13a)

b. The command—remove the wicked man from the church (v. 13b)

B. The church must deal with disputes among its members (6:1-8)

1. The reasons for not taking disputes before unbelieving judges (6:1-4)

a. Believers will judge the world—so why let unbelievers judge between believers now (v. 1-2)

i. The incredulous question (v. 1)

ii. The instructive questions (v. 2)

b. Believers will judge the angelic realm—so why let unbelievers judge believers in this life (v. 3-4)

i. The incredible reality—we will judge angels (v. 3)

ii. The incisive rebuke (v. 4)

c. Believers bring shame upon the church when they take other believers to unbelieving courts (v. 5-6)

i. It brings into question the wisdom of believers (v. 5)

ii. It brings into question the family relationship we have as believers (v. 6)

2. The results of taking disputes to unbelieving judges (6:5-8)
    a. *Dishonor in the realm of wisdom and fellowship (v. 5-6)*
        i. It brings into question the wisdom of believers (v. 5)
        ii. It brings into question the fellowship we have as believers (v. 6)
    b. *Defeat in the realm of witness and faith (v. 7)*
    c. *Damage in the realm of justice and love (v. 8)*

C. The church must discern that liberty does not lead to lawlessness—freedom does not lead to fornication (6:9-20)

1. The reminder concerning righteousness and the gospel that cleansed you from all unrighteousness (6:9-11)
    a. *Do not be deceived—the unrighteous will not inherit the kingdom of God (v. 9-10)*
        i. The rhetorical question (v. 9a)
        ii. The imperative—do not be deceived (v. 9b)
        iii. The illustrative list (v. 9c-10ab)
        iv. The repeated emphasis (v. 10c)
    b. *Delight in what God has done for you through the gospel (v. 11)*
        i. Remember who you were (v. 11a)
        ii. Remember what God has done for you (v. 11b)
            aa. You were washed
            bb. You were sanctified
            cc. You were justified
        iii. Remember how God accomplished this for you (v. 11c)
            aa. In the name of the Lord Jesus Christ
            bb. In the Spirit of God
2. The reality about our freedom in Christ (6:12-20)
    a. *Freedom is only freedom if it is exercised to keep you from the bondage of sin (v. 12)*
        i. You must use your freedom to benefit from it (v. 12a)
        ii. You must use your freedom to avoid becoming a slave to your own desires (v. 12b)
    b. *Freedom does not lead to fornication (v. 13-20)*
        i. The desires of the body are temporal (v. 13a)
        ii. The destiny of the body is eternal (v. 13b-14)
            aa. The body was not made for the purpose of immorality, but for the Lord (v. 13b)
            bb. The body will be resurrected as was the Lord (v. 14)

iii. The determinative factor for the use of the body is union with Christ (v. 15-20)

aa. Remember you are part of Christ's body (v. 15-17)

- A part of Christ's body should never be joined to the body of a prostitute (v. 15)
- One who is joins himself to a prostitute has an intimate union with her (v. 16)
- One who joins himself to the Lord has an intimate union spiritually with Him (v. 17)

bb. Repeatedly flee immorality—drunkenness and gluttony are sins of too much of something that is not sin in and of itself, but immorality is always sin, even in moderation (v. 18)

cc Remember that God the Holy Spirit dwells in you and owns you (v. 19)

dd. Remember that you were redeemed to glorify God in your body (v. 20)

IV. The wisdom of the cross and Christian marriage (7:1-40)

A. Serve one another sexually within marriage (7:1-7)

1. The confusion about abstinence in marriage expressed (7:1)

a. The correspondence cited (v. 1a)

b. The question stated (v. 1b)

2. The command concerning sexual relations in marriage explained (7:2-6)

a. The concern over abstinence in marriage (v. 2a)

b. The call to "have" one another within the marriage relationship (v. 2b)

c. The commitment to serve one another (v. 3)

d. The correct perspective on sexual oneness (v. 4)

e. The command (v. 5ac)

i. Stop depriving one another (v. 5a)

ii. So Satan will not tempt you because of a lack of self-control (v. 5c)

f. The concession (v. 5b-6)

i. For a short time, abstinence in marriage is permissible (v. 5b)

ii. For the purpose of prayer (v. 5b)

iii. Finalize this short abstinence by coming back together again (v. 5b)

iv. Forsaking sexual activity for the sake of prayer is a concession not a command (v. 6)

3. The comment about the gifts of singleness and marriage expressed (7:7)

a. Singleness is to be highly esteemed (v. 7a)

b. Singleness and marriage are both gifts from God (v. 7b)

B. Stay as you were called in Christ, whether married or single (7:8-24)

1. Stay as you are if you are single unless you must get married (7:8-9)
    - *a. Remaining single is an excellent choice—as the Apostle Paul's life illustrates (v. 8)*
    - *b. Requiring singleness is harmful—marriage is an honorable option (v. 9)*
2. Stay married if you have a believing spouse (7:10-11)
    - *a. Remain married to your spouse (v. 10)*
    - *b. Return to your spouse or remain single if you do get divorced (v. 11)*
3. Stay married if you have an unbelieving spouse who desires to remain married (7:12-16)
    - *a. Stay married if your unbelieving spouse desires to remain joined in marriage (v. 12-13)*
        - i. The Apostolic authority (v. 12a)
        - ii. The agreeable unbelieving wife (v. 12b)
        - iii. The agreeable unbelieving husband (v. 13)
    - *b. Staying married in this situation will bring God's sanctifying benefits to the entire family (v. 14)*
    - *c. Staying married is not required if the unbelieving spouse does not want to stay joined in marriage (v. 15)*
4. Stay as you were called in Christ—the principle stated, illustrated, and clarified (7:17-24)
    - *a. The principle stated—stay as you were called (v. 17)*
    - *b. The picture of circumcision (v. 18-19)*
        - i. Remain a Jew if you came to Christ as a Jew (v. 18a)
        - ii. Remain a Gentile if you came to Christ as a Gentile (v. 18b)
        - iii. Obey God's Word as a believer—whether Jew or Gentile (v. 19)
    - *c. The principle restated—stay as you were called (v. 20)*
    - *d. The picture of slave and free—a clarification (v. 21-23)*
        - i. Remain a slave unless you are able to obtain your freedom (v. 21)
        - ii. Remember that a believer who is a slave is free in the Lord (v. 22a)
        - iii. Remember that a believer who is free is Christ's slave (v. 22b)
        - iv. Remain free and don't become a slave of men—remember you were bought with a price (v. 23)
    - *e. The principle restated again—stay as you were called (v. 24)*

C. Stay focused on serving Christ whether married or single (7:25-40)

1. The recommendation of singleness and to remain as you are--single or married (7:25-35)
   a. *Respected advice rather than a requirement of the Lord (v. 25)*
   b. *Remain as you are—whether single or married (v. 26-28)*
      i. The reason (v. 26)
      ii. The repeated emphasis (v. 27)
      iii. The reality of marriage in a fallen world (v. 28)
         aa. Certainly it is no sin to get married (v. 28ab)
         bb. Certainly there will be trouble in this life (v. 28c)
   c. *Reckon the eternal as far more important than the temporal (v. 29-31)*
      i. Our spouse must not be our ultimate focus (v. 29)
      ii. Our circumstances must not be our ultimate focus (v. 30a)
      iii. Our possessions must not be our ultimate focus (v. 30b)
      iv. Our activities in this world must not be our ultimate focus (v. 31)
   d. *Restrict your ultimate devotion to the Lord and not your spouse (v. 32-35)*
      i. Paul's reason for recommending singleness (v. 32a)
      ii. Paul's reasoning in recommending singleness (v. 32b-34)
         aa. The devoted pursuit of a believer who is single (v. 32b, 34b)
         bb. The divided pursuit of a believer who is married (v. 33, 34a, 34c)
      iii. Paul's reason for recommending singleness restated (v. 35)
2. The recommendation for those who are engaged [or a father who has a daughter contemplating marriage] (7:36-38)
   a. *If there is an overriding desire for marriage, then get married (v. 36)*
   b. *If there is not an overriding desire for marriage, then don't (v. 37)*
   c. *It must be remembered that Christian marriage is good—and in some ways, singleness can be even better (v. 38)*
3. The requirement for those who are married and the recommendation to those who spouses have died (7:39-40)
   a. *The requirement of marriage—till death do us part (v. 39a)*
   b. *The right to remarry is open—only another believer (v. 39b)*
   c. *The recommendation from the Apostle Paul—remain single (v. 40)*

V. The wisdom of the cross and Christian liberty (8:1-11:1)

A. The instruction concerning our freedom in Christ (8:1-13)

1. Knowing the truth is not enough—it must be governed by love (8:1-3)
    - *a. A response to a question about our freedom (v. 1a)*
    - *b. A rebuke of knowledge without love regarding our freedom (v. 1b-2)*
    - *c. A relationship of love with God is the key to our freedom (v. 3)*
2. Knowing the truth *is* extremely important (8:4-8)
    - *a. The truth about an idol—it is neither a god nor alive (v. 4a)*
    - *b. The truth about God—He alone is God (v. 4b)*
    - *c. The truth about idolatry—there are many so-called gods and lords (v. 5)*
    - *d. The truth about saving faith—there is only One God and One Lord (v. 6)*
    - *e. The truth about the conscience—it is informed by knowledge (v. 7)*
    - *f. The truth about food—it can neither commend nor condemn before God (v. 8)*
3. Knowing the truth is sin if it is not governed by love (8:9-13)
    - *a. The caution concerning the exercise of your freedom (v. 9-12)*
        - i. Your freedom can be a stumbling block to others (v. 9)
        - ii. Your freedom can entice others to violate their conscience (v. 10)
        - iii. Your freedom would then actually be sin against a brother for whom Christ died (v. 11)
        - iv. Your freedom would ultimately be sin against Christ (v. 12)
    - *b. The care you must take when contemplating the use of your freedom (v. 13)*

B. The illustration concerning our freedom in Christ—the life of Paul (9:1-27)

1. The "rights" or freedoms Paul chose to forgo (9:1-14)
    - *a. The rights/freedoms of an Apostle examined (v. 1-7)*
        - i. The "free" position of Apostle (v. 1-3)
            - aa. The provocative questions (v. 1)
            - bb. The proof of Paul's authority as Apostle—the Corinthians church (v. 2-3)
        - ii. The "freedom" of partaking in food and drink (v. 4)
        - iv. The "freedom" of partnering with a spouse (v. 5)
        - v. The "freedom" of partaking of financial support (v. 6-7)
            - aa. The right to financial support implied (v. 6)
            - bb. The right to financial support illustrated (v. 7)
    - *b. The record of the Scripture confirms these rights (v. 8-14)*
        - i. The questions by way of introduction (v. 8)

- ii. The quotation and the clear instruction (v. 9-14)
  - aa. The quotation from Deuteronomy 25:4 (v. 9)
  - bb. The clear instruction (v. 9c-10)
  - cc. The consistent application (v. 11-12)
  - dd. The clear implication from the OT sacrificial system (v. 13-14)

2. The reason Paul chose to forgo those freedoms (9:15-18)

- *a. So that he might be a role model of integrity in ministry (v. 15)*
- *b. So that he might fulfill His responsibility (v. 16)*
- *c. So that he might receive a full reward (v. 17-18)*

3. The "rights" or freedoms Paul chose to freely exercise (9:19-27)

- *a. Freedom to serve everyone for the sake of the gospel (v. 19-23)*
  - i. Freedom to serve as a slave to all (v. 19)
  - ii. Freedom to serve Jews who are under the Law (v. 20)
  - iii. Freedom to serve Gentiles who are not under the Law (v. 21)
  - iv. Freedom to serve those who are weak concerning their "freedoms" (v. 22a)
  - v. Freedom to serve for the sake of the salvation of others (v. 22b)
- *b. Freedom to self-discipline and self-sacrifice for the sake of the reward of the gospel (v. 24-27)*
  - i. The analogy of running to win the prize (v. 24-25)
    - aa. Live out your freedoms with your eye on winning the prize (v. 24)
    - bb. Live out your freedoms knowing that the rewards are eternal (v. 25)
  - ii. The application of spiritual discipline to win the prize (v. 26-27)
    - aa. Don't let your "freedoms" let you drift off course or become lazy in the fight of faith (v. 26)
    - bb. Don't let your "freedoms" cause you to forfeit the honor given to those who win the prize (v. 27)

C. The idolatry to avoid that corrupts our freedom in Christ (10:1-33)

1. The biblical illustrations from the OT record (10:1-11)

- *a. Remember Israel's privileged position corporately did not exempt most of them from divine punishment (v. 1-5)*
  - i. Remember God's good gifts to Israel corporately (v. 1-4)
    - aa. They all benefited from God's miraculous presence and protection (v. 1)
    - bb. They all benefited from God's messenger—Moses (v. 2)
    - cc. They all benefited from God's manna (v. 3)
    - dd. They all benefited from God's Messiah (v. 4)

ii. Remember God's displeasure with most of them individually (v. 5)

b. Remember Israel's persistent idolatry in the face of God's good gifts (v. 6-11)

i. Freedom does not lead you to crave evil things (v. 6)

ii. Freedom does not lead you to into idolatry (v. 7)

iii. Freedom does not lead you to immorality (v. 8)

iv. Freedom does not lead you to test the Lord (v. 9)

v. Freedom does not lead you to dissatisfaction (v. 10)

vi. Freedom does not lead you to forget how God has dealt with His people in the past (v. 11)

2. The biblical imperatives from this NT epistle in light of Israel's history (10:12-11:1)

a. Take care as to where you stand with God (v. 12)

b. Take heed as you face temptation, and flee idolatry (v. 13-14)

i. Face temptation (v. 13)

aa. Remember it is common to man—your situation is not totally unique

bb. Remember the character of God

- Faithful
- Sovereign—will not allow you to be tempted beyond what you are able
- Compassionate—providing a way of escape, so that you may endure

ii. Flee idolatry (v. 14)

aa. Remember how to deal with temptation

bb. Remember that you are loved

cc. Remember to run

c. Take time to think about what your actions identify you with (v. 15-22)

i. The call to discernment (v. 15)

ii. The communion/identification involved in acts of worship (v. 16-18)

aa. The Lord's supper identifies believers with Christ (v. 16)

bb. The Lord's supper identifies believers with one another (v. 17)

cc. The Levitical priesthood is identified with its altar and sacrifices (v. 18)

iii. The conclusion—your actions in worship identify you either with God or idolatry (v. 19-22)

aa. Nothing created by God is inherently sinful in itself (v. 19)

bb. Nevertheless, spiritual realities are represented by our actions in worship (v. 20)

cc. Never confuse communion with pagan practice (v. 21-22)
- You cannot share the cup of Christ and the cup of demons (v. 21)
- You do not want to provoke All-mighty God to jealousy (v. 22)

d. *Take into account how your freedom will affect your neighbor and honor God (10:23-11:1)*

i. A slogan qualified (v. 23-24)

aa. All things are lawful (v. 23ac)

bb. Not all things profit or edify (v. 23bd)

cc. Selfishness is not freedom (v. 24)

ii. A scenario considered (v. 25-30)

aa. The freedom to eat of the Lord's creation (v. 25-27)
- As a consumer in the marketplace (v. 25)
- As a creature in God's good creation (v. 26)
- As a guest—not needing to question the host (v. 27)

bb. The forsaking of one's freedom for the sake of your neighbor's good and God's glory (v. 28-30)
- The conscience of the informant (v. 28)
- The concern for the informant's good (v. 29)
- The concern for your testimony for the glory of God (v. 30)

iii. A steadfast conviction and pursuit (v. 31-33)

aa. Glorify God in everything—even one's freedom (v. 31)

bb. Give no offence in your freedom—to Jew, Gentile or the church (v. 32)

cc. Glorify God by using your freedom to seek the salvation of all men—as Paul did (v. 33-11:1)
- Paul used his freedom to please others for the sake of gospel influence in their life (v. 33)
- Paul imitated Christ in this—so imitate Paul as He imitated Christ (11:1)

VI. The wisdom of the cross and Christian gender roles (11:2-16)

A. The proper order for worship explained (11:2-10)

1. Willing submission to apostolic instruction is to be praised (11:2)
2. Willing submission to God's order glorifies God's headship—but disregard brings dishonor (11:3-10)

a. *The proper perspective on headship and order (v. 3)*

i. Christ is the head of every man (v. 3a)

ii. Man is the head of a woman (v. 3b)

iii. God is the head of Christ (v. 3c)

b. *The problems that come from disregarding proper order and headship (v. 4-10)*

i. When a man disregards his proper role in worship it brings disgrace (v. 4)

ii. When a woman disregards her proper role in worship it brings disgrace (v. 5-6)

aa. Praying or prophesying with no symbol of authority on her head (v. 5)

bb. Prostitutes shaved their heads—similar shame belongs to those who refuse to submit to God's order (v. 6)

iii. Worship roles are reflected in the created order and glorify God in the angelic realm (v. 7-10)

aa. Man is the image and glory of God (v. 7ab)

bb. Woman is the glory of man (v. 7c)

cc. Woman originated from man (v. 8)

dd. Woman was created to be a helper suitable for man (v. 9)

ee. Angels are watching the worship of the church (v. 10)

B. The proper perspective on male/female equality asserted (11:11-12)

1. Mutual interdependence and equality asserted (11:11)
2. Mutual interdependence and equality affirmed (11:12)

C. The proper order for worship reaffirmed (11:13-16)

1. Most cultural norms affirm the proper order (11:13)
2. Men and women's hair affirm the proper order (11:14-15)

a. *The nature of men's hair growth (v. 14)*

b. *The nature of women's hair growth (v. 15)*

3. Make sure you submit to God's order of headship (11:16)

VII.The wisdom of the cross and communion/the Lord's Supper (11:17-34)

A. The rebuke of selfishness in regard to the Lord's Supper (11:17-22)

1. The problem summarized (11:17)

a. *Not praiseworthy*

b. *Not good*

2. The problem detailed (11:18-21)

a. *The people of the church were segmented/divided (v. 18-19)*

i. The report of divisions (v. 18)

ii. The result of divisions that could be deemed positive (v. 19)

   b. *The people of the church were selfish (v. 20-21)*
      i. A ceremony is not necessarily worship (v. 20)
      ii. A ceremony can actually be sin (v. 21)
3. The problem rebuked (11:22)
   a. *Think ahead (v. 22a)*
   b. *Think of others rather than yourself (v. 22b)*
   c. *Think about what is praiseworthy before God (v. 22c)*

B. The right practice and purpose of the Lord's Supper [commemoration, proclamation, anticipation] (11:23-26)

1. The practice of the Lord's Supper should be based on divine revelation (11:23a)
2. The purpose of the Lord's Supper includes commemoration, proclamation, and anticipation (11:23b-26)
   a. *The commemoration of the incarnation (v. 23b)*
   b. *The commemoration of the humiliation and substitution (v. 24)*
   c. *The commemorate of the ratification of the New Covenant in Jesus' blood (v. 25)*
   d. *The proclamation of the Lord's atonement (v. 26a)*
   e. *The anticipation of the Lord's return (v. 26b)*

C. The requirement of self-examination in regard to the Lord's Supper [self-examination] (11:27-32)

1. The call to self-examination (11:27-28)
   a. *Are you partaking of communion in an unworthy manner—i.e., without genuine care and concern for other believers? (v. 27a)*
   b. *If so, you are dishonoring Christ (v. 27b)*
   c. *If you pass the examination—celebrate the Lord's Supper (v. 28)*
2. The consequences of not judging oneself rightly (11:29-32)
   a. *Self-condemnation (v. 29)*
   b. *Sovereign discipline (v. 30-32)*
      i. In the form physical sickness and death (v. 30)
      ii. Is avoided when we examine ourselves rightly (v. 31)
      iii. Is for temporal training and mercy rather than eternal damnation (v. 32)

D. The requirement of selflessness in the practice of the Lord's Supper [unification] (11:33-34)

1. The command for mutual consideration (11:33)
   a. *Remember the relationship believers share (v. 33a)*
   b. *Recognize the reason we come together to eat (v. 33b)*
   c. *Respect God's command to wait for one another (v. 33c)*

2. The caution concerning a lack of preparation (11:34ab)
    - *a. Prepare yourself physically for worship (v. 34a)*
    - *b. Prepare yourself spiritually for worship (v. 34b)*
3. The call to teachability and flexibility in regard to worship (11:34c)

VIII. The wisdom of the cross and *charismata*/spiritual gifts (12:1-14:40)

A. Spiritual gifts should unify and build up the church—not divide and puff up (12:1-31)

1. The introductory principles concerning the gifts (12:1-3)
    - *a. Ignorance and idolatry must both be dealt with (v. 1-2)*
        - i. Ignorance is neither necessary nor desirable (v. 1)
        - ii. Idolatry in the past is evidence of a propensity toward spiritual ignorance (v. 2)
    - *b. Identifying the Source of the gifts and His sovereign purpose is essential (v. 3)*
        - i. The Spirit never denigrates the Person and work of Jesus (v. 3a)
        - ii. The Spirit is always the Source of a genuine profession of the Lordship of Jesus (v. 3b)
        - iii. The Spirit is supremely concerned with exalting Jesus as Lord (v. 3c)
2. The illustrative list demonstrating the diversity, yet unity of the gifts (12:4-11)
    - *a. Spiritual gifts reflect the diversity and unity of their Source—the Triune Godhead (v. 4-6)*
        - i. Diverse gifts—same Spirit (v. 4)
        - ii. Diverse ministries—same Lord (v. 5)
        - iii. Diverse effects—same God (v. 6)
    - *b. Spiritual gifts are diversely given for the unified good of God's people (v. 7-10)*
        - i. The Spirit gifts people for their unified good (v. 7)
        - ii. The Spirit gives differing gifts to different people (v. 8-10)
            - aa. Word of wisdom (v. 8a)
            - bb. Word of knowledge (v. 8b)
            - cc. Faith (v. 9a)
            - dd. Healing (v. 9b)
            - ee. Effecting of miracles (v. 10a)
            - ff. Prophecy (v. 10b)
            - gg. Distinguishing of spirits (v. 10c)
            - hh. Kinds of tongues (v. 10d)
            - ii. Interpretation of tongues (v. 10e)

c. *Spiritual gifts are distributed according to the Spirit's Sovereign wisdom and will (v. 11)*

3. The interdependent nature, yet individual uniqueness of the [gifted] body of Christ (12:12-31)

a. *The instruction concerning unity and diversity (v. 12-13)*

i. The instruction introduced by way of analogy (v. 12)

aa. The body has many members but is still one body (v. 12abc)

bb. The body of Christ has many members, but is still the one body of Christ (v. 12d)

ii. The instruction stated (v. 13)

aa. Unity in diversity is the work of the Spirit (v. 13a)

bb. Unity in diversity is seen in God's chosen (v. 13bc)

cc. Unity in diversity is the work of the Spirit (v. 13d)

b. *The illustration and instruction concerning unity and diversity (v. 14-26)*

i. The illustration introduced: The body is diverse, but interdependent (v. 14-17)

aa. The foot is not the hand, but is still an important part of the body (v. 15)

bb. The ear is not the eye, but is still an important part of the body (v. 16)

cc. Seeing, hearing, as well as the sense of smell are all important—but none of them can claim to be the whole body (v. 17)

ii. The instruction: God's sovereign will determines the giftedness of the body of Christ (v. 18-20)

aa. The will of God is determinative (v. 18)

bb. The wisdom of God is demonstrated (v. 19-20)

- It is apparent (v. 19)
- It is advantageous (v. 20)

iii. The illustration continued: The body parts need each other (v. 21-24a)

aa. The parts of the body need each other (v. 21-22)

bb. The "precious" or "private" parts of the body are honored by clothing or skeletal covering—but the public parts are not (v. 23-24a)

iv. The instruction: God's sovereign design calls for mutual care of the body of Christ among its members (v. 24b-26)

aa. The sovereign design (v. 24b-25)

bb. The suffering or success of one part affects the whole (v. 26)

c. *The instruction concerning the diversity within the unified body of Christ (v. 27-30)*

i. The illustration plainly applied (v. 27)

ii. The instruction concerning the diversity of gifts (v. 28-30)

aa. The sample list of gifts used as an example (v. 28)

- Apostles
- Prophets
- Teachers
- Miracles
- Healings
- Helps
- Administration
- Tongues

bb. The set reality that not everyone has the same gift (v. 29-30)

- Not all are Apostles
- Not all are prophets
- Not all are teachers
- Not all work miracles
- Not all have gifts of healing
- Not all speak in tongues
- Not all interpret

d. *The introduction of something more important and glorious than spiritual gifts (v. 31)*

i. The intense desire for greater gifts (v. 31a)

ii. The introduction of a greater way (v. 31b)

B. Spiritual gifts should manifest faith, hope, and love—not self-exaltation (13:1-13)

1. The hypothetical examples of ultimate giftedness without love (13:1-3)

a. *Without love, my tongues are nothing but a loud distraction (v. 1)*

b. *Without love, my prophecy, knowledge, and faith are of no account (v. 2)*

c. *Without love, my self-sacrificial service gains me nothing (v. 3)*

2. The higher essential attributes of love (13:4-13)

a. *Love's excellence described (v. 4-8a)*

i. Love suffers long [and waits expectantly] (v. 4)

ii. Love is kind [and good] (v. 4)

iii. Love is not envious [or covetous] (v. 4)

iv. Love is not self-aggrandizing (v. 4)

v. Love is not puffed up with pride (v. 4)

vi. Love does not act indecently [shamefully] (v. 5)

vii. Love is not selfish (v. 5)

viii. Love is not easily irritated (v. 5)

ix. Love does not keep a record of wrongs suffered (v. 5)

x. Love does not rejoice in what is not right (v. 6)

xi. Love rejoices in the truth (v. 6)

xii. Love covers all things (v. 7)

xiii. Love believes [and trust God in] all things (v. 7)

xiv. Love hopes [anticipates the fulfillment of God's promises in] all things (v. 7)

xv. Love remains standing under all things (v. 7)

xvi. Love never ends (v. 8a)

b. Love's exceeding greatness declared (v. 8b-13)

i. The spiritual gifts are temporal and temporary (v. 8b-12)

aa. The gifts are temporary (v. 8bcd)

- The gift of prophecies will be abolished (v. 8b)
- The gift of tongues will cease (v. 8c)
- The gift of knowledge will be abolished (v. 8d)

bb. The gifts are transitional and temporal (v. 9-12)

- The prophetic gifts are only partial and not complete (v. 9)
- The perfect/complete will put an end to the partial (v. 10)
- The picture of a child becoming a man and no longer needing childhood helps (v. 11)
- The picture of a mirror of burnished metal to see in contrast to perfect clarity (v. 12)

ii. The supreme virtues are eternal—faith, hope, and love—and the greatest is love (v. 13)

C. Spiritual gifts should prioritize the proclamation of truth to others in an orderly manner—not pacification of self (14:1-40)

1. The priority of prophecy over the gift of tongues (14:1-12)

a. Pursue love—and prioritize prophecy in your zeal for spiritual gifts (v. 1-5)

i. Constantly pursue love (v. 1a)

ii. Consciously prioritize prophecy in your zeal for spiritual gifts (v. 1bc-5)

aa. The command (v. 1bc)

bb. The comparison of prophecy and tongues (v. 2-5)

- One remains a mystery (v. 2)
- One reveals a message of edification to others (v. 3)

- One edifies self (v. 4a)
- One edifies the church (v. 4b)
- One is greater but both are desirable gifts (v. 5)

b. *Practice love as you use your spiritual gifts (v. 6-12)*

i. How will your speaking in tongues edify others? (v. 6)

ii. How will your speaking in tongues be understood by others? (v. 7-11)

aa. The illustration of a flute or harp—there must be a recognizable melody (v. 7)

bb. The illustration of a bugle—there must be an understood sound/signal (v. 8)

cc. The instruction and application concerning tongues (v. 9-11)

- Others need to be able to understand (v. 9)
- Other languages have meaning (v. 10)
- Other languages not understood alienate rather than edify (v. 11)

iii. Have it as your goal to edify the church as you use your spiritual gifts (v. 12)

2. The priority of interpretation when exercising the gift of tongues (14:13-19)

a. *The command to the tongue speaker—pray for the gift of interpretation (v. 13)*

b. *The concerns—personal understanding and the edification of others (v. 14-17)*

i. It is an issue of mental fruitfulness (v. 14)

ii. It is an issue of volition/choice (v. 15)

iii. It is an issue of concern for others (v. 16-17)

c. *The clear example of the Apostle Paul concerning the gift of tongues (v. 18-19)*

i. An appreciation for the gift of tongues (v. 18)

ii. An ardent pursuit of the edification of the church over self (v. 19)

3. The purpose and proper use of the gifts of tongues and prophecy (14:20-28)

a. *The plea to mature thinking (v. 20)*

b. *The purpose of the gifts of tongues and prophecy (v. 21-25)*

i. The public use of the gift of tongues without interpretation serves to confirm unbelievers in their unbelief (v. 21, 22a, 23)

aa. In Isaiah 28 the tongues signaled an unedified, unbelieving people's further alienation from God (v. 21)

bb. In using tongues without interpretation, it signals unedified, unbelieving people that will be further alienated from God (v. 22a) cc. In using tongues without interpretation, those without the gift of interpretation and unbelievers will only be further alienated from God and His people (v. 23)

ii. The public use of the gift of prophecy serves to correct and confirm God's glory to both believers and non-believers (v. 22b, 24, 25)

aa. Prophecy signals God's gracious call to believe and be restored (v. 22b)

bb. Prophecy brings conviction to the ungifted and the unbeliever (v. 24)

cc. Prophecy fosters worship and testifies of God's presence (v. 25)

c. *The proper use of the gift of tongues (v. 26-28)*

i. The repeated emphasis for all spiritual gifts—order and edification (v. 26)

ii. The requirements for the public use of tongues (v. 27-28)

aa. There may be three at most (v. 27a)

bb. There must be order, not simultaneous speaking (v. 27b)

cc. There must be an interpreter (v. 27c)

dd. There must be no public use if no interpreter (v. 28)

4. The proper ordering of the prophetic gifts (v. 14:29-40)

a. *The regulations concerning the use of prophecy in the church (v. 29-33a)*

i. To be limited—two or three per service (v. 29a)

ii. To be evaluated by others (v. 29b)

iii. To be yielding to new revelation during the service (v. 30)

iv. To be orderly—one by one, not simultaneously given (v. 31-33a)

aa. Must be one by one (v. 31a)

bb. Must be for the edification of others (v. 31b)

cc. Must be self-controlled in presentation and timing (v. 32)

dd. Must reflect God's character—order and peace, not confusion (v. 33)

b. *The role of women in regard to the use of prophecy in the church (v. 33b-38)*

i. The restriction: women are not to prophesy during the service (v. 33b-36)

aa. The scope of this mandate—all the churches (v. 33b)

bb. The silence in regard to prophecy in the church (v. 34-35)

- The directive (v. 34)
- The direction concerning instruction (v. 35)

cc. The strong censure of Corinthians laxity in this area (v. 36)

- ii. The requirement: agreement with apostolic authority on this matter (v. 37-38)
  - aa. Recognition of apostolic authority is a prerequisite for the godly (v. 37)
  - bb. Recognize that there is no divine recognition for those who reject apostolic authority (v. 38)

c. *The reminder of priorities and propriety in the use of spiritual gifts (v. 39-40)*

- i. The priority of prophecy (v. 39a)
- ii. The permission of tongues (v. 39b)
- iii. The propriety and orderliness of exercising the gifts in worship (v. 40)

IX. The wisdom of the cross and the Christian's resurrection (15:1-58)

A. The resurrection is certain (15:1-34)

1. Christ's resurrection is the crowning testimony of the gospel (15:1-11)

a. *Salvation rests entirely on the gospel message (v. 1-2)*

- i. The gospel is revealed in special revelation (v. 1a)
- ii. The gospel comes through biblical proclamation (v. 1b)
- iii. The gospel is received simply by faith (v. 1c)
- iv. The gospel provides a sure foundation (v. 1d)
- v. The gospel is the means salvation (v. 2a)
- vi. The gospel requires genuine faith (v. 2b)

b. *Scripture reveals the essentials of the gospel message (v. 3-4)*

- i. Christ's gospel is of primary importance (v. 3a)
- ii. <u>Christ died for our sins</u> according to the Scriptures [incarnation and substitutionary death/atonement] (v. 3b)
- iii. <u>Christ was buried</u> [literal, physical death] (v. 4a)
- iv. <u>Christ was raised on the third day</u> according to the Scriptures [literal physical resurrection] (v. 4b)

c. *Substantial eyewitness testimony confirms Christ's resurrection and affirms the gospel message (v. 5-11)*

- i. He appeared to Cephas (v. 5a)
- ii. He appeared to the Twelve (v. 5b)
- iii. He appeared to more than 500 at one time (v. 6)
- iv. He appeared to James (v. 7a)
- v. He appeared to all the apostles (v. 7b)
- vi. He appeared to Paul (v. 8-10)
  - aa. The last of the eyewitnesses (v. 8)
  - bb. The least of the apostles (v. 9)
  - cc. The laborer by God's grace (v. 10)

   - vii. He was accepted by faith through the preaching of these eyewitnesses (v. 11)

2. Christ's resurrection the key to the gospel and our resurrection (15:12-34)

- a. *The resurrection is the key to our salvation (v. 12-19)*
  - i. If Christ has not risen your faith is futile (v. 12-14)
    - aa. The contradiction—professed believers saying there is no resurrection from the dead (v. 12)
    - bb. The connection—if no resurrection, then Christ has not been raised (v. 13)
    - cc. The conclusion—if no resurrection, then your faith is futile/empty/full of nothing (v. 14)
  - ii. If Christ has not risen the gospel is false (v. 15-16)
    - aa. The conclusion—the eyewitnesses would be deceivers (v. 15)
    - bb. The connection—if no resurrection, then Christ has not risen (v. 16)
  - iii. If Christ has not risen your faith is fatal (v. 17-19)
    - aa. The consideration—if Christ is not raised then you are still in your sins (v. 17)
    - bb. The conclusion concerning death—those who die perish with the damned (v. 18)
    - cc. The conclusion concerning life—those who live for Christ now are to be most pitied as dreadfully deceived (v. 19)
- b. *The resurrection is the key to God's kingdom rule (v. 20-28)*
  - i. The representative headship of Christ and the first fruits of the resurrection [The first phase of the resurrection (first fruits)—Christ] (v. 20-22)
    - aa. The reality—Christ has been raised as the first fruits of the resurrection (v. 20)
    - bb. The representative headship (v. 21-22)
      - By man came death (v. 21a)
      - By man came resurrection from the death (v. 21b)
      - All in Adam die (v. 22a)
      - All in Christ will be made alive (v. 22b)
  - ii. The resurrection at the rapture of the church [The second phase of the resurrection (harvest)—the church] (v. 23)
    - aa. There is an order in which the resurrection will take place (v. 23a)
    - bb. The Christ's resurrection is first (v. 23b)
    - cc. Those in Christ will follow (v. 23c)

iii. The reign of Christ, the final defeat of death, and recognition of the supremacy of God over all [The third phase of the resurrection (the unsaved dead of all the ages) after the reign of Christ and before the eternal state] (v. 24-28)

aa. Then the end—the resurrection of unbelievers unto final judgment, after Christ has reigned and abolished all rule and authority (v. 24-25)

- "Then the end" follows the order of the resurrection—Christ first, then the church, then unbelievers (v. 24a)
- The resurrection of unbelievers will happen after Christ has reigned supreme and abolished all of God's enemies (v. 24b-25)

bb. The destroyer of the body—death—will itself be destroyed by the resurrection (v. 26)

cc. The Son will then present the Kingdom to the Father—and God will be all in all (v. 27-28)

- The functional submission of the Son as man's representative head (v. 27)
- The future Trinitarian glory of God (v. 28)

c. The resurrection is the key to perseverance in the Christian life (v. 29-34)

i. Without the resurrection why would people come to faith in Christ based upon the testimony of those who have died? (v. 29)

ii. Without the resurrection why would people put themselves in danger for the name of Christ? (v. 30-32)

aa. The principle in question form (v. 30)

bb. The Pauline example (v. 31-32ab)

cc. The proper perspective if there were no resurrection (v. 32c)

iii. When you keep associating with those who deny the truth, you will succumb to deception and sin (v. 33-34)

aa. Do not be deceived—if you associate with those given to error it will influence how you live (v. 33)

bb. Do not go on sinning—embracing those who deny the resurrection brings shame on you and dishonors God (v. 34)

B. The resurrection is supernatural (15:35-49)

1. A comparative analogy of resurrection from nature (15:35-38)

a. The skeptic's question (v. 35)

b. The stern correction of unbelief (v. 36a)

c. The simple comparison (v. 36b-38)

i. The resurrection of a seed is preceded by its death and burial (v. 36b)

ii. The resurrected life produced by that seed far exceeds the single seed sown (v. 37)

iii. The Ruler/God is sovereign over the process (v. 38)

2. A comparative analogy of the differences between the glory of the earthly and heavenly (15:39-41)
    a. *An illustration from nature of different kinds of flesh (v. 39)*
    b. *And illustration from nature of different kinds of glory (v. 40-41)*
        i. There is heavenly glory and earthly glory (v. 40)
        ii. There are even differences in glory among the heavenly bodies (v. 41)
3. A commentary on how the comparisons apply to the resurrection (15:42-49)
    a. *The resurrection contrast (v. 42-44)*
        i. Sown perishable—raised imperishable (v. 42)
        ii. Sown in dishonor and weakness—raised in glory and power (v. 43)
        iii. Sown as a natural body—raised as a spiritual body (v. 44)
    b. *The representative head correspondence (v. 45-49)*
        i. The reference from Scripture (v. 45)
        ii. The resurrection order (v. 46)
        iii. The representative head correspondence (v. 47-49)
            aa. The first Adam—from earth (v. 47a)
            bb. The last Adam—from heaven (v. 47b)
            cc. The identification (v. 48)
            dd. The resurrection (v. 49)

C. The resurrection is our sure hope and motivation (15:50-58)

1. The resurrection is necessary to inherit the Kingdom of God (15:50)
    a. *Our current physical makeup is not fit inherit the Kingdom of God (v. 50a)*
    b. *Our corruptible bodies cannot inherit that which is incorruptible (v. 50b)*
2. The resurrection and transformation at the last trumpet will be the capstone of our victory over sin and death (15:51-57)
    a. *A mystery revealed—the resurrection will be accompanied by the transformation of the rapture (v. 51-53)*
        i. The truth about physical death—not every believer will die physically (v. 51a)
        ii. The truth about physical transformation—every believer will be transformed (v. 51b)
        iii. The timing of the resurrection and transformation (v. 53)
            aa. It will be instantaneous (v. 52a)
            bb. It will be eschatologically determined (v. 52b)
            cc. It will be a forever—permanent transformation to incorruptibility (v. 52c-53)

   b. *A majestic reality—absolute and eternal victory over sin and death (v. 54-57)*
      i. The Scripture's promises will be fulfilled (v. 54-55)
         aa. The future incorruptible state (v. 54a)
         bb. The fulfillment of Isaiah 28:5 (v. 54b)
         cc. The final reversal of Hosea 13:14 (v. 55)
      ii. The Savior will give us victory over sin and death through the resurrection (v. 56-57)
         aa. The painful sting of death is removed (v. 56a)
         bb. The power of sin, the condemnation of the law, is removed (v. 56b)
         cc. The praise belongs to God, Who gives us the victory through our Lord Jesus Christ (v. 57)
3. The resurrection is our motivation to persevere and abound in the work of the Lord (15:58)
   a. *Because of our victorious resurrection ... (v. 58a)*
   b. *Be steadfast, immoveable, always abounding in the work of the Lord (v. 58b)*
   c. *Be ever mindful of the glorious fruit and future to come in the Lord (v. 58c)*

X. The wisdom of the cross and the collection for the saints (16:1-4)

A. The Pauline directive on the collection (16:1)

1. A ministry of relief for the saints (16:1a)
2. A multi-church relief effort (16:1b)

B. The particular directions for the collection (16:2)

1. The period determined—every Sunday until Paul came (16:2a)
2. The people involved—each one of you (16:2b)
3. The preparation needed—set apart and save (16:2c)
4. The proportion requested—as he may prosper (16:2d)

C. The painstaking discretion for the administration and distribution of the collection (16:2e-4)

1. Avoid even the appearance of coercion (16:2e)
2. Actively involve people who are approved as trustworthy in the congregation (16:3a)
3. Actively seek propriety in every step of the process 16:3b-4)

XI. The wisdom of the cross and the concluding remarks (16:5-24)

A. Plans and their communication are important for an effective gospel ministry (16:5-12)

1. Clarity and flexibility communicated—the plan concerning Paul's intended visit (16:5-9)
   a. *The plan was unambiguous but not inflexible (v. 5-7)*
      i. Clarity of intention (v. 5)
      ii. Conveyance of desire (v. 6-7a)
      iii. Cognizant of God's sovereignty (v. 7b)
   b. *The plan was intentional in pursuing the outcome but not ignorant of the opposition (v. 8-9)*
      i. The place and time—Ephesus until Pentecost (v. 8)
      ii. The purpose—effective ministry (v. 9a)
      iii. The problems—extensive opposition (v. 9b)
2. Concern and preparation communicated—the plan concerning Timothy's probable visit (16:10-11)
   a. *A probable visit to Corinth (v. 10a)*
   b. *A possibility of fear in Corinth (v. 10b)*
   c. *A peaceful and respectful sendoff from Corinth (v. 11)*
3. Confidence in the Spirit's leading of others communicated—the plan concerning Apollos's future visit (16:12)
   a. *The ministry direction Paul gave Apollos (v. 12a)*
   b. *The ministry decision Apollos made (v. 12b)*

B. Personal relationships and their communication are important for an effective gospel ministry (16:13-24)

1. Exhortations to foster relational harmony and effective ministry (16:13-18)
   a. *Stay alert spiritually (v. 13a)*
   b. *Stand firm in the faith (v. 13b)*
   c. *Show yourself to be spiritually courageous (v. 13c)*
   d. *Stay strong in the Lord (v. 13d)*
   e. *Saturate everything you do with love (v. 14)*
   f. *Submit to those who have devoted themselves to the ministry of the saints (v. 15-16)*
      i. The call to remember the longevity and devotion of Stephanis's household's ministry (v. 15)
      ii. The call to be subject to such men (v. 16)

g. *Show honor to those who encourage others and meet ministry needs (v. 17-18)*
    i. The ministry of support and encouragement (v. 17-18a)
    ii. The mandate to recognize such men (v. 18b)

2. Epistolary greetings and prayers to foster relational unity and eschatological anticipation (16:19-24)
    a. The encouragement of final greetings (v. 19-21)
        i. They were embraced by a large coalition of churches (v. 19a)
        ii. They were embraced by Aquila and Prisca and the church in their house (v. 19b)
        iii. They were embraced by all true believers (v. 20b)
        iv. Therefore, they were to embrace each other (v. 21)
    b. The encouragement of final prayers (v. 22-24)
        i. A prayer of imprecation—justice (v. 22a)
        ii. A prayer of anticipation—glory (v. 22b)
        iii. A prayer of intercession—grace (v. 23)
        iv. A personal encouragement—the Apostle's love (v. 24)

2 Corinthians

Kress Biblical Resources

Overview Outline of 2 Corinthians

Defending the New Covenant Gospel Ministry of Grace and the Sufficiency of Christ

I. Introduction (1:1-2)

A. The writer (1:1a)

B. The recipients (1:1b)

C. The reasons (see detailed outline)

D. The requisite greeting (1:2)

II. Gospel ministry and the sufficiency of Christ (1:3-7:16)

A. A change in plans explained and defended (1:3-2:11)

1. Comfort in suffering, fellowship, and mutual concern should be more important than a change of plans (1:3-11)
2. Changing plans should not necessarily be equated with sinister motives or weak leadership (1:12-22)
3. Changing plans may indicate godly motives and spiritual discernment (1:23-2:11)

B. A Christ-sufficient ministry explained and defended (2:12-7:16)

1. The Christ-sufficient ministry promotes Spirit-enabled, New Covenant worship and liberty—not legalism (2:12-3:18)
2. A Christ-sufficient ministry will be marked by difficulty and satanic opposition—not temporal ease (4:1-15)
3. A Christ-sufficient ministry seeks to please Christ with a view to the eternal reward—not earthly reward (4:16-5:10)
4. A Christ-sufficient ministry is motivated by faith, Christ's love, and the desire to honor Him—not the love and honor of self (5:11-6:10)
5. A Christ-sufficient ministry is characterized by a deep concern for spiritual well-being of others—not personal profit (6:11-7:3)
6. A Christ-sufficient ministry is characterized by divine comfort, joy, and holy optimism—not pessimism and defeat (7:4-16)

III. Giving principles concerning the collection for the saints and the sufficiency of Christ (8:1-9:15)

A. The call for grace giving concerning the needs of the saints (8:1-15)

1. The example of the churches in Macedonia (8:1-5)
2. The exhortation to the church at Corinth (8:6-8)
3. The example of the Lord Jesus (8:9)
4. The exhortation continued (8:10-12)
5. The explanation of divine provision (8:13-15)

B. The concern for propriety in regard to the handling of the collection and the distribution of the funds (8:16-9:5)

1. Integrity and accountability are essential in the collection and distribution of God's resources (8:16-23)
2. Intentionality, preparation, and commitment are essential in the giving of God's resources (8:24-9:5)

C. The corollary principles and precepts for grace giving (9:6-15)

1. The principle of sowing and reaping in grace giving[1]—be generous in your giving (9:6)
2. The proper perspective of grace giving—be joyful, not grudging in your giving (9:7)
3. The power and purposes of God's grace in grace giving—be confident in God's power and purposes in your giving (9:8-14)
4. The praise of God's glorious gift of grace—be thankful and amazed by God's grace (9:15)

IV. God-ordained authority and the sufficiency of Christ (10:1-13:10)

A. Christ-sufficient authority is self-restrained and employs spiritual means—not worldly tactics and self-exaltation (10:1-6)

1. Spiritual authority is characterized by both meekness and might (10:1-2)
2. Spiritual authority wields spiritual weapons—which are divinely powerful to both deliver and destroy (10:3-6)

B. Christ-sufficient authority will, when necessary, speak in self-defense (boast) for the sake of gospel and those under its care (10:7-12:13)

1. Boasting in Christ-sufficient authority—not self-acclamation (10:7-18)
2. Boasting in Christ-sufficient ministry support (11:1-15)
3. Boasting in Christ-sufficient service (11:16-33)
4. Boasting in Christ-sufficient gifting and power (12:1-13)

C. Christ-sufficient authority is willing, when necessary, to personally and painfully confront error, and call for repentance (12:14-13:10)

1. Confronting false accusations (12:14-18)
2. Confronting a lack of repentance (12:19-21)
3. Calling for self-examination and corporate action (13:1-10)

V. Conclusion (13:11-14)

A. Practicing fellowship and experiencing the presence of God (13:11-13)

B. Praying for fellowship with the triune Person of God (13:14)

[1] The following context makes it clear that spiritual blessing is the harvest, not primarily a monetary reciprocity.

Introductory Matters

I. **The author (1:1a)**

A. The human author (1:1a)[1]

1. His name
2. His office
3. His authority
3. His ministry representative[2]

A. The divine Author (2 Tim. 3:16; 2 Pet. 1:21; 3:15-16)

II. **The audience (1:1b)**

A. The original recipients (cf. Acts 18:1-18; 19:1)

1. The church of God in Corinth
2. The wider audience of believers throughout Achaia

B. The current recipients (2 Tim. 3:16; 2 Pet. 3:15-16)

III. **The aim**

A. To explain why Paul had decided to change his previously planned visit to Corinth (1:8, 15-19, 23-24; 2:1)

B. To encourage the church to forgive a penitent offender who had sinned publicly [against Paul] (2:5-11; cf. 7:8-12)

C. To defend the superiority of the New Covenant gospel ministry of grace against those who would denigrate Paul's ministry (2:15-17; 3:1-18; 4:3-6; 5:11-21; 6:1, 3-10)

D. To encourage the church to embrace Paul's ministry wholeheartedly and separate from those who taught contrary doctrine (6:11-7:7)

E. To encourage the church to complete the collection for the needy saints in Jerusalem (8:1-9:15)

F. To defend Paul's authority as an Apostle so that the purity and simplicity of the gospel would be preserved against false apostles (10:1-13:10)

G. Summary reason: **Defending the New Covenant gospel ministry of grace and the sufficiency of Christ**

---

[1] For a biblical biography of the Apostle Paul see Acts 7:58; 8:1; 9:1-30; 11:25-30; 12:25-28:31; 1 Cor. 15:30-32; 2 Cor. 6:4-5; 11:23-30; Gal. 1:13-2:16; Phil. 3:4-14; 2 Thes. 3:8

[2] For a biblical biography of Timothy see Acts 16:1; 17:14-15; 18:5; 1 Cor. 4:17; 16:10; Phil. 2:19-23; 1 Thes. 3:2, 6; 1 Tim. 1:2; 5:23; Heb. 13:23

Detailed Outline of 2 Corinthians

Defending the New Covenant Gospel Ministry of Grace and the Sufficiency of Christ

I. Introduction (1:1-2)

A. The writer (1:1a)

1. The human author (1:1a)[1]
   - *a. His name*
   - *b. His office*
   - *c. His authority*
   - *d. His ministry representative*[2]
2. The divine Author (2 Tim. 3:16; 2 Pet. 1:21; 3:15-16)

B. The recipients (1:1b)

1. The original recipients (cf. Acts 18:1-18; 19:1)
   - *a. The church of God in Corinth*
   - *b. The wider audience of believers throughout Achaia*
2. The current recipients (2 Tim. 3:16; 2 Pet. 3:15-16)

C. The requisite greeting (1:2)

1. The salutation of grace and peace
2. The Source of grace and peace

II. Gospel ministry and the sufficiency of Christ (1:3-7:16)

A. A change in plans explained and defended (1:3-2:11)

1. Comfort in suffering, fellowship, and mutual concern should be more important than a change of plans (1:3-11)
   - *a. Extolling God before the explanation of the change of plans (v. 3-7)*
     - i. The praise proffered to the God of all comfort (v. 3-4a)
       - aa. The God and Father of our Lord Jesus Christ (v. 3a)
       - bb. The Father of mercies (v. 3b)
       - cc. The God of all comfort (v. 3c-4a)
     - ii. The practical purpose of His comfort (v. 4b-7)
       - aa. To comfort others in their afflictions (v. 4b)
       - bb. To demonstrate the sufficiency of Christ's comfort in the midst of suffering (v. 5)

---

[1] For a biblical biography of the Apostle Paul see Acts 7:58; 8:1; 9:1-30; 11:25-30; 12:25-28:31; 1 Cor. 15:30-32; 2 Cor. 6:4-5; 11:23-30; Gal. 1:13-2:16; Phil. 3:4-14; 2 Thes. 3:8

[2] For a biblical biography of Timothy see Acts 16:1; 17:14-15; 18:5; 1 Cor. 4:17; 16:10; Phil. 2:19-23; 1 Thes. 3:2, 6; 1 Tim. 1:2; 5:23; Heb. 13:23

cc. To foster fellowship with other believers in suffering and comfort (v. 6-7)

b. *Explaining the circumstances that led to the change plans (v. 8-11)*

i. A desperate situation arose (v. 8)

ii. A deepening dependence on God resulted (v. 9)

iii. A deliverance from death was experienced (v. 10)

iv. A deliberate prayer request is now petitioned (v. 11)

2. Changing plans should not necessarily be equated with sinister motives or weak leadership (1:12-22)

a. *Plans can be made and changed with a clear conscience (v. 12-16)*

i. The testimony of a good conscience (v. 12)

ii. The truth plainly communicated as intended (v. 13)

iii. The trust that should issue from godly relationships (v. 14)

iv. The thinking behind the initial plan (v. 15-16)

aa. The intention (v. 15)

bb. The itinerary (v. 16)

b. *Plans can be made and changed and still reflect the faithfulness of God (v. 17-22)*

i. The plan was not made flippantly (v. 17-19)

aa. The plan was made in good faith (v. 17)

bb. The plan was founded on God's faithfulness (v. 18)

cc. The preaching of Christ is evidence of good faith and God's faithfulness (v. 19)

ii. The Providence that directs believers' lives is faithful (v. 20)

iii. The pledge of the Spirit and the redemption of God in Christ is proof of God's faithfulness (v. 21-22)

aa. The firm foundation is God Himself (v. 21)

bb. The future is secured by God's Spirit (v. 22)

3. Changing plans may indicate godly motives and spiritual discernment (1:23-2:11)

a. *The spiritual reasons for the change in plans (1:23-2:2)*

i. An expression of grace (v. 23)

ii. An expression of humility (v. 24)

iii. An expression of wisdom [after an initial painful visit] (v. 1)

iv. And expression of hope (v. 2)

b. *The sorrowful letter that was sent instead of a second painful visit (v. 3-11)*

i. The sorrowful letter was sent in the hope of repentance (v. 3)

ii. The sorrowful letter was personally painful but sent out of love (v. 4)

iii. The sorrowful letter was for the good of the whole body—not just the offending party (v. 5)

iv. The sorrowful letter was intended to foster faithfulness, forgiveness and restoration within the church (v. 6-11)
  aa. The response of the church was church discipline (v. 6)
  bb. The response of the church to the repentant must be comfort and forgiveness (v. 7)
  cc. The restored must receive charity [love] and affirmation (v. 8)
  dd. The reason for the letter was to prove the church's faithfulness to the truth (v. 9)
  ee. The response of Paul to the offense was not personal, but rather due to the public nature of the offense (v. 10ab)
  ff. The response of Paul was forgiveness from the heart before Christ and public acknowledgement of that forgiveness (v. 10c)
  gg. The refusal to forgive and restore is a satanic scheme to destroy people and the church (v. 11)

B. A Christ-sufficient ministry explained and defended (2:12-7:16)

1. The Christ-sufficient ministry promotes Spirit-enabled, New Covenant worship and liberty—not legalism (2:12-3:18)

a. *The Lord's sovereign grace that triumphs through the ministry of frail men (v. 12-17)*
  i. The unlocked/open door for ministry in the Lord (v. 12)
  ii. The unsettled spirit in the minister and the concern over a ministry partner (v. 13ab)
  iii. The unexpected change in ministry location (v. 13c)
  iv. The undeserved grace of God manifested to and through frail men (v. 14-16)
    aa. The triumph of God's sovereign grace (v. 14a)
    bb. The truth of Christ honors God regardless of man's response (v. 14b-16)
      - The apostolic proclamation of Christ (v. 14b-15)
      - The aroma of death to the perishing (v. 16a)
      - The aroma of life to the believing (v. 16b)
      - The adequacy is in the message not men (v. 16c)
  v. The untainted motives of those who minister for God—not mammon (v. 17)

b. *The life change that comes from the sufficiency of Christ and the ministry of the Spirit (v. 1-6)*
  i. Letters of commendation written in ink are limited in scope (v. 1)
  ii. Lives changed are living letters that reveal the commendation of the Spirit of God (v. 2-3)
    aa. The life-change in the Corinthians themselves is the living letter of recommendation (v. 2)

bb. The life-giving Spirit is the author and the Apostle was its courier (v. 3)

iii. Life comes from the Holy Spirit and the ministry of the sufficiency of Christ (v. 4-6)

aa. Confidence in ministry is rooted in the sufficiency of Christ (v. 4-5)

bb. Confidence in ministry is found in the superiority of the New Covenant and the life-giving power of the Holy Spirit (v. 6)

c. *The liberty that comes from the Spirit-enabled, New Covenant ministry of glory (v. 7-18)*

i. The glory of the New Covenant far exceeds that of the Old Covenant (v. 7-11)

aa. The Mosaic covenant was glorious as a ministry of death (v. 7)

bb. The ministry of the Spirit cannot fail to exceed in glory [as a ministry of life] (v. 8)

cc. The Mosaic covenant was glorious as a ministry of condemnation (v. 9a)

dd. The ministry of the Spirit far exceeds in glory as a ministry of righteousness (v. 9b)

ee. The Mosaic covenant's glory cannot even begin to be compared to the glory of the New Covenant (v. 10)

ff. The Mosaic covenant and its glory has faded away, but the New Covenant and its glory is forever (v. 11)

ii. The glory of the New Covenant frees and is forever transforming those who turn to the Lord in faith (v. 12-18)

aa. The glory of the New Covenant is accessible (v. 12)

bb. The glory of the Old Covenant is veiled and fading away (v. 13-15)

- The glory was fading (v. 13)
- The glory is veiled by unbelief (v. 14-15)

cc. The glory of the New Covenant is accessed by turning to the Lord (v. 16)

dd. The glory of the New Covenant frees from bondage (v. 17)

ee. The glory of the New Covenant is forever transforming those who have turned to the Lord in faith (v. 18)

2. A Christ-sufficient ministry will be marked by difficulty and satanic opposition—not temporal ease (4:1-15)

a. *The preaching of Jesus as Lord is the singular message and focus of a Christ-sufficient ministry—but will be opposed by Satan (v. 1-6)*

i. The source of encouragement for the Christ-sufficient ministry (v. 1)

aa. Having received a ministry that frees and transforms

bb. Having received mercy from God

- ii. The sincerity and integrity of the Christ-sufficient minister (v. 2)
  - aa. No secret agenda
  - bb. No slick manipulation of God's Word
  - cc. Notable sincerity and honesty in revealing the truth to men and before God
- iii. The supernatural nature of the Christ-sufficient message (v. 3-6)
  - aa. The minds of unbelievers are naturally blinded to the message (v. 3-4)
    - The gospel is veiled to those who are perishing (v. 3)
    - The god of this age has blinded the minds of the unbelieving to the glory of Christ (v. 4)
  - bb. The message proclaimed is Jesus as Lord (v. 5)
    - The Sovereignty of Jesus as Lord
    - The servants of the church for Jesus' sake
  - cc. The miracle of illumination and regeneration creates light, life, and love for Christ in a once darkened heart (v. 6)
    - The power of God in creation
    - The power of God in conversion

b. The power of God is sufficient to sustain God's ministers amid opposition and difficulty (v. 7-15)

- i. The priceless treasure of the gospel (v. 7a)
- ii. The power of God in frail messengers of the gospel (v. 7b-12)
  - aa. The purpose—to reveal the surpassing power of God (v. 7b)
  - bb. The paradox and peculiar perseverance (v. 8-12)
    - Hard pressed but not crushed (v. 8a)
    - At a loss but not lost (v. 8b)
    - Hunted but not hopeless (v. 9a)
    - Down but not destroyed (v. 9b)
    - Suffering for Christ but showing He is alive (v. 10-11)
    - Loss and death producing life and disciples (v. 12)
- iii. The principle convictions produced by the gospel (v. 13-15)
  - aa. The conviction of faith (v. 13)
    - Faith that is comparable to Psalm 116:10—hope in the midst of persecution
    - Faith that compels you to speak to others of the gospel
  - bb. The conviction of the resurrection (v. 14)
    - The power of God in raising Jesus
    - The power of God in raising us
    - The power of God to present us together before Him

- cc. The conviction of the praiseworthiness of God (v. 15)
  - Suffering is to strengthen others
  - Suffering is serving to spread the gospel of grace, and the praiseworthiness of God

3. A Christ-sufficient ministry seeks to please Christ with a view to the eternal reward—not earthly reward (4:16-5:10)

- a. *The reality of eternal glory fortifies in present suffering (v. 16-18)*
  - i. Faith focused on the coming glory will encourage and spiritually renew us day-by-day (v. 16)
    - aa. The reason we do not lose heart (v. 16a)
    - bb. The reality of life in a fallen world (v. 16b)
    - cc. The renewal and encouragement (v. 16c)
  - ii. Faith focused on the coming glory will reckon present suffering as temporary and light by comparison (v. 17-18)
    - aa. Present affliction is momentary in light of eternity (v. 17)
    - bb. Present affliction is light in comparison to the eternal weight of glory (v. 17b)
    - cc. Present affliction must be seen through eyes of faith (v. 18)
- b. *The reality of the resurrection and eternal reward fosters passion to please Christ (v. 1-10)*
  - i. The truth we know about the resurrection (v. 1)
    - aa. Our current body is earthly and temporary, like a tent (v. 1a)
    - bb. Our resurrection body prepared by God is eternal and heavenly (v. 1b)
  - ii. The triumph we long for while still groaning in this earthly tent (v. 2-4)
    - aa. The temporal reality we live in—longing for what we don't currently have (v. 2)
    - bb. The triumph of the resurrection we long for (v. 3-4)
      - We long to be clothed with our resurrection body (v. 3)
      - We long to conquer death fully in the resurrection (v. 4)
  - iii. The treasured down payment we have now of future glory (v. 5)
    - aa. God has sovereignly prepared us for this triumphant future (v. 5a)
    - bb. God's Spirit is the pledge/down payment of our triumphant future (v. 5b)
  - iv. The tenacity that results from the Spirit's presence and the resurrection promise (v. 6-8)
    - aa. The courage to face the present realities of life (v. 6)
    - bb. The conviction to walk by faith not by sight (v. 7)
    - cc. The conviction that our home is not here, but rather with the Lord (v. 8)

v. The target we aim for in light of the resurrection and our eternal reward (v. 9-10)

aa. To be pleasing to Christ (v. 9)

- In life
- In death
- In everything

bb. To be positively evaluated by Christ (v. 10)

- The exhaustive scope of the judgment seat of Christ
- The examination of the believers works—good and bad

4. A Christ-sufficient ministry is motivated by faith, Christ's love, and the desire to honor Him—not the love and honor of self (5:11-6:10)

a. The motivation of faith issues in evangelism (v. 11)

i. Faith in the reality of Christ's holiness and holy examination of our lives (v. 11a)

ii. Faith that is approved by God (v. 11b)

iii. Faith that should be approved by other believers (v. 11c)

iv. Faith that should be defended by other believers (v. 12-13)

aa. Genuine faith is to be commended—not questioned (v. 12)

bb. Genuine faith may come across as crazy by some—but is actually concerned for the well-being of others (v. 13)

b. The motivation of Christ's love issues in love for Christ and a life lived for Him (v. 14-17)

i. The compelling nature of Christ's love (v. 14-15)

aa. The love of Christ (v. 14a)

bb. The logical conclusion concerning His sacrifice (v. 14b-15a)

cc. The life of love that issues from the love of Christ (v. 15b)

ii. The complete transformation of those in Christ (v. 16-17)

aa. A completely new perspective (v. 16)

bb. A completely new person (v. 17)

c. The message issues in a ministry of reconciliation (v. 18-21)

i. The message issues in a ministry of reconciliation (v. 18-20)

aa. The Source of the gospel message and the ministry of reconciliation (v. 18-19)

- God Himself in Christ (v. 18a, 19a)
- God's message preached through God's messengers (v. 18b, 19b)

bb. The summons of the gospel message and ministry of reconciliation—be reconciled to God in Christ (v. 20)

- ii. The message is summarized by God's plan of substitution and imputation in Christ (v. 21)
  - aa. The Sovereign plan
  - bb. The sinless Savior
  - cc. The substitutionary sacrifice
  - dd. The saving righteousness (imputation)

d. *The ministry of this message issues in a passion for souls and a passion to honor Christ no matter the cost (v. 1-10)*

- i. A passion for souls/people (v. 1-3a)
  - aa. Co-laboring with God (v. 1a)
  - bb. Calling people to embrace the grace of God (v. 1b-2)
    - The solemn concern (v. 1b)
    - The Scripture quotation (v. 2ab)
    - The short expository exhortation (v. 2c)
  - cc. Conducting oneself uprightly so that the ministry is not discredited (v. 3)
- ii. A passion to honor Christ no matter the cost (v. 4-10)
  - aa. The summary desire stated (v. 4a)
  - bb. The suffering and difficulty faced (v. 4b-5)
    - In very trying times (v. 4b)
    - In pressure situations (v. 4c)
    - In need (v. 4d)
    - In sorrow (v. 4e)
    - In beatings (v. 5a)
    - In imprisonments (v. 5b)
    - In riots (v. 5c)
    - In overwork (v. 5d)
    - In sleeplessness (v. 5e)
    - In hunger (v. 5f)
  - cc. The supernatural character revealed (v. 6-7ab)
    - In purity (v. 6a)
    - In knowledge (v. 6b)
    - In kindness (v. 6c)
    - In the Holy Spirit (v. 6d)
    - In sincere love (v. 6e)
    - In the word of truth (v. 7a)
    - In the power of God (v. 7b)
  - dd. The spiritual opposition noted (v. 7c-8)
    - Through weapons of righteousness in both hands (v. 7c)
    - Through glory and dishonor (v. 8a)

- Through slander and praise (v. 8b)
- Treated as imposters yet true (v. 8c)

ee. The Scriptural perspective embraced (v. 9-10)

- Though strangers here—yet intimately known by the Lord (v. 9a)
- Though dying here—yet behold alive to the Lord (v. 9b)
- Though beaten here—yet not being put to death before the Lord (v. 9c)
- Though grieving here—yet rejoicing in the Lord (v. 10a)
- Though beggars here—yet enriching others in the Lord (v. 10b)

5. A Christ-sufficient ministry is characterized by a deep concern for spiritual well-being of others—not personal profit (6:11-7:3)

a. *A concern for restored fellowship with other believers expressed (v. 11-13)*

i. The concern of an open heart (v. 11)

ii. The constraints of a closed heart (v. 12)

iii. The call to reciprocal openness and spiritual fellowship (v. 13)

b. *A concern for a right perspective of fellowship with the world detailed (6:14-7:1)*

i. The call for consecration/separation—do not be in spiritual partnership with unbelievers (v. 14a)

ii. The questions confirming the obvious (v. 14b-16a)

aa. How can right and wrong be partners? (v. 14b)

bb. What do light and darkness have in common? (v. 14c)

cc. How can Christ and the Devil be in harmony? (v. 15a)

dd. What inheritance does one who trusts God share in with one who does not trust God? (v. 15b)

ff. How can the Temple of God come to an agreement with idols? (v. 16a)

iii. The quotation confirming the need for separation (v. 16b-18)

aa. The spiritual reality of the church stated (v. 16b)

bb. The scriptural principle for sonship and separation cited (v. 16c-18)

- A principle illustrated from Leviticus 26:11-12; Ezekiel 37:27; Isaiah 52:11; Ezekiel 20:41 (v. 16c-17a)
- A paraphrastic principle from Isaiah 43:6; 2 Samuel 7:14; Jeremiah 3:19

iv. The call for consecration/separation to God (v. 1)

c. *A concern for restored fellowship with other believers repeated (v. 2-3)*

i. The call for an open heart of fellowship (v. 2)

aa. The call for unhindered fellowship (v. 2a)

bb. The claim of unsoiled conduct (v. 2b)

ii. The concern of love—not condemnation (v. 3)

6. A Christ-sufficient ministry is characterized by divine comfort, joy, and holy optimism—not pessimism and defeat (7:4-16)

a. *Confidence in the face of questions (v. 4)*

b. *Comfort from God in the wake of confrontation (v. 5-16)*

i. Conflicts and concern are a reality in relationships (v. 5)

ii. Comfort can come through providence (v. 6)

iii. Comfort can come through confrontation (v. 7-13a)

aa. The report that brought joy—a longing and a zeal for Paul (v. 7)

bb. The repentance that brought joy[3] (v. 8)

- The confrontation via a sorrowful letter (v. 8)
- The contrast between worldly and godly sorrow (v. 9-10)

  Sorrow producing repentance and salvation (v. 9-10a)

  Sorrow producing death (v. 10b)
- The contrition/repentance produced by godly sorrow (v. 11)

  Diligence to make a defense [of Paul as God's representative; cf. v 7]

  Displeasure [over being complicit in the offense against Paul as God's representative]

  Dismay [over allowing the offense against Paul as God's representative to go unchecked]

  Desire [for Paul as God's representative to be honored]

  Devotion [to Paul's reputation as God's representative]

---

[3] The expositor must be careful to note the context of this passage on repentance and not simply make it a blanket template for all repentance. The qualities used to describe the Corinthians' repentance as a church, or a large portion of the church are corporate and somewhat specific to the nature of the offense. Not all sin demands the exact same nuances of repentance—but rather repentance should be specific to the offense committed. Examples here include "defense" and "demonstration of innocence" in the matter (evidently of not appropriately disciplining a member who challenged Paul's Apostolic authority). There seems to be a "defense" of Paul and a "demonstration" they had not actually agreed with the one who had been slandering him, though they were at first complicit by not rebuking the man.

A change in thinking will result in changed attitudes and actions. God ultimately evaluates repentance and certainly there will be evidence of repentance seen by the church. But to strictly apply every quality listed here in order to evaluate or even self-evaluate one's repentance was not likely the Apostle Paul's purpose in writing this section.

Determination [to see the injustice against Paul as God's representative rectified]

Demonstration of innocence [in regard to the offense against Paul as God's representative]

- The concern for others—not vengeance or self-vindication (v. 12)
- The comfort of reconciliation and repentance (v. 13a)

iii. Confidence and joy through affectionate fellowship and obedience to God's truth (v. 13b-16)

aa. Fellowship and obedience bring spiritual refreshment (v. 13b)

bb. Fellowship and obedience affirm sanctified optimism (v. 14)

cc. Fellowship and obedience increase spiritual affection (v. 15)

dd. Fellowship and obedience supply joy and further confidence (v. 16)

III. Giving principles concerning the collection for the saints and the sufficiency of Christ (8:1-9:15)

A. The call for grace giving concerning the needs of the saints (8:1-15)

1. The example of the churches in Macedonia (v. 1-5)

a. Not wealthy, but willing to give out of what they had (v. 1-2)

i. The grace of God was the basis of their giving (v. 1)

ii. The great hardship they faced did not keep them from giving (v. 2)

b. Not sparingly, but sacrificially and joyously, giving themselves to God and others (v. 3-5)

i. Beyond their ability (v. 3)

ii. Begging for the privilege to help (v. 4)

iii. Bondservants of God and others (v. 5)

2. The exhortation to the church at Corinth (v. 6-8)

a. The coming of Titus as an apostolic representative (v. 6)

b. The call to abound in the gracious work of giving (v. 7)

c. The concern for genuine love—not grudging obedience to a command (v. 8)

3. The example of the Lord Jesus (v. 9)

a. Consider His grace—a summary statement

b. Consider His glory (heavenly riches in pre-incarnate glory)

c. Consider His gift and what it cost Him

d. Consider your gain from His costly gift

4. The exhortation continued (v. 10-12)

a. Good intentions are no substitute for actually giving (v. 10-11)

i. Paul was not demanding they give—but encouraging them for their good (v. 10)

ii. Paul was encouraging them to finish what they had begun (v. 11)

b. Giving, however, should be out of what one has—not beyond one's capacity (v. 12)

5. The explanation of divine provision (v. 13-15)

a. God calls for reciprocity—not absolute economic equality (v. 13-14)

i. This was not to penalize the wealthy (v. 13)

ii. This was a temporary relief for a church in need (v. 14)

b. God confirmed His ability to provide for His people in Exodus 16:18 (v. 15)

B. The concern for propriety in regard to the handling of the collection and the distribution of the funds (8:16-9:5)

1. Integrity and accountability are essential in the collection and distribution of God's resources (v. 16-23)

a. A man with a passion for God's people—Titus (v. 16-17)

i. A passion that is wrought by God in the heart (v. 16)

ii. A passion that is willing to serve (v. 17)

b. A man with the approval of God's people—unnamed but well-known (v. 18-19a)

i. He was well-known by God's people (v. 18)

ii. He was approved by God's people (v. 19a)

c. A ministry of generosity, grace and glory—above reproach in the sight of God and men (v. 19b-21)

i. A ministry of grace (v. 19b)

ii. A ministry of glory (v. 19c)

iii. A ministry of honesty and caution (v. 20)

iv. A ministry of honor before God and men (v. 21)

d. A man with a record of faithfulness—unnamed but tested and approved by Paul (v. 22)

e. A ministry team summary in regard to the collection (v. 23)

i. The Apostle's representative—Titus (v. 23a)

ii. The approved messengers of the churches (v. 23b)

iii. The appropriate motive and purpose (v. 23c)

2. Intentionality, preparation, and commitment are essential in the giving of God's resources (v. 24-9:5)

a. Purposeful giving testifies of God's glory to those who administrate the offering (v. 24)

b. Purposeful giving is the fulfillment of the initial desires to help (v. 1-2)

i. Reminders can be helpful to those who have already purposed to give (v. 1)

ii. Readiness to give can be an encouragement to others to give (v. 2)

c. *Preparedness beforehand guarantees the fulfillment of the initial desire to give (v. 3-5)*
    i. A pledge to give may need follow-up (v. 3)
    ii. A pledge unfulfilled is disappointing and very possibly dishonorable (v. 4)
    iii. A pledge may be subject to second-guessing due to covetousness (v. 5)

C. The corollary principles and precepts for grace giving (9:6-15)

1. The principle of sowing and reaping in grace giving[4]—be generous in your giving (v. 6)
    a. *Limited sowing makes for limited reaping (v. 6a)*
    b. *Lavish sowing makes for lavish reaping (v. 6b)*
2. The proper perspective of grace giving—be joyful, not grudging in your giving (v. 7)
    a. *Freely, not forced*
    b. *Full of joy, knowing God loves a cheerful giver*
3. The power and purposes of God's grace in grace giving—be confident in God's power and purposes in your giving (v. 8-14)
    a. *The surety of God's provision (v. 8)*
        i. The power of God to make all grace abound to you
        ii. The purpose of this grace—spiritual sufficiency in everything for every good work
    b. *The Scripture confirming God's spiritual provision and purposes (v. 9)*
    c. *The Sovereign supply of both spiritual and physical resources (v. 10-11)*
        i. God will supply physical resources for the purpose of a spiritual harvest (v. 10)
        ii. God supplies physical and spiritual resources for His glory (v. 11)
    d. *The service of giving supplies both physical and spiritual needs—and ultimately issues in worship (v. 12-14)*
        i. A giving ministry meets physical needs (v. 12a)
        ii. A giving ministry issues in thanksgiving to God (v. 12b)
        iii. A giving ministry confirms the truth of the gospel to the glory of God (v. 13)
        iv. A giving ministry fosters prayer, and a holy longing for mutual fellowship (v. 14)

[4] The following context makes it clear that spiritual blessing is the harvest, not primarily a monetary reciprocity.

4. The praise of God's glorious gift of grace—be thankful and amazed by God's grace (v. 15)
    - *a. Say grace—because of God's giving ministry of grace (v. 15a)*
    - *b. Stand in awe—because of God's indescribable giving ministry of grace (v. 15b)*

IV. God-ordained authority and the sufficiency of Christ (10:1-13:10)

A. Christ-sufficient authority is self-restrained and employs spiritual means—not worldly tactics and self-exaltation (10:1-6)

1. Spiritual authority is characterized by both meekness and might (v. 1-2)
    - *a. An appeal based on the meekness and gentleness of Christ (v. 1a)*
    - *b. An accusation implicitly referenced (v. 1b)*
    - *c. An appeal for a spiritual response of obedience (v. 2)*
        - i. The request for humble obedience (v. 2a)
        - ii. The response would be bold/mighty if the gentle request was disregarded (v. 2b)
2. Spiritual authority wields spiritual weapons—which are divinely powerful to both deliver and destroy (v. 3-6)
    - *a. The spiritual war introduced (v. 3)*
    - *b. The spiritual weapons introduced (v. 4ab)*
        - i. Man-made or fleshly--no (v. 4a)
        - ii. Mighty weapons of God—divinely powerful (v. 4b)
    - *c. The spiritual weapons for destruction and deliverance (v. 4c-6)*
        - i. The destruction of strongholds (v. 4c-5ab)
            - aa. The destruction summarized (v. 4c)
            - bb. The destruction of speculations (v. 5a)
            - cc. The destruction of every thought opposed to God's truth (v. 5b)
        - ii. The deliverance of thinking that is captive to the Word of God/the obedience of Christ (v. 5c-6)
            - aa. The principle (v. 5c)
            - bb. The practical application for the Corinthians Church (v. 6)

B. Christ-sufficient authority will, when necessary, speak in self-defense (boast) for the sake of gospel and those under its care (10:7-12:13)

1. Boasting in Christ-sufficient authority—not self-acclamation (v. 7-18)

a. The proper perspective on authority (v. 7-11)

i. Do not rely on a superficial/external perspective of authority (v. 7a)

ii. Determine to assess authority with a spiritual perspective (v. 7b-11)

aa. Spiritual authority necessitates salvation in Christ (v. 7b)

bb. Spiritual authority is exercised for edification—even when it involves self-defense (v. 8-11)

- The summary—self-defense is necessary if it builds other believers up in the faith (v. 8)
- The specific accusation—his writing is powerful, but his personal presence is insignificant (v. 9-10)
- The solemn truth—actions confirm character and words written in letters (v. 11)

b. The proper practice of authority (v. 12-18)

i. It does not constantly compare itself to others (v. 12)

ii. It does not constantly seek to extend its authority beyond its God-assigned sphere of influence (v. 13-14)

aa. The testimony (v. 13)

bb. The witnesses—the Corinthian Church itself (v. 14)

iii. It does not credit itself for the accomplishments of others (v. 15-16)

aa. The declaration (v. 15a)

bb. The desire—Corinthians encouragement and support to properly extend their God-given ministry authority (v. 15b-16)

iv. It does consistently concern itself with honoring the Lord and desires the approval of the Lord (v. 17-18)

aa. The proper perspective on boasting and ministry (v. 17)

bb. The proper perspective on commendation in ministry (v. 18)

2. Boasting in Christ-sufficient ministry support (v. 1-15)

a. The biblical concern for the gospel and God's people (v. 1-4)

i. Holy sarcasm about wisdom and folly (v. 1)

ii. Holy jealousy over Christ and His Bride (v. 2)

iii. Honest concerns about satanic deception and tolerating false teaching and teachers (v. 3-4)

aa. Satanic deception of targets thinking (v. 3a)

bb. Satanic deception seeks to lead people astray from the simplicity of devotion to Christ (v. 3b)

cc. Sanctioning false teaching and false teachers [by allowing it/them to go unchallenged] is true foolishness (v. 4)

b. The boasting necessary to rebuke the enemies of a Christ-sufficient approach to ministry support (v. 5-15)

i. A necessary boast/defense of ministry authority (v. 5-6)

aa. The self-assessment given—not inferior in authority to the self-proclaimed "super-apostles" (v. 5)

bb. The self-evident proof manifested—irrefutable fruit of ministry (v. 6)

ii. A necessary boast/defense of waiving direct ministry support (v. 7-12)

aa. Offering the gospel without charge—is that a sin? (v. 7)

bb. Other churches supported the missionary effort (v. 8-9)

cc. Others who want to compete for ministry authority will not silence this boast (v. 10-12)

- Waiving direct support will continue in Achaia (v. 10)
- Why?—because I love you (v. 11)
- Why?—to give no opportunity to those who desire an opportunity to exalt themselves by comparing ministries (v. 12)

iii. A necessary denunciation of those who oppose Christ's sufficiency in regard to ministry authority and support (v. 13-15)

aa. Such men are false apostles (v. 13)

bb. Satan disguises himself as a messenger of truth (v. 14)

cc. Such men are Satan's servants and will be judged according to their deeds (v. 15)

3. Boasting in Christ-sufficient service (v. 16-33)

a. Boasting rebuked and yet required (v. 16-21)

i. Asking for forbearance concerning the foolishness to follow (v. 16)

ii. Acknowledging that Jesus did not boast (v. 17)

iii. Answering a fool according to his folly (v. 18)

iv. Asserting the foolishness of embracing the arguments of those who oppose Christ-sufficient ministry (v. 19-20)

aa. The folly of seeing yourself as wise in your tolerance (v. 19)

bb. The folly of submitting to legalism and authoritarian exploitation (v. 20)

v. Acknowledging the wisdom of weakness and assuming the argument of the foolish—for the sake of the gospel (v. 21)

b. Boasting required for the sake of the gospel and the good of God's people (v. 22-33)

i. The ethnic issue addressed (v. 22)

ii. The evidence of being a servant of Christ detailed (v. 23-33)

aa. The insane comparison via holy sarcasm (v. 23a)

bb. The introductory evidence summarized (v. 23b)

cc. The irrefutable evidence of service to Christ detailed (v. 24-29)

- Many beatings (v. 24-25a)
- Many dangers nearing death (v. 25b-26)
- Many hardships (v. 27)
- Many pastoral concern (v. 28-29)

dd. The insufficiency of self and the sufficiency of Christ (v. 30-33)

- The weakness of self (v. 30)
- The witness of God (v. 31)
- The watch in Damascus (v. 32)
- The window in the wall and the escape from Damascus (v. 33)

4. Boasting in Christ-sufficient gifting and power (v. 1-13)

a. The required boasting continued (v. 1a)

b. The revelation of God experienced (v. 1b-6)

i. Divine revelation introduced (v. 1b)

ii. Dispatched to the third heaven (v. 2-4a)

aa. Who—a man Paul knew (v. 2a, 3a)

bb. When—fourteen years ago (v. 2b)

cc. How—I don't know (v. 2c, 3b)

dd. Where—the third heaven/paradise (v. 2d, 4a)

iii. Disallowed to repeat the specifics of the revelation (v. 4)

iv. Determined to boast in weakness rather than wonders (v. 5-6)

aa. The rhetorical device used

bb. The reason for the rhetorical device

c. The reward of the exceeding revelations and exceptional gifting from God explained—a thorn in the flesh for the sake of humility (v. 7-10)

i. Privilege may necessitate painful trials (v. 7)

ii. Prayer may not always receive what is specifically requested (v. 8)

iii. Power from God is perfected in weakness (v. 9-10)

aa. Christ's power in our weakness (v. 9)

bb. Contentment in Christ in our weakness (v. 10)

- *d. The response to Christ-affirmed authority solicited (v. 11-13)*
  - i. Commendation rather than compelling the foolishness of boasting (v. 11)
  - ii. Confidence and celebration rather than consternation and questioning (v. 12-13)
    - aa. The proofs of a true Apostle (v. 12)
    - bb. The privilege of being led by a true Apostle—without any financial burden (v. 13)

C. Christ-sufficient authority is willing, when necessary, to personally and painfully confront error, and call for repentance (12:14-13:10)

1. Confronting false accusations (v. 14-18)

- *a. Relationships are more important that remuneration (v. 14)*
- *b. Return on investment in love should be expected among believers (v. 15)*
- *c. Recognize false accusations of deceit by considering the truth (v. 16-18)*
  - i. Consider the accusations in light of what actually happened (v. 16)
  - ii. Consider the accusations in light of the apostolic representatives' actions (v. 17-18)
    - aa. Did any take advantage? (v. 17)
    - bb. Did Titus take advantage? (v. 18)

2. Confronting a lack of repentance (v. 19-21)

- *a. The defense has not been for self, but rather for the sake of those who are in danger of defection, and for the glory of God in Christ (v. 19)*
- *b. The danger of unrepentance involves the devastating consequences of sin and the demonstration of divine discipline (v. 20-21)*
  - i. Demonstration of apostolic power to discipline (v. 20a)
  - ii. Demonstration of unrepentant attitudes and actions (v. 20b)
  - iii. Divine discipline for those who are unrepentant (v. 21)

3. Calling for self-examination and corporate action (v. 1-10)

- *a. The potential for corporate discipline is a call to action (v. 1-4)*
  - i. The witness/confirmation process concerning sin and discipline (v. 1)
  - ii. The warning (v. 2-3)
    - aa. The previous warning mentioned
    - bb. The proof of Christ's authority through the Apostle
  - iii. The weakness of Christ crucified and His life-giving power (v. 4)
- *b. The proof of faith will be self-examination and appropriate action (v. 5-10)*
  - i. The test of the new birth (v. 5)
  - ii. The test of acknowledging apostolic truth (v. 6)

iii. The test of doing what is right in accordance with the truth (v. 7-8)
iv. The test of maturity—strength in weakness (v. 9)
v. The test of repentance in conjunction with the truth (v. 10)

V. Conclusion (13:11-14)

A. Practicing fellowship and experiencing the presence of God (13:11-13)

1. The commands concerning fellowship issued (13:11)
   - *a. The context (v. 11a)*
   - *b. The commands (v. 11b)*
     - i. Be joyful
     - ii. Be made mature
     - iii. Be comforted/encouraged
     - iv. Be of the same mind (the glory of God)
     - v. Be in peace
2. The comfort of God's presence promised (13:11)
   - *a. The comfort of the presence of the God of love*
   - *b. The comfort of the presence of the God of peace*
3. The common affection of God's people (13:12-13)
   - *a. The command to embrace God's people with affection (v. 12)*
   - *b. The comfort of the embrace of all of God's people (v. 13)*

B. Praying for fellowship with the triune Person of God (13:14)

1. The prayer concerning the Persons of the Godhead
   - *a. The grace of the Lord Jesus Christ*
   - *b. The love of God*
   - *c. The fellowship of the Holy Spirit*
2. The prayer for the presence of divine fellowship

Galatians

Kress Biblical Resources

Overview Outline of Galatians

The True Gospel Boasts in Christ Alone Rather Than Mixing Law with Grace

I. The Gospel of Grace Defended Personally (1:1-2:21)

A. The damning consequences of distorting the gospel of grace introduced (1:1-10)
   1. The author (1:1-2a)
   2. The audience (1:2b)
   3. The address/salutation and ascription (1:3-5)
   4. The aim (1:6-10)

B. The Divine origin of the gospel of grace defended (1:11-2:21)
   1. Jesus Christ is the source of the gospel—not man (1:11-12)
   2. Jesus Christ is the source of Paul's gospel authority—not any of the other Apostles (1:13-2:21)

II. The Gospel of Grace Delineated Doctrinally (3:1-4:31)

A. An examination of personal salvation and the gospel of grace (3:1-6)
   1. The questions about the Galatians' salvation (3:1-5)
   2. The quotation about Abraham's salvation (3:6)

B. An exposition of the biblical data concerning salvation by faith rather than law-keeping (3:7-4:7)
   1. The promised blessings of Abraham—salvation by faith to the nations (3:7-14)
   2. The purpose of the Law (3:15-25)
   3. The privileged position of those who trust in Christ [rather than law-keeping] (3:26-29)
   4. The proper relationship between the law and salvation by grace through faith (4:1-7)

C. An exhortation to turn away from legalism and turn back to the gospel of grace (4:8-31)
   1. Recognize that legalism/Law-keeping is just as much slavery as paganism (4:8-11)
   2. Remember the blessings of coming to Christ and the freedom of gospel-based fellowship (4:12-20)
   3. Recognize the distinction between children of the flesh and children of the promise—between fleshly means and faith (4:21-31)

III. The Gospel of Grace Displayed Practically (5:1-6:18)

A. Stand firm in your freedom in Christ (5:1-12)
   1. Christ is our freedom—not Law-keeping (5:1-6)
   2. Combining Law-keeping and "Christianity" abolishes the scandal of the cross and perverts the gospel (5:7-12)

B. Serve one another in love because of your freedom in Christ (5:13-15)
   1. Love-inspired service is the anecdote for sin—not legalism (5:13)
   2. Love is the truth fulfillment of the Law (5:14)
   3. Legalism leads to spiritual cannibalism and self-destruction (5:15)

C. Seek sanctification by the Spirit—not Law-keeping (5:16-26)
   1. Walking by the Spirit introduced (5:16-18)
   2. Walking by the flesh evidenced (5:19-21)
   3. Walking by the Spirit evidenced (5:22-23)
   4. Walking by the Spirit summarized (5:24-26)

D. Serve one another with humility and generosity (6:1-10)
   1. Serve those who are struggling spiritually (6:1-5)
   2. Serve those who serve/minister to you (6:6-9)
   3. Serve everyone—but especially believers (6:10)

E. Seek to glory in the cross of Christ and His grace—rather than the flesh (6:11-18)
   1. Legalism demands emphatic Apostolic intervention (6:11)
   2. Legalism makes a good showing in the flesh, but does not satisfy the true demands of the Law (6:12-13)
   3. Learning to glory in Christ's Person and work alone is the only path to freedom and peace (6:14-18)

Introductory Matters

I. The author (1:1-2a)

A. The human author[1]

1. The man—Paul (v. 1a)
2. His mandate from God (v. 1b)
3. The mention of "all the brethren" with him (v. 2a)

B. The Divine Author (2 Tim. 3:16; 2 Pet. 3:15-16)

II. The audience (1:2b)

A. The original recipients (cf. 3:1; 4:19-20)

1. Their identification as churches
2. Their location in Galatia (Acts 13-14; cf. 16:6-8; 18:23)

B. The current recipients (2 Tim. 3:16-17; 2 Pet. 3:15-16)

III. The aim

A. To confront desertion from the true gospel (1:6-10)

1. The concern over desertion from the gospel (v. 6-7)
   a. *Anything other than the grace of Him who called you is a different gospel (v. 6)*
   b. *Anything other than the grace of Him who called you is a distorted gospel (v. 7)*
2. The condemnation of those who preach a different gospel (v. 8-9)
   a. *Anyone—even if an Apostle or Angel—preaching a gospel contrary to what was originally preached is to be accursed (v. 8)*
   b. *Again, anyone preaching a gospel contrary to what you have received is to be accursed (v. 9)*
3. The commendation of God as the goal—not the commendation of men (v. 10)

B. To call believers to stand firm in the true gospel of grace—and turn away from the deadly mixture of law and grace

1. Personally (1:11-2:21)
2. Doctrinally (3:1-4:31)
3. Practically (5:1-6:18)

---

[1] For a biblical biography of the Apostle Paul see Acts 7:58; 8:1; 9:1-30; 11:25-30; 12:25-28:31; 1 Cor. 15:30-32; 2 Cor. 6:4-5; 11:23-30; Gal. 1:13-2:16; Phil. 3:4-14; 2 Thes. 3:8

Detailed Outline of Galatians

The True Gospel Boasts in Christ Alone Rather Than Mixing Law with Grace

I. The Gospel of Grace Defended Personally (1:1-2:21)

A. The damning consequences of distorting the gospel of grace introduced (1:1-10)

1. The author (1:1-2a)[1]
    - *a. The human author*
        - i. The man—Paul (v. 1a)
        - ii. His mandate from God (v. 1b)
        - iii. The mention of "all the brethren" with him (v. 2a)
    - *b. The Divine Author (2 Tim. 3:16; 2 Pet. 3:15-16)*
2. The audience (1:2b)
    - *a. The original recipients (cf. 3:1; 4:19-20)*
        - i. Their identification as churches
        - ii. Their location in Galatia (Acts 13-14; cf. 16:6-8; 18:23)
    - *b. The current recipients (2 Tim. 3:16-17; 2 Pet. 3:15-16)*
3. The address/salutation and ascription (1:3-5)
    - *a. The salutation of grace to you and peace (v. 3a)*
    - *b. The Source of grace and peace (v. 3b)*
    - *c. The sacrifice that obtained our grace and peace (v. 4)*
    - *d. The splendor of God to be acknowledged forever (v. 5)*
4. The aim (1:6-10)
    - *a. To confront desertion from the true gospel (v. 6-10)*
        - i. The concern over desertion from the gospel (v. 6-7)
            - aa. Anything other than the grace of Him who called you is a different gospel (v. 6)
            - bb. Anything other than the grace of Him who called you is a distorted gospel (v. 7)
        - ii. The condemnation of those who preach a different gospel (v. 8-9)
            - aa. Anyone—even if an Apostle or Angel—preaching a gospel contrary to what was originally preached is to be accursed (v. 8)
            - bb. Again, anyone preaching a gospel contrary to what you have received is to be accursed (v. 9)

---

[1] For a biblical biography of the Apostle Paul see Acts 7:58; 8:1; 9:1-30; 11:25-30; 12:25-28:31; 1 Cor. 15:30-32; 2 Cor. 6:4-5; 11:23-30; Gal. 1:13-2:16; Phil. 3:4-14; 2 Thes. 3:8

iii. The commendation of God as the goal—not the commendation of men (v. 10)

b. *To call believers to stand firm in the true gospel of grace—and turn away from the deadly mixture of law and grace*

i. Personally (1:11-2:21)

ii. Doctrinally (3:1-4:31)

iii. Practically (5:1-6:18)

B. The Divine origin of the gospel of grace defended (1:11-2:21)

1. Jesus Christ is the source of the gospel—not man (1:11-12)

a. *The gospel of grace is not a gospel invented by man (v. 11)*

b. *The gospel of grace was received through divine revelation (v. 12)*

2. Jesus Christ is the source of Paul's gospel authority—not any of the other Apostles (1:13-2:21)

a. *Paul was previously opposed to the gospel (v. 13-14)*

i. He was a radical persecutor of the church (v. 13)

ii. He was a rising star in his sect of Judaism (v. 14)

b. *Paul was powerfully transformed into a preacher of the gospel (v. 15-24)*

i. He was chosen and called by God as a preacher to the Gentiles—not by men (v. 15-16b)

aa. Sovereign grace (v. 15)

bb. Special revelation (v. 16a)

cc. Selected to be a preacher to the Gentiles (v. 16b)

ii. He was commissioned to preach in obscurity in the early portions of his ministry (v. 16c-24)

aa. Did not consult with flesh and blood (v. 16c)

bb. Did not go up to Jerusalem for years (v. 17)

cc. After three years, spent 15 days in Jerusalem with Peter and saw James, but no other Apostle (v. 18-20)

dd. Ministered in Syria and Cilia after that (v. 21)

ee. Was unknown by sight to the churches of Judea (v. 22)

ff. Testimony was known by those churches however (v. 23)

gg. God was glorified because of that testimony (v. 24)

c. *Paul was publicly recognized at the Jerusalem Council as an Apostle to the Gentiles (v. 1-10)*

i. The context of the visit to Jerusalem (v. 1-2)

aa. The persons and timing (v. 1)

bb. The purpose (v. 2)

ii. The conflict at the visit (v. 3-5)

aa. The freedom of Titus exhibited (v. 3)

bb. The false brethren exposed (v. 4-5)

- Their deceptive purpose—slavery to legalism
- Their defeat—steadfastness in grace

iii. The confirmation of Paul's Apostolic authority (v. 6-10)

aa. The other Apostles and leaders added nothing to Paul's gospel or his gospel authority (v. 6)

bb. The other Apostles and leaders acknowledged Paul's gospel authority and ministry to the Gentiles (v. 7-9)

- A comparable and complimentary ministry to Peter's (v. 7-8)
- A confirmed partnership in the gospel ministry (v. 9)

cc. The other Apostles and leaders asked Paul to remember the poor—which he was already eager to do (v. 10)

d. Paul was publicly faithful to confront Peter on his failure to properly represent the gospel (v. 11-21)

i. The context of the confrontation (v. 11-13)

aa. The condemnation of Cephas in Antioch (v. 11)

bb. The cowardice and change in Cephas' fellowship because of those of the circumcision (v. 12)

cc. The change in all the Jewish believers there—including Barnabas—because of Cephas' example (v. 13)

ii. The content of the confrontation (v. 14-21)

aa. The exposing of Peter's practical hypocrisy (v. 14)

bb. The exposition of justification by faith rather than works of the law (v. 15-21)

- Jews by birth vs. Gentile lawbreakers (v. 15)
- Justification is by faith in Christ, not works of the law (v. 16)
- Justification by faith does not lead to a sinful life (v. 17)
- Going back to the law will only reveal one is a lawbreaker (v. 18)
- Leaning on Christ's death under the law results in life lived for God by faith (v. 19-20)
- Righteous comes by grace—going back to law keeping communicates disregard for Christ's sacrifice (v. 21)

II. The Gospel of Grace Delineated Doctrinally (3:1-4:31)

A. An examination of personal salvation and the gospel of grace (3:1-6)

1. The questions about the Galatians' salvation (3:1-5)

a. Did someone entice you to turn your focus away from the cross of Christ [the redemptive work of Christ]? (3:1)

i. Law-keeping religion is devoid of wisdom (v. 1a)

ii. Law-keeping religion is demonic (v. 1b)

iii. Law-keeping religion is damning (v. 1c)

b. *Did your regeneration come by works of the Law or by hearing with faith? (3:2)*

i. The means of regeneration is of singular importance (v. 2a)

ii. The means of regeneration is hearing with faith—not works of the law (v. 2b)

c. *Does your sanctification come through works of the Law or through living by faith? (3:3-4)*

i. Sanctification comes through living by faith (v. 3)

ii. Suffering for Christ is vain if you are relying on works of the law (v. 4)

d. *Does God's power come through law-keeping or hearing by faith? (3:5)*

2. The quotation about Abraham's salvation (3:6)

a. *Abraham's salvation is typical of all believers' salvation (v. 6a)*

b. *Abraham's salvation came through faith (v. 6b)*

B. An exposition of the biblical data concerning salvation by faith rather than law-keeping (3:7-4:7)

1. The promised blessings of Abraham—salvation by faith to the nations (3:7-14)

a. *An exposition of justification from Genesis 12:3 (v. 7-9)*

i. The proposition—those who are of faith are sons of Abraham (v. 7)

ii. The proof from Scripture that God would justify Gentiles by faith—Genesis 12:3 (v. 8)

iii. The pronouncement—those of faith are blessed with Abraham, the believer (v. 9)

b. *An exposition of judgment based on law-keeping from the Pentateuch and the Prophets (v. 10-14)*

i. The proposition—law-keepers are under a curse (v. 10a)

ii. The proof from Scripture—Deuteronomy 27:26 (v. 10b)

iii. The proposition—no one is justified by law-keeping (v. 11a)

iv. The proof from Scripture—Habakkuk 2:4 and Leviticus 18:5 (v. 11b-12)

v. The proposition—Christ redeemed us from the curse of the Law (v. 13a)

vi. The proof from Scripture—Deuteronomy 21:23 (v. 13b)

vii. The pronouncement—the blessing of Abraham and the Spirit of God do not come through law-keeping, but rather through faith (v. 14)

2. The purpose of the Law (3:15-25)

a. *The covenant with Abraham is not nullified by the coming of the Law (v. 15-18)*
   i. The explanation of covenants in general—binding and unalterable (v. 15)
   ii. The explanation of the Abrahamic covenant promises—the Law could not negate or alter it (v. 16-18)
      aa. The promises were to Abraham and His Seed (singular)—that is Christ (v. 16)
      bb. The previously ratified covenant could not be changed by the coming of the law—which was 430 years later (v. 17)
      cc. The promised inheritance of the Abrahamic covenant is not based on Law, but on the promise itself (v. 18)

b. *The coming of the Law was a temporary addition to help identify sin and mediate between God and man until Christ would come (v. 19-20)*
   i. The Law was added to identify sin (v. 19ab)
   ii. The Law was given via angelic and mosaic mediation (v. 19c)
   iii. The Law was a temporary addition until Christ (v. 19d)
   iv. The Law was bi-lateral, whereas the Abrahamic covenant was unilaterally given by God (v. 20)

c. *The contribution of the Law was not to impute righteousness, but rather to convict everyone as under sin and in need of a Savior (v. 21-25)*
   i. The Law was not contrary to the Abrahamic promises, but rather complimentary (v. 21)
   ii. The lesson from Scripture is that all are under sin—and the promise of faith comes to those who believe (v. 22)
   iii. The Law acted as legal guardian of the people of God until the faith was revealed (v. 23)
   iv. The Law acted as a tutor to lead people to faith in Christ (v. 24)
   v. The Law is no longer the guardian-tutor for those who trust in Christ (v. 25)

3. The privileged position of those who trust in Christ [rather than law-keeping] (3:26-29)

a. *Those who believe in Christ are sons of God (v. 26)*

b. *Those who are baptized into Christ are clothed with Christ (v. 27)*

c. *Those who are in Christ are one in Him—equal status before God in Christ (v. 28)*

d. *Those who belong to Christ are beneficiaries of the Abrahamic promises (v. 29)*

4. The proper relationship between the law and salvation by grace through faith (4:1-7)
   a. *The illustration introduced—a child heir under a tutor has the same rights as a slave until the father's appointed time (v. 1-2)*
      i. As long as the heir is a minor, he has the same rights as a slave, though he is the owner of all (v. 1)
      ii. He is under guardians and managers until the appointed time (v. 2)
   b. *The illustration applied to believers in Christ—we were under bondage to the Law until God gave us the Spirit of His Son (v. 3-7)*
      i. Our position before Christ—under bondage (v. 3)
      ii. Our position because of Christ—sons and heirs of God (v. 4-7)
         aa. The plan of redemption (v. 4)
         bb. The purchase of redemption (v. 5)
         cc. The privileges of redemption (v. 6-7)
            - Intimacy with the Father (v. 6)
            - Inheritance from the Father (v. 7)

B. An exhortation to turn away from legalism and turn back to the gospel of grace (4:8-31)

1. Recognize that legalism/Law-keeping is just as much slavery as paganism (4:8-11)
   a. *When you were a pagan, you were in bondage (v. 8)*
   b. *Why now—after coming to know God—would you turn back to bondage? (v. 9-10)*
      i. The leading question (v. 9)
      ii. The legalistic observances (v. 10)
   c. *Was my gospel work among you in vain? (v. 11)*
2. Remember the blessings of coming to Christ and the freedom of gospel-based fellowship (4:12-20)
   a. *The call to follow Paul's example and gospel (v. 12)*
   b. *The call to remember the blessing of gospel fellowship (v. 13-15)*
      i. The reason Paul originally preached to them (v. 13)
      ii. The reception he had with them (v. 14)
      iii. The reversal now of that sense of gospel blessing they originally had (v. 15)
   c. *The concern over influences that lead to bondage to the flesh rather than truth that leads to Christlikeness (v. 16-20)*
      i. A question of truth (v. 16)
      ii. A quest for personal influence (v. 17)

iii. A quest for proper influence (v. 18-20)
 aa. Seeking influence is good if it's for the right reason (v. 18)
 bb. Seeking others out of a desire to help them see their identity in Christ is good (v. 19)
 cc. Seeking confirmation of grace in others is good (v. 20)

3. Recognize the distinction between children of the flesh and children of the promise—between fleshly means and faith (4:21-31)

 a. *The admonition to would be law keepers to really understand the Scriptures (v. 21)*
 b. *The analogy of Abraham's two sons and the two covenants—to illustrate fleshly means vs. faith (v. 22-31)*
  i. Two sons of Abraham—one born because of human effort and reasoning, the other because of God's promise (v. 22-23)
   aa. Two sons by two wives (v. 22)
   bb. Two means—the flesh and the promise of God (v. 23)
  iii. Two covenants (as applied to those seeking to live by law and those seeking to live by faith)—Mosaic and Abrahamic (v. 24-31)
   aa. The illustration introduced (v. 24a)
   bb. The illustration explained (v. 24b-27)
    - Abraham's two wives represent two covenants (v. 24b)
    - Hagar represents those who are slaves to Law (v. 24c)
    - Present Jerusalem/Judaizers are slaves to the Law (v. 25)
    - Heavenly Jerusalem signifies those of us who are gospel children—those who trust the promise not the flesh (v. 26)
    - Isaiah 54:1 confirms this (v. 27)
   cc. The illustration applied (v. 28-30)
    - Again, believers are comparable to Isaac—children of promise, not children of the flesh (v. 28)
    - Just as Ishmael persecuted Isaac, so Law-keepers will persecute gospel believers (v. 29)
    - Just as God called for separation from the slave-son, so gospel believers must not allow Law-keepers to continue to influence them (v. 30)
    - Believers are not slaves bound by the Mosaic covenant—but free from the Law (v. 31)

III. The Gospel of Grace Displayed Practically (5:1-6:18)

A. Stand firm in your freedom in Christ (5:1-12)

1. Christ is our freedom—not Law-keeping (5:1-6)
   a. *Christ set us free—so stand firm and don't look to legalism for freedom (v. 1)*
   b. *Circumcision as a requirement [Law-keeping] negates the freedom you have in Christ (v. 2-4)*
      i. Legalism rejects Christ's righteousness (v. 2)
      ii. Legalism requires keeping the whole Law (v. 3)
      iii. Legalism results in a falling away from grace (v. 4)
   c. *Christ will perfect us in righteousness at His coming (v. 5)*
   d. *Circumcision or uncircumcision is of no value for sanctification—only faith working through love (v. 6)*
2. Combining Law-keeping and "Christianity" abolishes the scandal of the cross and perverts the gospel (5:7-12)
   a. *Be careful who you let influence you (v. 7-9)*
      i. The legalist hinders you from obeying the truth (v. 7)
      ii. The Lord does not persuade you away from the truth (v. 8)
      iii. The leaven of legalism will affect everyone and everything (v. 9)
   b. *Be cognizant that legalism abolishes the scandal of the cross and perverts the gospel (v. 10-12)*
      i. Paul's confidence—grace will be the focus of genuine believers rather than legalism (v. 10)
      ii. Paul's concern—circumcision/legalism perverts the gospel (v. 11)
      iii. Paul's condemnation—damning doctrine is serious (v. 12)

B. Serve one another in love because of your freedom in Christ (5:13-15)

1. Love-inspired service is the anecdote for sin—not legalism (5:13)
2. Love is the true fulfillment of the Law (5:14)
3. Legalism leads to spiritual cannibalism and self-destruction (5:15)

C. Seek sanctification by the Spirit—not Law-keeping (5:16-26)

1. Walking by the Spirit introduced (5:16-18)
   a. *The command and the promise to those who obey (v. 16)*
      i. Live life in submission to the Spirit of God (v. 16a)
      ii. You will not carry out the lusts of the flesh (v. 16b)
   b. *The conflict between the Spirit and the flesh (v. 17)*
      i. The flesh and the Spirit are at conflict (v. 17ab)
      ii. The result is a struggle in the believer's life (v. 17c)

c. *The control of the Spirit vs. the confines of the Law (v. 18)*
   i. The condition—if you are led by the Spirit (v. 18a)
   ii. The promise—you are not under the Law (v. 18b)

2. Walking by the flesh evidenced (5:19-21)
   a. *The deeds of the flesh introduced (v. 19a)*
   b. *The deeds of the flesh exemplified (v. 19b-21a)*
      i. Examples of sexual sins (v. 19b)
         aa. Immorality
         bb. Impurity
         cc. Sensuality
      ii. Examples of religious sins (v. 20a)
         aa. Idolatry
         bb. Sorcery
      iii. Examples of attitudinal sins (v. 20b-21a)
         aa. Enmities
         bb. Strife
         cc. Jealousy
         dd. Outbursts of anger
         ee. Disputes
         ff. Dissensions
         gg. Factions
         hh. Envying
      iv. Examples of social sins (v. 21a)
         aa. Drunkenness
         bb. Carousing
      v. Examples as examples—not an exhaustive list [and things like these] (v. 21a)
   c. *The deeds of the flesh assessed (v. 21b)*
      i. Their presence is a reality in a fallen world
      ii. Their practice will result in exclusion from the kingdom of God

3. Walking by the Spirit evidenced (5:22-23)
   a. *The fruit is produced by the Spirit (v. 22a)*
   b. *The fruit is focused on attitudes of the heart (v. 22b-23)*
      i. Love
      ii. Joy
      iii. Peace
      iv. Patience
      v. Kindness
      vi. Goodness
      vii. Faithfulness

viii. Gentleness

ix. Self-control

4. Walking by the Spirit summarized (5:24-26)

   a. *As a believer you have the guarantee of victory over the flesh—your flesh was crucified with Christ [Focus on your victory in Christ] (v. 24)*

   b. *As a believer you have the responsibility to follow the Spirit [Follow the Spirit] (v. 25)*

   c. *As a believer you have the responsibility to turn away from conceit, provoking others, and envy [Forsake comparing yourself to others] (v. 26)*

D. Serve one another with humility and generosity (6:1-10)

1. Serve those who are struggling spiritually (6:1-5)

   a. *By helping to restore the sinning brother (v. 1)*

      i. You must be a believer

      ii. You must be sure that your brother is actually in sin

      iii. You must be walking by the Spirit

      iv. You must seek his restoration in a spirit of gentleness

      v. You must be humble and careful not to fall into sin yourself

   b. *By helping to carry the difficult burdens of your fellow believers (v. 2)*

      i. The command

      ii. The consequence—love/fulfilling the Law

   c. *By humbly examining ourselves and carrying out the responsibilities Christ allotted to each of us (v. 3-5)*

      i. The self-deceptive nature of pride (v. 3)

      ii. The self-examination that leads to confidence (v. 4-5)

         aa. Examine yourself alone before the Lord (v. 4)

         bb. Each person has his own assignment from the Lord (v. 5)

2. Serve those who serve/minister to you (6:6-9)

   a. *Share all good things with those who teach you (v. 6)*

   b. *Sow to the Spirit rather than to the flesh (v. 7-8)*

      i. It is self-deceptive to think you can honor God, but not support His ministry (v. 7)

      ii. It is certain that what you support will have eternal consequences (v. 8)

   c. *Stay steadfast in doing what is good—and in due time you will reap (v. 9)*

3. Serve everyone—but especially believers (6:10)

E. Seek to glory in the cross of Christ and His grace—rather than the flesh (6:11-18)

1. Legalism demands emphatic Apostolic intervention (6:11)
2. Legalism makes a good showing in the flesh, but does not satisfy the true demands of the Law (6:12-13)
   a. *There is a pretense of good—but an avoidance of embracing the scandal of the cross of Christ (v. 12)*
   b. *There is a personal failure to fulfill the Law—but a personal agenda to aggrandize self (v. 13)*
3. Learning to glory in Christ's Person and work alone is the only path to freedom and peace (6:14-18)
   a. *The perspective of faith—boast in nothing but Christ (v. 14-16)*
      i. The commitment to glory in the cross will lead you to sanctification (v. 14)
      ii. The concern isn't whether you are circumcised or not—it's whether you are a new creation in Christ (v. 15)
      iii. The cross-committed life will issue in peace and mercy—even for Jewish believers (v. 16)
   b. *The proof of Paul's desire to glory in Christ alone (v. 17)*
   c. *The prayer for grace for God's people (v. 18)*

Ephesians

Kress Biblical Resources

Overview Outline of Ephesians

Our Riches in Christ Unify the Church, and Manifest His Glory in the Heavenly Realm

I. Introduction (1:1-2)

A. The author (1:1a)
   1. The human author
   2. The Divine Author (2 Tim. 3:16; 2 Pet. 3:15-16)

B. The audience (1:1b)
   1. The original recipients
   2. The current recipients (2 Tim. 3:16-17; 2 Pet. 3:15-16)

C. The address/prayer—grace and peace (1:2)
   1. The salutation of grace to you and peace
   2. The Source of grace and peace

D. The aim
   1. To prepare the church with the truth (cf. Acts 20:29-30)
   2. To promote love (Eph. 1:4, 6; 6:23-24; cf. Rev. 2:1-7)
   3. To promote faith-strengthened, holy living in the Church (4:1; 6:10)
   3. To promote the cosmic glory of God through a unified Church comprised of redeemed Jewish and Gentile believers (1:3, 9-10, 20-21; 2:6, 14-22; 3:6, 10; 6:12)

II. Worshipping in Light of Our Riches as the Church (Eph. 1-3)

A. Rejoice in the Triune God for what He has done for you (1:3-14)
   1. Praise the Father Who planned your redemption (1:3-6)
   2. Praise the Son Who purchased your redemption (1:7-12)
   3. Praise the Spirit Who personally guarantees your redemption (1:13-14)

B. Recognize the surpassing greatness of God's power toward you (1:15-23)
   1. God's power can be made known through the intercessory prayers of other believers (1:15-16, 18-19)
   2. God's power is connected to knowing the Person of God (1:17)
   3. God's power is connected to knowing the promises of God (1:18-19)
   4. God's power is connected to understanding the preeminence of Christ (1:20-23)

C. Remember who you were before Christ and who you are now in Christ (2:1-22)
   1. You were dead spiritually—but now you are alive in Christ (2:1-10)
   2. You were hopeless, without God—but now you are part of the Holy Temple of God (2:11-22)

D. Recognize the unique purpose of the Church, Christ's love, and God's power toward you (3:1-21) [see v. 10]
   1. The purpose of the Church and the Church itself had been a mystery prior to the Apostolic age and Paul's ministry (3:1-13)

2. The prayer of the Apostle is that the Church comprehend and experience the love of Christ and the power of God—to the glory of God (3:14-21)

III. Walking in Light of Our Responsibilities as the Church (Eph. 4-6)

A. Walk worthy of your calling in Christ (4:1-16)
   1. We reveal God's wisdom, power, and love by walking in love and unity (4:1-6)
   2. We reveal God's wisdom, power and love by doing the work of the ministry (4:7-16)

B. Walk with renewed thinking in Christ (4:17-32)
   1. The Sovereign directive concerning our thinking in Christ (4:17a)
   2. The summary and sequence of the world's thinking (4:17b-19)
   3. The sanctified mindset of those who are in Christ (4:20-24)
   4. The sacred responsibilities that exemplify renewed thinking in Christ (4:25-32)

C. Walk in love as God in Christ has loved you (5:1-6)
   1. The precept: Be imitators of God and walk in love (5:1-2)
   2. The practice of love fleshed out (5:3-6)

D. Walk in truth and holiness as children of the light (5:7-14)
   1. Don't partner with those characterized by disobedience to God (5:7-10)
   2. Don't participate in the deeds of those characterized by disobedience to God (5:11-14)

E. Walk in wisdom (5:15-6:9)
   1. Being careful and diligent about living for Christ (5:15-16)
   2. Being cognizant of the will of the Lord (5:17)
   3. Being controlled by the Spirit (5:18-6:9)

F. Walk as warriors for Christ, with the full armor of God (6:10-20)
   1. The Christian warrior[1] (6:10-11)
   2. The Christian's warfare (6:12)
   3. The Christian's weapons (6:13-20)

IV. Conclusion (6:21-24)

A. A faithful messenger commended (6:21-22)

B. A final prayer offered (6:23-24)

---

[1] The Christian warrior; The Christian's warfare; and The Christian's weapons are taken from W. Graham Scroggie, *Scroggie's Bible Handbook*, Revel, p. 429.

Introductory Matters

I. The author (1:1a)

A. The human author[1]

1. The man—Paul
2. His mandate

B. The Divine Author (2 Tim. 3:16; 2 Pet. 3:15-16)

II. The audience (1:1b)

A. The original recipients (cf. Acts 18:19-20:1, 16-38; 1 Cor. 15:32)

1. Their position
2. Their place of residence
3. Their profession and practice

B. The current recipients (2 Tim. 3:16-17; 2 Pet. 3:15-16)

III. The aim

A. To prepare the church with the truth (cf. Acts 20:29-30)

B. To promote love (Eph. 1:4, 6; 6:23-24; cf. Rev. 2:1-7)

C. To promote faith-strengthened, holy living in the Church (4:1; 6:10)

D. To promote the cosmic glory of God through a unified Church comprised of redeemed Jewish and Gentile believers (1:3, 9-10, 20-21; 2:6, 14-22; 3:6, 10; 6:12)

[1] For a biblical biography of the Apostle Paul see Acts 7:58; 8:1; 9:1-30; 11:25-30; 12:25-28:31; 1 Cor. 15:30-32; 2 Cor. 6:4-5; 11:23-30; Gal. 1:13-2:16; Phil. 3:4-14; 2 Thes. 3:8

Detailed Outline of Ephesians

Our Riches in Christ Unify the Church, and Manifest His Glory in the Heavenly Realm

I. Introduction (1:1-2)

A. The author (1:1a)

1. The human author[1]
   a. *The man—Paul*
   b. *His mandate*
2. The Divine Author (2 Tim. 3:16; 2 Pet. 3:15-16)

B. The audience (1:1b)

1. The original recipients (cf. Acts 18:19-20:1, 16-38; 1 Cor. 15:32)
   a. *Their position*
   b. *Their place of residence*
   c. *Their profession and practice*
2. The current recipients (2 Tim. 3:16-17; 2 Pet. 3:15-16)

C. The address/prayer—grace and peace (1:2)

1. The salutation of grace to you and peace
2. The Source of grace and peace

II. Worshipping in Light of Our Riches as the Church (Eph. 1-3)

A. Rejoice in the Triune God for what He has done for you (1:3-14)

1. Praise the Father Who planned your redemption (1:3-6)
   a. *His Person—worthy of praise (v. 3a)*
   b. *His present to us in Christ (v. 3b)*
   c. *His predetermined plan (v. 4-5)*
      i. Election in Christ (v. 4)
         aa. An eternal plan
         bb. An excellent purpose
      ii. Predestination in love (v. 4d-5)
         aa. Adoption as sons through Jesus Christ
         bb. According to grace
   d. *His purpose—**to the praise of the glory of His grace** (v. 6)*

[1] For a biblical biography of the Apostle Paul see Acts 7:58; 8:1; 9:1-30; 11:25-30; 12:25-28:31; 1 Cor. 15:30-32; 2 Cor. 6:4-5; 11:23-30; Gal. 1:13-2:16; Phil. 3:4-14; 2 Thes. 3:8

2. Praise the Son Who purchased your redemption (1:7-12)
   a. *In Him we have redemption through His blood (v. 7a)*
   b. *In Him we have the free and full forgiveness of sins (v. 7b-8a)*
   c. *In Him the Father has made known the mystery of His will (v. 8b-10)*
      i. The provision of wisdom into this mystery (v. 8b-9)
      ii. The purpose of God's revealed mystery—Christ as over all (v. 10)
   d. *In Him we have been sovereignly allotted an eternal inheritance (v. 11-12)*
      i. The reality of our inheritance (v. 11a)
      ii. The reason for our inheritance (v. 11b)
      iii. The result of this redemption in Christ and inheritance we have (v. 12) [**note—to the glory of His grace**]
3. Praise the Spirit Who personally guarantees your redemption (1:13-14)
   a. *The Holy Spirit seals you in Christ, through the gospel you received by faith (v. 13)*
      i. He seals the believer in Christ (v. 13a)
      ii. He does so through the gospel message, to those who listen and believe (v. 13b)
   b. *The Holy Spirit is the down payment of our inheritance (v. 14)*
      i. The pledge of our inheritance and ultimate redemption (v. 14a)
      ii. The purpose of our Spirit-sealed redemption (v. 14b) [**note—to the praise of His glory**]

B. Recognize the surpassing greatness of God's power toward you (1:15-23)

1. God's power can be made known through the intercessory prayers of other believers (1:15-16, 18-19)
   a. *Prayer based on the glorious truths of redemption (v. 15a; cf. v. 3-14)*
   b. *Prayer because of the evident faith and love of those prayed for (v. 15)*
   c. *Prayer bathed in thanksgiving and thoughtfulness (v. 16)*
   d. *Prayer based on the sovereign power and promises of God (v. 18-19)*
2. God's power is connected to knowing the Person of God (1:17)
   a. *The God of our Lord Jesus Christ*
   b. *The God Who is the Father of Glory*
   c. *The Giver of wisdom and of the revelation of the knowledge of Him*
3. God's power is connected to knowing the promises of God (1:18-19)
   a. *Concerning the past (the hope of your calling) (v. 18a)*
   b. *Concerning the future (the inheritance of the saints) (v. 18b)*
   c. *Concerning the present (His power toward us) (v. 19)*

4. God's power is connected to understanding the preeminence of Christ (1:20-23)
    a. *God's power is preeminently displayed in the resurrection and exaltation of Christ (v. 20-21)*
        i. God's power and Christ's resurrection (v. 20a)
        ii. God's power and Christ's ascension to the right hand of God (v. 20b)
        iii. God's power and Christ's exaltation over all authority, power, and dominion—in every age and for all time (v. 21)
    b. *God's power has put all things in subjection to Christ and made Him head over the Church, which is His body (v. 22-23)*
        i. God's power and Christ's rule over all things (v. 22a)
        ii. God's power and Christ's rank in regard to the church as His body (v. 22b-23)

C. Remember who you were before Christ and who you are now in Christ (2:1-22)

1. You were dead spiritually—but now you are alive in Christ (2:1-10)
    a. *You were spiritually dead (v. 1-3)*
        i. The declaration (v. 1)
        ii. The details (v. 2-3)
            aa. You walked in the ways of the world (v. 2a)
            bb. You walked under the influence of Satan (v. 2b)
            cc. You lived out the desires of your fallen nature (v. 3)
    b. *You were made alive in Christ (v. 4-10)*
        i. The Source of your spiritual resurrection (v. 4)
        ii. The stunning reality of your spiritual resurrection (v. 5-6)
            aa. Life came out of death by the sheer grace of God (v 5)
            bb. Now you share the resurrected life and exaltation of Christ Jesus (v. 6)
        iii. The stunning purpose for your spiritual resurrection (v. 7-10)
            aa. To reveal the surpassing riches of His grace in the ages to come (v. 7)
            bb. To reveal that the grace at work in your spiritual resurrection eliminates any human boasting (v. 8-9)
            cc. To reveal that the grace at work in your spiritual resurrection produces divinely ordained good works that we are responsible to walk in (v. 10)

2. You were hopeless, without God—but now you are part of the Holy Temple of God (2:11-22)
   a. *You were separated from God's people and hopeless apart from the gospel (v. 11-12)*
      i. Without the sign of the covenant—circumcision (v. 11)
      ii. Without the covenant promises (v. 12)
   b. *You are now are united to God's people in Christ (v. 13-18)*
      i. Brought near by the blood of Christ (v. 13)
      ii. Barriers removed by Christ, Who is our peace (v. 14-18)
         aa. The summary—Jews and Gentiles are one in Christ (v. 14)
         bb. He fulfilled the demands of the Law that separated (v. 15)
         cc. His death puts the division to death (v. 16)
         dd. His message is peace to both Jew and Gentile (v. 17)
         ee. He is the means by which we have access in one Spirit to the Father (v. 18)
   c. *You are now in the family of God and part of the Holy Temple of God (v. 19-22)*
      i. No longer strangers and aliens—but rather fellow citizens and family (v. 19)
      ii. Now part of the holy temple of God (v. 20-22)
         aa. The foundation—the apostles and prophets (v. 20)
         bb. The Cornerstone—Christ Himself (v. 20b)
         cc. The community being constructed into a living, holy Temple of God in the Spirit (v. 21-22)

D. Recognize the unique purpose of the Church, Christ's love, and God's power toward you (3:1-21) [see v. 10]

1. The purpose of the Church and the Church itself had been a mystery prior to the Apostolic age and Paul's ministry (3:1-13)
   a. *Paul's ministry and the mystery of Gentile inclusion in the body as fellow partakers of Christ (v. 1-6)*
      i. The ministry given to Paul (v. 1-3)
         aa. As a prisoner of Christ (v. 1a)
         bb. As an apostle to the Gentiles (v. 1b-2)
         cc. As a recipient of divine revelation (v. 3)
      ii. The mystery revealed to Paul (v. 4-6)
         aa. Its communication (v. 4-5)
            - Paul had previously written about the divine revelation he had received concerning the mystery (v. 4)
            - It had not been known to prior generations (v. 5)
         bb. Its content—Gentile inclusion in the body and fellow partakers of Christ (v. 6)

b. *Paul's ministry of grace and the magnification of God's glory in the heavenly realm (v. 7-13)*
   i. The gift of gospel ministry (v. 7)
   ii. The gift of Gentile ministry (v. 8)
   iii. The gift of a revelatory ministry (v. 9-12)
      aa. Revealing the administration of the mystery (v. 9)
      bb. Revealing the wisdom of God in the heavenly realm through the church (v. 10)
      cc. Realizing God's eternal purpose in Christ (v. 11)
      dd. Resulting in confident access to the heavenly realm in Christ (v. 12)
   iv. The gift of a suffering ministry (v. 13)

2. The prayer of the Apostle is that the Church comprehend and experience the love of Christ and the power of God—to the glory of God (3:14-21)

a. *The recognition of God's grace, wisdom and sovereign authority (v. 14-15)*
   i. The resumption of thought—"for this reason" (v. 14a)
   ii. The reverence before the Father (v. 14b)
   iii. The recognition of the Father as Source and sovereign over all (v. 15)

b. *The request for God's empowering and illuminating grace, and sovereign glory (v. 16-19)*
   i. Praying for spiritual strength in Christ (v. 16-17a)
      aa. Spiritual strength that has no limit (v. 16a)
      bb. Spiritual strength that is divinely wrought (v. 16b)
      cc. Spiritual strength that is inextricably bound to faith in Christ (v. 17a)
   ii. Praying for supernatural comprehension of Christ's love (v. 17b-19)
      aa. The reality is that love is already your foundation (v. 17b)
      bb. The request is for a unified grasp of the infinite and incomprehensible love of Christ (v. 18-19a)
      cc. The result culminates in being filled up to the fullness of Christ (v. 19b)

c. *The recognition and reverence of God's wisdom, power, and glory (v. 20-21)*
   i. Recognize His incomprehensible wisdom and power (v. 20)
   ii. Reverence His glory in the Church and in Christ Jesus forever and ever (v. 21)

III. Walking in Light of Our Responsibilities as the Church (Eph. 4-6)

A. Walk worthy of your calling in Christ (4:1-16)

1. We reveal God's wisdom, power, and love by walking in love and unity (4:1-6)
   - a. *The example of Paul as a prisoner (v. 1a)*
   - b. *The exhortation to walk worthy of your calling (v. 1b)*
   - c. *The explanation of the worthy walk (v. 2-3)*
     - i. Forbearing with one another in humility, gentleness and love (v. 2)
     - ii. Fastidiously protecting unity and peace within the body (v. 3)
   - d. *The expansion on the basis for our unity in Christ (v. 4-6)*
     - i. One Spirit, one body, one hope (v. 4)
     - ii. One Lord, one faith, one baptism (v. 5)
     - iii. One God and Father, who is over, in and through all (v. 6)
2. We reveal God's wisdom, power and love by doing the work of the ministry (4:7-16)
   - a. *Every believer has a gift—not just pastors or church leaders (v. 7-10)*
     - i. God's grace has gifted a unified body with a diversity of gifts (v. 7)
     - ii. God's Word has revealed this beforehand (v. 8-10)
       - aa. The citation from Psalm 68 (v. 8)
       - bb. The commentary from Paul (v. 9-10)
         - The incarnation, death, burial and resurrection of Christ is assumed within the citation (v. 9-10a)
         - The exaltation and sovereign rule that verifies His right to bestow gifts is implicit in the text (v. 10b)
   - b. *Every believer is to do the work of the ministry—not just pastors or church leaders (v. 11-16)*
     - i. The leaders equip believers to do the work of the ministry (v. 11-12a)
     - ii. Church members do the work of the ministry by building one another up in truth and love (v. 12b-13)
       - aa. The ministry of building up the body (v. 12b)
       - bb. The mission/goal of this ministry (v. 13)
     - iii. Spiritual stability and maturity should be the combined result of this biblical approach to ministry (v. 14-16)
       - aa. No longer children in regard to false teaching (v. 14)
       - bb. Now growing in Christ (v. 15-16)

B. Walk with renewed thinking in Christ (4:17-32)

1. The Sovereign directive concerning our thinking in Christ (4:17a)
2. The summary and sequence of the world's thinking (4:17b-19)
   a. *Thinking that is empty/futile/confused (v. 17b)*
   b. *Thinking that is dark, hard-hearted, and excluded from the life of God (v. 18)*
   c. *Thinking that can no longer sense shame (v. 19)*
3. The sanctified mindset of those who are in Christ (4:20-24)
   a. *A disciple of Christ thinks differently than the world (v. 20-21)*
      i. The reality stated—a disciple has a different mindset than the world (v. 20a)
      ii. The reflection required—have you heard and been taught this (v. 21ab)
      iii. The revelation summarized—the truth is in Jesus (v. 21c)
   b. *A disciple of Christ pursues sanctification (v. 22-24)*
      i. Because of the truth in Jesus a disciple sheds his old way of life (v. 22)
      ii. Because of the truth in Jesus a disciple allows himself to be renewed in his thinking (v. 23)
      iii. Because of the truth in Jesus a disciple pursues righteousness and holiness in the truth (v. 24)
4. The sacred responsibilities that exemplify renewed thinking in Christ (4:25-32)
   a. *Put off lying and put on speaking the truth (v. 25)*
      i. The responsibility (v. 25ab)
      ii. The reason (25c)
   b. *Put off sinful anger and put on being quick to forgive (v. 26-27)*
      i. The responsibility (v. 26)
      ii. The reason (v. 27)
   c. *Put off theft and put on an ethic of hard work and generosity (v. 28)*
      i. The responsibility (v. 28ab)
      ii. The reason (v. 28c)
   d. *Put off corrupt speech and put on edifying speech (v. 29-30)*
      i. The responsibility (v. 29ab)
      ii. The reasons (v. 29c-30)
   e. *Put off hostility and hatred and put on kindness and forgiveness (v. 31-32)*
      i. The responsibility (v. 31-32a)
      ii. The reason (v. 32b)

C. Walk in love as God in Christ has loved you (5:1-6)

1. The precept: Be imitators of God and walk in love (5:1-2)
   - *a. Walk in the ways of your Father (v. 1)*
     - i. Kindness, tenderness, forgiveness (v. 1a)
     - ii. Fatherly love (v. 1b)
   - *b. Walk in the ways of Christ your Savior (v. 2)*
     - i. Redemptive love (v. 2ab)
     - ii. Worshiping love (v. 2c)
2. The practice of love fleshed out (5:3-6)
   - *a. Thanksgiving rather than taking or tearing down (v. 3-4)*
     - i. Immorality, impurity, and greed are not fitting for holy people (v. 3)
     - ii. Filthiness, foolish talk, and foul jokes are not fitting for a thankful people (v. 4)
   - *b. Taking seriously the eternal consequences of not having God as your Father, and therefore not walking in love (v. 5-6)*
     - i. It is certain that no immoral, impure, covetous, idolaters [those who do not walk in love] will enter the kingdom of Christ and God (v. 5)
     - ii. It is clear that the wrath of God comes upon those who are characterized by disobedience to God [those who do not have God as their Father] (v. 6)

D. Walk in truth and holiness as children of the light (5:7-14)

1. Don't partner with those characterized by disobedience to God (5:7-10)
   - *a. Because your Father forbids it (v. 7)*
   - *b. Because your Father has transformed you (v. 8)*
   - *c. Because your fruit confirms who you belong to (v. 9)*
   - *d. Because your fervor is to please the Lord (v. 10)*
2. Don't participate in the deeds of those characterized by disobedience to God (5:11-14)
   - *a. Expose sin as sin rather than participate in it (v. 11)*
   - *b. Even talking about what they do in secret is a disgrace (v. 12)*
   - *c. Expose sin by walking in the light of God's Word (v. 13-14)*
     - i. The truth stated (v. 13)
     - ii. The truth supported (v. 14)

E. Walk in wisdom (5:15-6:9)

1. Being careful and diligent about living for Christ (5:15-16)
   - *a. Careful to live according to God's wisdom (v. 15)*
   - *b. Concerned about taking every opportunity to honor Christ (v. 16)*
2. Being cognizant of the will of the Lord (5:17)

3. Being controlled by the Spirit (5:18-6:9)
   - *a. The Spirit's control introduced (v. 18-21)*
     - i. Drunkenness vs. divine control (v. 18)
     - ii. Devotion to edification, praise and thanksgiving (v. 19-20)
       - aa. Edifying others (v. 19a)
       - bb. Exalting the Lord (v. 19b)
       - cc. Ever giving thanks for all things to the Father through Christ (v. 20)
     - iii. Deference to one another in the fear of Christ (v. 21)
   - *b. The Spirit's control illustrated (v. 22-6:9)*
     - i. In the relationship of wives and husbands (v. 22-32)
       - aa. The Spirit-filled wife's mandate (v. 22-24)
         - The responsibility stated—submission (v. 22)
         - The reason stated (v. 23)
         - The responsibility restated (v. 24)
       - bb. The Spirit-filled husband's mandate (v. 25-32)
         - The responsibility stated—sacrificial love (v. 25)
         - The reflection of Christ and the church elaborated (v. 26-27)
         - The responsibility restated (v. 28-29)
         - The reflection of Christ and the church expanded (v. 30-32)
       - cc. The summary (v. 33)
     - ii. In the relationship of children and parents (v. 1-4)
       - aa. The Spirit-filled child's mandate (v. 1-3)
         - The responsibility stated—obey your parents in the Lord (v. 1)
         - The reason stated—for this is right (v. 1b)
         - The reason supported with Scripture (v. 2)
         - The reward supported by implication in the Scripture (v. 3)
       - bb. The Spirit-filled father's mandate (v. 4)
         - Don't provoke them to anger
         - Discipline/train them to trust the Lord
     - iii. In the relationship of slaves and masters (v. 5-9)
       - aa. The Spirit-filled slave's mandate (v. 5-8)
         - The responsibility stated (v. 5a)
         - The reason—service to Christ (v. 5b-7)
         - The reward (v. 8)

bb. The Spirit-filled master's mandate (v. 9)

- The responsibility stated—treat them in a way that is pleasing to the Lord (v. 9a)
- The reason and reward—their master and yours will reward to each without partiality (v. 9b)

F. Walk as warriors for Christ, with the full armor of God (6:10-20)

1. The Christian warrior[2] (v. 10-11)

a. The call to be empowered by the Lord (v. 10)

b. The call to be equipped for spiritual battle (v. 11)

2. The Christian's warfare (v. 12)

a. A war not against flesh and blood (v. 12a)

b. A war against spiritual forces that are fighting for darkness and depravity in the heavenly realm (v. 12b)

3. The Christian's weapons (v. 13-20)

a. The warrior's mandate reemphasized—stand firm (v. 13-14a)

b. The weapons represented (v. 14b-20)

i. The belt of truth—integrity/faithfulness (v. 14b)

ii. The breastplate of righteousness—trusting in Christ's righteousness and doing what is right (v. 14c)

iii. The boots of the gospel of peace—standing firm knowing you have peace with God (v. 15)

iv. The broad shield of faith—to take cover from the weapons of the adversary (v. 16)

v. The battle-helmet of salvation—focus on the final salvation to be brought at the revelation of Jesus Christ (v. 17a)

vi. The blade/dagger of the Spirit—the specific Word of God for that battle situation (v. 17b)

c. The warrior's prayers requested (v. 18-20)

i. "All" prayer (v. 18)

ii. Apostolic prayer—that the Word of God would go forth and accomplish its purposes (v. 19-20)

Clarity (v. 19a)

Boldness (v. 19b-20)

---

[2] The Christian warrior; The Christian's warfare; and The Christian's weapons are taken from W. Graham Scroggie, *Scroggie's Bible Handbook*, Revel, p. 429.

IV. Conclusion (6:21-24)

A. A faithful messenger commended (6:21-22)

1. Tychicus' mission to the Ephesians introduced (v. 21a, c)
2. Tychicus' character commended (v. 21b)
3. Tychicus' mission reiterated (v. 22)

B. A final prayer offered (6:23-24)

1. A prayer for peace and love with faith (v. 23)
2. A prayer for grace (v. 24)

Philippians

Kress Biblical Resources

Overview Outline of Philippians

Living as Citizens of Heaven brings Unity and Joy, No Matter the Circumstances

I. The introduction (1:1-2)

A. The writer (1:1a)

B. The recipients (1:1b)

C. The reasons (see detailed outline)

D. The requisite greeting (1:2)

II. Praying for fellow participants in the gospel of grace (1:3-11)

A. The practice and perspective of intercessory prayer (1:3-8)

B. The petition of intercessory prayer (1:9-11)

III. Promoting Christ's exaltation no matter the circumstances, whether by life or by death (1:12-26)

A. Joy in the painful circumstances (1:12-18b)

B. Joy in the prospects of the future (1:18c-26)

IV. Practically living out humility, love, and obedience in a manner worthy of the gospel of Christ (1:27-2:30)

A. Keep on conducting yourselves as citizens worthy of the gospel (1:27-30)

B. Keep on considering one another as more important than yourselves (2:1-11)

C. Keep on conforming to the Word of God, as children of God (2:12-18)

D. Keep on cherishing fellowship relationships, and those who model humility, love, and submission to God's will (2:19-30)

V. Pressing on in faith toward the goal of Christlikeness (3:1-4:1)

A. Living by faith as opposed to putting confidence in the flesh [You must avoid the error of the legalists] (3:1-16)

B. Living by faith as opposed to pursuing earthly satisfaction [You must avoid the error of the earthly-minded] (3:17-4:1)

VI. Pursuing unity and peace within the fellowship (4:2-9)

A. The call to be of the same mind (4:2-3)

B. The command to rejoice in the Lord (4:4)

C. The command to reveal kindness/gentleness to all men (4:5a)

D. The comfort that the Lord is near (4:5b)

E. The command to stop worrying and start praying (4:6-7)

F. The command to dwell on that which reflects the character of God (4:8)

G. The command to practice/obey the truth of God (4:9)

VII.Praising God for His provision through His people (4:10-20)

A. Rejoicing in the perfect provision of God (4:10-13)
B. Rejoicing in the partnership that believers have in the gospel and the worship of God (4:14-18)
C. Reaffirming the promised provision and pre-eminent glory of God (4:19-20)

VIII.Conclusion (4:21-23)

A. Greetings—fellowship of the saints [a reminder of unity] (4:21-22)
B. Grace—favor from the Lord Jesus Christ [a request for undeserved favor] (4:23)

Alternate Macro-Structure

Intro (1:1-2)
  Prayer (1:2-11)
    Personal circumstances (1:12-26)
      Plea for a worthy walk and unity (1:27-2:18)
        Partners who seek Christ's interests above all else (2:19-30)
        Pursuing Christ above all else (3:1-4:1)
      Pursuing Peace (4:2-9)
    Personal provisions (4:10-19)
  Prayer (4:20)
Conclusion (4:21-23)

Introductory Matters

I. The author (1:1a)

A. The human author (1:1a)

1. The men [fellow bond-slaves in the gospel ministry]

    a. *Paul*[1]

    b. *Timothy*[2]

2. Their ministry [unified in their service of Christ Jesus]

B. The divine Author (2 Tim. 3:16-17; 2 Pet. 1:12-21, 3:15-16; cf. Col. 4:16; 1 Thes. 2:13; 5:27; 2 Thes. 3:1-4; 1 Tim. 5:18 in which Paul quotes Luke alongside Deut. 25:4 and calls them "Scripture")

II. The audience (1:1b)

A. The original recipients (1:1b; cf. 4:15; Acts 16:12-40; 1 Thes. 2:2)

1. All the saints in Christ Jesus in Philippi
2. Including the overseers and deacons

B. The current recipients (cf. 2 Pet. 3:15-16)

III. The aim

A. To thank and encourage the Philippians in their participation in the gospel ministry and support of Paul (1:3, 5; 2:25, 30; 4:10-20)

B. To inform the Philippians of his current circumstances and the furtherance of the gospel ministry (1:12-14)

C. To inform the Philippians of Timothy's planned visit in the future, and explain why Epaphroditus was returning to them [i.e., gospel ministry relationships] (2:19-29)

D. To exhort the Philippians in unity as they strive together for the faith of the gospel—even in the midst of difficulty and suffering (1:27-2:18; 4:1-2)

E. To warn against false teachers who trust something other than Christ for their righteousness before God [i.e., warning against those who oppose the gospel of Christ] (3:2-21)

F. To encourage true joy based on the furtherance of the gospel, and relationships based on the gospel (1:4-5, 18, 25; 2:2, 17-18, 28-29; 3:1; 4:1, 4, 10)

---

[1] For a biblical biography of the Apostle Paul see Acts 7:58; 8:1; 9:1-30; 11:25-30; 12:25-28:31; 1 Cor. 15:30-32; 2 Cor. 6:4-5; 11:23-30; Gal. 1:13-2:16; Phil. 3:4-14; 2 Thes. 3:8

[2] For a biblical biography of Timothy see Acts 16:1; 17:14-15; 18:5; 1 Cor. 4:17; 16:10; Phil. 2:19-23; 1 Thes. 3:2, 6; 1 Tim. 1:2; 5:23; Heb. 13:23

G. To encourage believers as to the great hope of Christ's return (1:6, 10; 2:9-11, 16; 3:20-21; 4:5)

H. To promote an all-consuming passion for the Person and glory of the Lord Jesus Christ (1:2, 11, 19-23; 2:5-11, 21; 3:3, 7-14, 20-21; 4:23)

I. Summary theme: Stand firm in unity and joy no matter the opposition, through an all-consuming passion for the Person and glory of Christ, the furtherance of the gospel, and the fellowship of the saints—until the day of Christ

Detailed Outline of Philippians

Living as Citizens of Heaven brings Unity and Joy, No Matter the Circumstances

- **I. The introduction (1:1-2)**
  - **A. The writer (1:1a)**
    1. The human author (1:1a)
       - *a. The men [fellow bond-slaves in the gospel ministry]*
         - i. Paul[1]
         - ii. Timothy[2]
       - *b. Their ministry [unified in their service of Christ Jesus]*
    2. The divine Author (2 Tim. 3:16-17; 2 Pet. 1:12-21, 3:15-16; cf. Col. 4:16; 1 Thes. 2:13; 5:27; 2 Thes. 3:1-4; 1 Tim. 5:18 in which Paul quotes Luke alongside Deut. 25:4 and calls them "Scripture")
  - **B. The recipients (1:1b)**
    1. The original recipients (1:1b; cf. 4:15; Acts 16:12-40; 1 Thes. 2:2)
       - *a. All the saints in Christ Jesus in Philippi*
       - *b. Including the overseers and deacons*
    2. The current recipients (cf. 2 Pet. 3:16)
  - **C. The requisite greeting (1:2)**
    1. The greeting/prayer of grace to you and peace (1:2a)
    2. The Giver of grace and peace (1:2b)
- **II. Praying for fellow participants in the gospel of grace (1:3-11)**
  - **A. The practice and perspective of intercessory prayer (1:3-8)**
    1. The practice and perspective of <u>thankfulness</u> (1:3)
       - *a. Thanking God (v. 3a)*
         - i. It was a personal thanksgiving
         - ii. It was a persistent thanksgiving
       - *b. Thinking of others (v. 3b)*
    2. The practice of prayer with the perspective of <u>joy</u> (1:4-6)
       - *a. The many entreaties (v. 4a)*

---

[1] For a biblical biography of the Apostle Paul see Acts 7:58; 8:1; 9:1-30; 11:25-30; 12:25-28:31; 1 Cor. 15:30-32; 2 Cor. 6:4-5; 11:23-30; Gal. 1:13-2:16; Phil. 3:4-14; 2 Thes. 3:8

[2] For a biblical biography of Timothy see Acts 16:1; 17:14-15; 18:5; 1 Cor. 4:17; 16:10; Phil. 2:19-23; 1 Thes. 3:2, 6; 1 Tim. 1:2; 5:23; Heb. 13:23

b. *The manifold joy (v. 4b)*

c. *The ministry partnership (v. 5)*

d. *The marked confidence (v. 6)*

3. The presence and perspective of affection (1:7-8)

a. *Because of their participation in grace (v. 7)*

b. *Because of Paul's perspective in Christ (v. 8)*

B. The petition of intercessory prayer (1:9-11)

1. Growth in biblical love, wisdom, and righteous character (1:9-11a)

a. *Love that abounds more and more, yet is governed by knowledge and discernment (v. 9)*

b. *Discernment that issues in sincerity and integrity (v. 10)*

c. *Righteous character through Jesus Christ (v. 11a)*

2. God's glory (1:11b)

III. Promoting Christ's exaltation no matter the circumstances, whether by life or by death (1:12-26)

A. Joy in the painful circumstances (1:12-18b)

1. Relating the progress of the gospel in and through imprisonment (1:12-17)

a. *Christ's glory revealed to the Philippians (v. 12)*

b. *Christ's glory revealed to the Praetorian Guard and everyone else (v. 13)*

c. *Christ's glory revealed by the brethren (v. 14)*

d. *Christ's glory revealed by those with pure motives and those who witness out of selfish ambition (v. 15-17)*

i. The truth about those preaching Christ (v. 15)

ii. The true preachers' motives examined more closely (v. 16)

iii. The treacherous preachers' motives examined more closely (v. 17)

2. Rejoicing in the proclamation of Christ no matter what (1:18a, b)

a. *The cause of joy (v. 18a)*

b. *The choice of joy (v. 18b)*

B. Joy in the prospects of the future (1:18c-26)

1. Paul's passionate conviction concerning His life's ambition—Christ's exaltation (1:18c-21)

a. *Christ's exaltation certified Paul's future rejoicing (1:18c)*

b. *Christ's exaltation could be accomplished in Paul's life through the prayers of others and the provision of the Spirit of Christ (v. 19)*

c. *Christ's exaltation characterized Paul's life ambition (v. 20-21)*

i. His confidence (v. 20a)

ii. His concern stated negatively (v. 20b)
iii. His concern stated positively (v. 20c)
iv. His creed (v. 21)

2. Paul's precious conundrum/quandary concerning life and death (1:22-24)
   a. *To live on for Christ—fruitful labor (v. 22)*
   b. *To depart and be with Christ—far better personally (v. 23)*
   c. *To remain on in the flesh for the sake of the Philippians—quite needful (v. 24)*
3. Paul's personal conviction concerning the future (1:25-26)
   a. *The knowledge that he would remain for their sake (v. 25)*
   b. *The next reunion that would bring even greater confidence in Christ (v. 26)*

IV. Practically living out humility, love, and obedience in a manner worthy of the gospel of Christ (1:27-2:30)

A. Keep on conducting yourselves as citizens worthy of the gospel (1:27-30)

1. The command (1:27a)
2. The commitment (1:27b-30)
   a. *Standing firm in unity (v. 27b)*
   b. *Striving together for the faith of the gospel (v. 27c)*
   c. *Standing strong in the face of opposition and suffering (v. 28-30)*
      i. The sign of salvation—courage in the face of opposition (v. 28ab)
      ii. The gift of God—not only faith in Christ but also suffering for His sake (v. 28c-29)
      iii. The fellowship of Paul—the fight/agony of faith (v. 30)

B. Keep on considering one another as more important than yourselves (2:1-11)

1. The exhortation to biblical love and humility (2:1-4)
   a. *The motivations behind biblical love and humility (v. 1-2a)*
      i. Encouragement in Christ (v. 1a)
      ii. Consolation of love (v. 1b)
      iii. Fellowship of the Spirit (v. 1c)
      iv. Affection and compassion (v. 1d)
      v. Apostolic joy (v. 2a)
   b. *The manifestations of biblical love and humility (v. 2b-4)*
      i. Unity (v. 2b-e)
         aa. Same mind (v. 2b)
         bb. Same love (v. 2c)
         cc. United in spirit (v. 2d)

dd. Intent on one purpose (v. 2e)

ii. Humility (v. 3)

aa. Doing nothing from selfishness or empty conceit (v. 3a)

bb. Regarding one another as more important than self (v. 3b)

iii. Love/concern for others (v. 4)

2. The Example of biblical love and humility (2:5-11)

a. The mind of Christ is required to live out biblical love and humility (v. 5)

b. The mind of Christ is revealed when you understand who He is, what He did, and the final result of His sacrificial love and self-humbling (v. 6-11)

i. Understand His sovereignty as God (v. 6)

ii. Understand His Self-emptying in becoming a man (v. 7)

iii. Understand His Self-humiliation, submission, sacrifice on the cross (v. 8)

iv. Understand His super-exaltation as Lord of all, which followed His submission and sacrifice (v. 9-11)

aa. The reason for His exaltation (v. 9a)

bb. The Source of His exaltation (v. 9b)

cc. The supremacy of His exaltation (v. 9c)

dd. The result of His exaltation (v. 10-11a)

ee. The purpose of His exaltation (v. 11b)

C. Keep on conforming to the Word of God, as children of God (2:12-18)

1. The paradox of faith-driven obedience (2:12-13)

a. The believer's responsibility—"work out your salvation" (v. 12)

i. The commitment of obedience (v. 12abc)

aa. Based on Christ's submission and obedience (v. 12a)

bb. Based on their relationship with Paul (v. 12b)

cc. Based on a pattern of obedience (v. 12c)

ii. The command of obedience (v. 12d)

iii. The concern of obedience (v. 12e)

b. The believer's rest—"for it is God who is at work in you" (v. 13)

i. The Person who ultimately works out your salvation—God (v. 13a)

ii. The place where He is at work—in you (v. 13b)

iii. The process by which He is at work—to will and to work (v. 13c)

iv. The purpose for which He is at work (v. 13d)

2. The practice of faith-driven obedience (2:14-16)

a. Obey without grumbling or disputing (v. 14)

- b. *Obey so that you may shine forth as children of God, as lights in a dark world (v. 15)*
- c. *Obey by holding fast [holding forth] the word of life (v 16a)*
- d. *Obey so that those who proclaimed the Word to you will not have toiled in vain (v. 16b)*

3. The Pauline example of faith-driven obedience (2:17-18)
   - a. *The drink-offering—a picture of pouring oneself out completely in the worship of God (v. 17a)*
   - b. *The delight of unified worship (v. 17b-18)*

D. Keep on cherishing fellowship relationships, and those who model humility, love, and submission to God's will (2:19-30)

1. The example of Paul (2:19-30)
   - a. *In sending Timothy (v. 19-24)*
     - i. Concern for the welfare of others (v. 19-21)
       - aa. A desire to know of the spiritual condition of friends in Christ (v. 19)
       - bb. A desire to see them grow in Christ (v. 20-21)
     - ii. Concern for the furtherance of the gospel (v. 22)
     - iii. Concern for giving of oneself in order to bless friends in Christ (v. 23-24)
       - aa. Proper communication pursued (v. 23)
       - bb. Personal coming planned (v. 24)
   - b. *In sending Epaphroditus (v. 25-30)*
     - i. Concern for the welfare of others (v. 25-28)
       - aa. The welfare of Epaphroditus (v. 25-27)
       - bb. The welfare of the Philippians (v. 25-26, 28)
     - ii. Concern for the proper response to those who sacrifice of themselves for the sake of the gospel (v. 29-30)
2. The example of Timothy (2:19-24)
   - a. *His personal history (v. 19, 22)*
   - b. *His passionate concern (v. 20-21)*
     - i. The interests/welfare of the Philippians (v. 20)
     - ii. The interests of Christ Jesus (v. 21)
   - c. *His proven worth (v. 22)*
   - d. *His particular mission in regard to the Philippians (v. 23-24)*
     - i. Information (v. 23)
     - ii. Reservations (v. 24)
3. The example of Epaphroditus (2:25-30)
   - a. *His ministry (v. 25)*
     - i. In relation to Paul (v. 25a,b,c)
       - aa. Brother (v. 25a)

bb. Co-worker (v. 25b)

cc. Co-soldier (v. 25c)

ii. In relation to the Philippians (v. 25d,e)

aa. An apostle from the Philippians (v. 25d)

bb. An attendant from the Philippians to meet Paul's need (v. 25e)

b. His mindset (v. 26)

c. His malady and merciful recovery (v. 27)

d. His mission in returning to Philippi (v. 28)

e. His much deserved honor (v. 29-30)

i. The reception he is to be given (v. 29a)

ii. The regard he is to be held in (v. 29b)

iii. The reason for this honor (v. 30)

V. Pressing on in faith toward the goal of Christlikeness (3:1-4:1)

A. Living by faith as opposed to putting confidence in the flesh [You must avoid the error of the legalists] (3:1-16)

1. The summary command for living by faith—"Rejoice in the Lord" (3:1)

a. The prescription—"Keep rejoicing in the Lord" (v. 1a)

b. The protection it brings (v. 1b)

2. The surpassing value of knowing Christ Jesus by faith (3:2-11)

a. The caution concerning legalists (v. 2)

i. Their character is unclean (v. 2a)

ii. Their conduct is evil (v. 2b)

iii. Their confidence (faith) is misplaced [Their circumcision is really mutilation] (v. 2c)

b. The comfort and confession of all true believers (v. 3)

i. We belong to the true people of God (v. 3a)

ii. We bring worship in the Spirit of God (v. 3b)

iii. We boast only in Christ Jesus and put no confidence in the flesh (v. 3c)

c. The contrast between Paul's former life, and his life of faith (v. 4-11)

i. His former life remembered—Valuing religious credentials (v. 4-6)

aa. Paul's argument (v. 4)

bb. Paul's accomplishments and religious credentials (v. 5-6)

ii. His life of faith revealed—Valuing Christ above all else (v. 7-11)

aa. His repentance in regard to former religious achievements (v. 7)

bb. His re-evaluation of all things in light of knowing Christ (v. 8) cc. His reception of Christ's righteousness by faith (v. 9)

dd. His relationship with Christ—the all-consuming passion (v. 10)

ee. His resurrection hope (Christlikeness)—the sanctifying prize (v. 11)

3. The steadfast pursuit of the prize, which is Christlikeness (3:12-16)

a. The personal perspective and pursuit of the Apostle Paul (v. 12-14)

i. His personal perspective—not yet perfected (v. 12a)

ii. His personal pursuit—pressing on in pursuit of Christlikeness (v. 12b)

iii. His public profession—not yet perfected (v. 13a)

iv. His preeminent pursuit—pressing on for the prize of Christlikeness (v. 13b-14)

aa. Choosing to forget what is behind and reaching forward to what is ahead (v. 13b)

bb. Chasing the finish line and the prize of the upward call of God in Christ Jesus (v. 14)

b. The proper perspective and pursuit for all believers (v. 15-16)

i. We must continue to meditate on Christ's infinite value and pursue the heavenly prize of Christlikeness above all else (v. 15)

ii. We must continue to live according to the same standard by which we have come—faith (v. 16)

B. Living by faith as opposed to pursuing earthly satisfaction [You must avoid the error of the earthly-minded] (3:17-4:1)

1. The examples to imitate and observe (3:17)

a. Be continually imitating Paul's example (v. 17a)

b. Be continually observing those who walk according to the Apostolic pattern (v. 17b)

2. The enemies to contemplate and avoid (3:18-19)

a. The reminder of the enemies (v. 18)

i. They are many (v. 18a)

ii. They are mentioned frequently by Paul (v. 18b)

iii. They are enemies of the cross of Christ (v. 18c)

b. The reminder of their condemnation and character (v. 19)

i. Their end is destruction (v. 19a)

ii. Their god is their appetite (v. 19b)

iii. Their glory is their shame (v. 19c)

iv. Their minds are set on earthly things (v. 19d)

VI. Pursuing unity and peace within the fellowship (4:2-9)

A. The call to be of the same mind (4:2-3)

1. The exhortation to Euodia and Syntyche to be of the same mind (4:2)
2. The entreaty to Paul's "yoke fellow" to help in these women (4:3a)
3. The encouragement concerning these two women (4:3b)

B. The command to rejoice in the Lord (4:4)

1. The repeated command to keep on rejoicing (4:4a,d)
2. The root of one's rejoicing (4:4b)
3. The range of times when one is to rejoice (4:4c)

C. The command to reveal kindness/gentleness to all men (4:5a)

D. The comfort that the Lord is near (4:5b)

E. The command to stop worrying and start praying (4:6-7)

1. Stop worrying (4:6a)
   - a. *The exhortation*
   - b. *The exceptions—there are none*
2. Start praying (4:6b)
   - a. *What we are to pray about*
   - b. *How we are to pray*
     - i. Prayer
     - ii. Supplication
     - iii. With thanksgiving
     - iv. Requests
   - c. *To Whom we are to pray*
3. Supernatural results promised (4:7)
   - a. *The peace of God, which surpasses all comprehension (v. 7a)*
   - b. *The protection of your hearts and minds in Christ Jesus (v. 7b)*

F. The command to dwell on that which reflects the character of God (4:8)

1. The concluding remark (4:8a)
2. The character to contemplate (4:8b)
   - a. *Whatever is true*
   - b. *Whatever is honorable*
   - c. *Whatever is right*
   - d. *Whatever is pure*
   - e. *Whatever is lovely*

f. *Whatever is of good repute*
g. *If there is any excellence*
h. *If there is anything worthy of praise*

3. The command to contemplate them (4:8c)

G. The command to practice/obey the truth of God (4:9)

1. Following Paul's teaching and example (4:9a)
2. Fellowshipping with the God of peace (4:9b)

VII.Praising God for His provision through His people (4:10-20)

A. Rejoicing in the perfect provision of God (4:10-13)

1. The concern of God's people enhances joy in the Lord (4:10)
   a. *Paul rejoiced greatly in the Lord because of the Philippians' gift (v. 10a)*
   b. *Paul recognized the Philippians' thoughtfulness of him (v. 10b,c)*
      i. Because of the gift (v. 10b)
      ii. Before the gift (v. 10c)
2. The contentment of Christ's sufficiency is the secret of joy in the Lord (4:11-13)
   a. *The satisfaction of contentment is available in any and every circumstance (v. 11-12)*
      i. Contentment is a learned spiritual discipline (v. 11)
      ii. Contentment is available regardless of one's temporal prosperity or poverty (v. 12)
   b. *The secret of contentment is resting in the sufficiency of Christ (v. 13)*

B. Rejoicing in the partnership that believers have in the gospel and the worship of God (4:14-18)

1. Rejoicing in the partnership of giving and receiving for the sake of the gospel (4:14-17)
   a. *The present partnership and gift (v. 14)*
   b. *The past partnership and previous gifts (v. 15-16)*
   c. *The profit [future reward] of sacrificial giving (v. 17)*
2. Rejoicing in the provision and worship of God through sacrificial giving (4:18)

C. Reaffirming the promised provision and pre-eminent glory of God (4:19-20)

1. The promise for those who sacrifice for Christ's sake (4:19)
2. The praise and prayer of every sacrificial worshipper (4:20)

VIII.Conclusion (4:21-23)

A. Greetings—fellowship of the saints [a reminder of unity] (4:21-22)

1. Greetings from Paul (v. 21a)
2. Greetings from the brethren with Paul (v. 21b)
3. Greetings from all the saints [in Rome] (v. 22a)
4. Greetings from those saints from Caesar's household (v. 22b)

B. Grace—favor from the Lord Jesus Christ [a request for undeserved favor] (4:23)

Colossians

Kress Biblical Resources

Overview Outline of Colossians

Completeness in Christ Guards Against the Counterfeits of Mysticism, Legalism, and Traditionalism

I. Introduction: Greetings of grace and peace to those complete in Christ (1:1-2)

A. The writer (1:1)
   1. The human author
   2. The Divine author

B. The recipients (1: 2a)
   1. The original recipients
   2. The current recipient (cf. 2 Tim. 3:16-17; 2 Pet. 3:15-16)

C. The reasons
   1. Confirmation: Paul confirmed his care for the Colossian believers, and assured them of their standing in Christ (1:2-12, 24-29; 2:1-5)
   2. Refutation: Paul refuted the error of integrating human wisdom/philosophy with Christianity (2:2-4, 8-23)
   3. Exhortation: Paul exhorted the Colossians to live in light of the supremacy and sufficiency in Christ (2:6-7; 3:1-4:6)
   4. Information: Paul sent information concerning himself, his fellow-workers, and even another epistle (4:7-18)
   5. Summation/Theme: Paul's theme in Colossians is the sufficiency and supremacy of Christ/Complete in Christ (1:13-23, 28-29; 2:2-3, 8-10; 3:3-4, 11c)

D. The requisite greeting (2:2b)

II. Intercession/Edification: Encouragement through thanksgiving and prayer for those in Christ (1:3-14)

A. Paul thanked God for the Colossians' faith: Completeness in Christ begins with true conversion (1:3-8)

B. Paul prayed for the Colossians growth: Completeness in Christ is experienced through living in light of God's revealed will (1:9-14)

III. Instruction: Completeness in Christ starts with understanding the supremacy and sufficiency of Christ (1:15-2:5)

A. The supremacy and sufficiency of Christ's Person and work (1:15-23)

B. The supremacy and sufficiency of Christ in Paul's ministry (1:23c-2:5)

IV. Refutation: Completeness in Christ cannot be obtained by human wisdom, religious tradition, mystical experience, or human effort—it is a gift of grace received by faith (2:6-23)

A. You are complete in Christ—do not be taken captive by philosophical deception (2:6-15)

B. You are complete in Christ—do not be subject to ritualism [religious traditionalism] (2:16-17)

C. You are complete in Christ—do not be defrauded by mysticism (2:18-19)

D. You are complete in Christ—do not be subject to asceticism/self-made religion [rule-keeping religion] (2:20-23)

V. Exhortation: Completeness in Christ is a gift of God that should shape all of life (3:1-4:6)

A. The root of your life: Your thinking and desires should reflect your completeness in Christ (3:1-4)

B. The fruit of your life in general character: Your character should reflect your completeness in Christ (3:5-17)

C. The fruit of your life in specific social relationships: Your relationships should reflect your completeness in Christ (3:18-4:1)

D. The fruit of your life in prayer and evangelism: Your prayer life and witness should reflect your completeness in Christ (4:2-6)

VI. Information/Participation: Completeness in Christ brings fellowship, love and concern for the brethren (4:7-18)[1]

A. Paul sent two representatives to both inform and encourage the Colossians because of his fellowship, love and concern for them—and they for him (4:7-9)

B. Paul sent greetings from other believers of note to the Colossians because of their mutual fellowship, love and concern (4:10-14)

C. Paul sent his final instructions, and personal greetings to promote mutual fellowship, love and concern (4:15-18)

[1] These weren't superficial closing remarks, but were meant to foster fellowship, love and mutual care for those complete in Christ—between both Jewish and Gentile believers.

Introductory Matters

I. The writer (1:1)

A. The human author

1. Paul[1]
2. In association with Timothy[2]

B. The Divine author

II. The recipients (1:2a; cf. 1:7; 2:1; 4:12)

A. The original recipients

1. Their position in Christ
   a. *Set apart in Christ*
   b. *Faithful in Christ*
   c. *Brothers in Christ*
2. Their place of residence

B. The current recipients (2 Tim. 3:16-17; 2 Pet. 3:15-16)

III. The reasons

A. Confirmation: To confirm care for the Colossian believers, and assured them of their standing in Christ (1:2-12, 24-29; 2:1-5)

B. Refutation: To refute the error of integrating human wisdom/philosophy with Christianity (2:2-4, 8-23)

1. Philosophy/so-called knowledge (2:2-4, 8)
2. Traditional legalism (2:11-17)
3. Mysticism (2:18-19)
4. Self-made legalism/asceticism (2:20-23)

C. Exhortation: To exhort the Colossians to live in light of the supremacy and sufficiency in Christ (2:6-7; 3:1-4:6)

D. Information: To inform the Colossians about Paul's situation, his fellow-workers, and even another epistle (4:7-18)

---

[1] For a biblical biography of the Apostle Paul see Acts 7:58; 8:1; 9:1-30; 11:25-30; 12:25-28:31; 1 Cor. 15:30-32; 2 Cor. 6:4-5; 11:23-30; Gal. 1:13-2:16; Phil. 3:4-14; 2 Thes. 3:8

[2] For a biblical biography of Timothy see Acts 16:1; 17:14-15; 18:5; 1 Cor. 4:17; 16:10; Phil. 2:19-23; 1 Thes. 3:2, 6; 1 Tim. 1:2; 5:23; Heb. 13:23

E. **Summation/Summary purpose**: To exalt the sufficiency and supremacy of Christ and thus believers are complete in Christ (1:13-23, 28-29; 2:2-3, 8-10; 3:3-4, 11c)

1. He is Savior (1:14, 20-22; 2:11-15)
2. He is Supreme (1:15b, 17-18; 2:10, 19; 3:1)
3. He is Creator (1:16)
4. He is God (1:1:15a, 16, 19; 2:9)
5. He is life and all the believer needs (2:9-10; 3:3-4, 11)

Detailed Outline of Colossians

Completeness in Christ Guards Against the Counterfeits of Mysticism, Legalism, and Traditionalism

I. Introduction: Greetings of grace and peace from an Apostle of Christ (the All-sufficient One) to those complete in Christ (1:1-2)

A. The writer (1:1)

1. The human author
    a. *Paul*[1]
    b. *In association with Timothy*[2]
2. The Divine author

B. The recipients (1:2a; cf. 1:7; 2:1; 4:12)

1. Their position in Christ
    a. *Set apart in Christ*
    b. *Faithful in Christ*
    c. *Brothers in Christ*
2. Their place of residence

C. The requisite greeting (1:2b)

II. Intercession/Edification: Encouragement through thanksgiving and prayer for those in Christ (1:3-14)

A. Paul thanked God for the Colossians' faith: Completeness in Christ begins with true conversion (1:3-8)

1. He verified that they evidenced true conversion (1:3-5a)
    a. *The evidence of true conversion compels godly ministers of the gospel to thank God for His saving work—Is that true of your life? (v. 3)*
        i. Paul and Timothy consistently gave thanks for the Colossian believers (v. 3a)
        ii. God, the Father of our Lord Jesus Christ was the One to be thanked [The true God was the source of their conversion/salvation] (v. 3b)
    b. *True conversion is evidenced by faith in Christ Jesus—Do others "hear" of your faith and see it?] (v. 4a)*
    c. *True conversion is evidenced by love for other believers—Is that evidenced in your life? (v. 4b)*

---

[1] For a biblical biography of the Apostle Paul see Acts 7:58; 8:1; 9:1-30; 11:25-30; 12:25-28:31; 1 Cor. 15:30-32; 2 Cor. 6:4-5; 11:23-30; Gal. 1:13-2:16; Phil. 3:4-14; 2 Thes. 3:8

[2] For a biblical biography of Timothy see Acts 16:1; 17:14-15; 18:5; 1 Cor. 4:17; 16:10; Phil. 2:19-23; 1 Thes. 3:2, 6; 1 Tim. 1:2; 5:23; Heb. 13:23

   d. *True conversion is evidenced as springing from the promised hope of perfect intimacy with God—Do our goals evidence such hope (5a)*

2. He verified that their conversion was based on the true gospel (1:5b-8)
   a. *The true gospel is a message of hope and "the word of truth" (v. 5b-6a)*
      i. It is a message of hope
      ii. It is a message of truth
      iii. It is a message of good news preached
   b. *The true gospel of grace changes lives [bears fruit] wherever it is received (v. 6)*
      i. In all the world (it is a universal gospel)
      ii. In you also (it is a personal gospel)
      iii. Through hearing and understanding the grace of God in truth
   c. *The true gospel is proclaimed by faithful servants of Christ (v. 7-8)*
      i. Epaphras was a beloved, fellow-slave [a respected fellow-worker with Paul]
      ii. Epaphras was a faithful minister in regard to the Apostolic message
      iii. Epaphras was convinced of the Colossians' conversion as evidenced by love (v. 8)

B. Paul prayed for the Colossians growth: Completeness in Christ is experienced through living in light of God's revealed will (1:9-14)

1. The cause and commitment of their intercession: Paul and his associates consistently prayed for the Colossians as believers (1:9a)
   a. *The reason for their prayers was the evidence of conversion*
   b. *The people who prayed*
   c. *The consistency of their prayers*
2. The content of their intercession: Paul and his associates consistently prayed for the spiritual growth of the Colossians as believers (1:9b-14)
   a. *True spiritual growth begins with the knowledge of God's will (v. 9b)*
      i. That you may be filled with the knowledge of His will
      ii. In all spiritual wisdom and understanding
   b. *The true knowledge of God's will leads to a life conducted in a manner worthy of the Lord (v. 10-14)*
      i. A desire to please Him in all respects (v. 10b)
      ii. Bearing fruit in every good work (v. 10c)
      iii. Increasing in the knowledge of God (v. 10d)

- iv. Walking in God's strength, which results in perseverance and patience (v. 11a)
- v. Joyously giving thanks to God (v. 11b-14)
  - aa. Because He makes us righteous/worthy: He qualified us for the inheritance of the saints in Light (v. 12)
  - bb. Because He has given us a new citizenship in the Kingdom of His beloved Son (v. 13)
  - cc. Because He has forgiven and redeemed us in Christ (v. 14)

III. Instruction: Completeness in Christ starts with understanding the supremacy and sufficiency of Christ (1:15-2:5)

A. The supremacy and sufficiency of Christ's Person and work (1:15-23)

1. The supremacy and sufficiency of Christ's Person (1:15-18)

- *a. He is the visible manifestation of the invisible God (v. 15a)*
- *b. He holds the ownership rights over all creation (v. 15b-16)*
  - i. He is pre-eminent over all creation (v. 15b)
  - ii. He created all things (v. 16)
    - aa. In the heavens and on earth
    - bb. Visible and invisible
    - cc. Thrones, dominions, rulers, authorities
  - iii. He is the One for whom all things have been created (v. 16c)
- *c. He is eternal, and sovereign over the universe (v. 17a)*
  - i. His eternality
  - ii. His sovereignty over the universe
- *d. He is the sovereign Lord of the Church—so that He might come to have first place in everything (v. 18)*
  - i. He is the head of the body, the church (v. 18a)
  - ii. He is the beginning and pre-eminent One of the resurrection (v. 18b)
    - aa. He is the beginning
    - bb. He is the pre-eminent One of the resurrection
    - cc. He is to have the highest rank in everything

2. The supremacy and sufficiency of Christ's redemptive work (1:19-23)

- *a. God's perspective of Christ's redemptive work (v. 19-20)*
  - i. God was pleased to become incarnate in His Son (v. 19)
    - aa. A sovereign choice of "good pleasure"
    - bb. The fullness
    - cc. To dwell in Him
  - ii. God was reconciling all things to Himself in Christ (v. 20)
    - aa. Separation: Reconciliation

bb. Enmity/Wrath: Peace

cc. Atonement/propitiation: The blood of His cross

b. The believer's/Colossians' perspective of Christ's redemptive work (v. 21-23)

i. Your standing before coming to Christ (v. 21)

aa. Alienated

bb. Hostile in mind

cc. Engaged in evil deeds

ii. Your reconciliation in Christ (v. 22)

aa. The substitution

bb. The purpose

iii. Your responsibility until the coming of Christ (v. 23)

B. The supremacy and sufficiency of Christ in Paul's ministry (1:23c-2:5)

1. Paul's ministry to the church in general (1:23c-29)

a. It was a ministry of salvation/good news in Christ (v. 23c)

b. It was a ministry of joyful suffering for Christ and His church (v. 24)

c. It was a ministry of service to Christ and His church (v. 25a)

d. It was a ministry of revelation of the glory of Christ and the mystery of His church (v. 25b-27)

i. The Word of God and the mystery hidden from past generations (v. 25b-26a)

ii. The sovereign revelation of that mystery (v. 26b-27)

iii. The riches of the glory of this mystery (v. 27b)

e. It was a ministry of proclaiming Christ, and discipling His church (v. 28-29)

i. The message of Paul's ministry: Christ (v. 28a)

ii. The methods of Paul's ministry: Admonishing and teaching concerning Christ (v. 28b)

iii. The purpose [motive] of Paul's ministry: Worship through presenting men complete in Christ (v. 28c)

iv. The power [might] of Paul's ministry: Christ's power energizing Paul's intense labor (v. 29)

2. Paul's ministry to the local church [Colossae and Laodicea] specifically (2:1-5)

a. It was a ministry of deep concern for the people of Christ (v. 1-2)

i. The concern revealed (v. 1a)

ii. The reason for the concern (v. 1b-4)

b. It was a ministry of prayer and teaching the sufficiency of Christ (v. 2-3)

i. The sufficiency of Christ brings comfort/encouragement

ii. The sufficiency of Christ brings unity in love

- iii. The sufficiency of Christ brings the experience of full assurance
- iv. The sufficiency of Christ is bound to the true knowledge of Christ
- v. The sufficiency of Christ means, in Him all the treasures of wisdom and knowledge are found (v. 3)

c. *It was a ministry of warning against error and errorists who denied the sufficiency of Christ (v. 4)*

d. *It was a ministry of joyous fellowship because of the Colossians' faith in Christ (v. 5)*

IV. Refutation: Completeness in Christ cannot be obtained by human wisdom, religious tradition, mystical experience, or human effort—it is a gift of grace received by faith (2:6-23)

A. You are complete in Christ—do not be taken captive by philosophical deception (2:6-15)

1. Continue as you started—trusting solely in Christ Jesus the Lord (2:6-7)

a. *By faith you received Him (v. 6a)*

b. *By faith you are to walk in Him (v. 6b-7)*

- i. Rooted and built up in Him (v. 7a)
- ii. Established in the faith just as you were instructed (v. 7b)
- iii. Overflowing with gratitude (v. 7c)

2. Captivity to human philosophy is slavery—captivity to Christ is freedom and completeness (2:8-15)

a. *Captivity to human philosophy is slavery (v. 8)*

- i. The means of slavery: Philosophy and empty deception
- ii. The 1st slave master: Tradition of men
- iii. The 2nd slave master: Elementary principles of the world

b. *Captivity to Christ is freedom and completeness/fullness (v. 8d-15)*

- i. Because He is God in human flesh (v. 9)
- ii. Because in Him you have been made complete (v. 10a)
- iii. And He is Lord of all (v. 10b)
- iv. Because in Him you have been born again (v. 11-15)
  - aa. Spiritually circumcised—identified with the true people of God (v. 11)
  - bb. Spirit baptized—identified with Christ in His baptism of death and resurrection from the dead (v. 12)
  - cc. Regenerated from death to life (v. 13a)
  - dd. Forgiven/Debt free (v. 13b-14)
  - ee. Triumphant over Satan and his forces (v. 15)

B. You are complete in Christ—do not be subject to ritualism [religious traditionalism] (2:16-17)

1. Because you've been born again—a new creature, complete in Christ ["Therefore"] (2:16a)
2. Because it is commanded (2:16b)
    - a. *In regard to what you eat or drink*
    - b. *In respect to days of worship and holidays*
3. Because rituals ["religious" observances] cannot make you "more" complete in Christ (2:17)

C. You are complete in Christ—do not be defrauded by mysticism (2:18-19)

1. Because it is commanded (2:18a)
2. Because mysticism subtly exalts self (2:18b)
    - a. *False humility and the worship of the messengers*
    - b. *"Private revelations" resulting in fleshly pride*
3. Because mysticism subtly disregards the supremacy and sufficiency of Christ (2:19)
    - a. *It turns the focus away from Christ*
    - b. *It creates spiritual poverty and division—only Christ can bring true provision and unity*
    - c. *It does not foster true growth—only Christ can bring divine growth*

D. You are complete in Christ—do not be subject to asceticism/self-made religion [rule-keeping religion] (2:20-23)

1. Because asceticism [and rule-keeping religion] disregards the work of Christ [in Christ you died to what holds the world captive] (2:20-22a)
    - a. *You died with Christ to the elementary principles of the world (v. 20a)*
    - b. *Why would you live like you belonged to the world, and under its authority (v. 20b-22a)*
        - i. Some representative decrees of self-made religion (v. 21)
            - aa. Do not handle
            - bb. Do not taste
            - cc. Do not touch
        - ii. The truth about such religious taboos (v. 22a)
2. Because asceticism [and rule-keeping religion] finds its authority in the commandments and teachings of men, not God (3:22b)

3. Because asceticism [and rule-keeping religion] is of no value against fleshly indulgence (3:23)
    - *a. It has the appearance of wisdom (v. 23a)*
        - i. Self-made religion
        - ii. Self-abasement
        - iii. Severe treatment of the body
    - *b. But it is of no value against fleshly indulgence (v. 23b)*

V. Exhortation: Completeness in Christ is a gift of God that should shape all of life (3:1-4:6)

A. The root of your life: Your thinking and desires should reflect your completeness in Christ (3:1-4)

1. Continually pursue the glory and worship of God in Christ (3:1)
    - *a. Because of your life union with Christ*
    - *b. Because it is commanded by God's Word*
    - *c. Because Christ is your exalted Lord, Savior and Intercessor*
2. Continually purpose to meditate on the glory of God in Christ, and the vindication to come—not earthly "religion", earthly circumstances, or earthly desires (3:2-4)
    - *a. Because it is commanded by God's Word (v. 2)*
    - *b. Because Christ is the source and summation of your life (v. 3-4a)*
    - *c. Because of the final vindication and glory to come at the revelation of our Lord and Savior—the Christ (v. 4)*

B. The fruit of your life in general character: Your character should reflect your completeness in Christ (3:5-17)

1. Put off your old way of life (3:5-11)
    - *a. Slay [put to death] the things that formerly controlled your physical pursuits (v. 5-7)*
        - i. The command to put to death the things that formerly controlled you physically (v. 5a)
        - ii. The description of what formerly controlled you (v. 5)
            - aa. Immorality
            - bb. Impurity
            - cc. Passion
            - dd. Evil desire
            - ee. Greed, which is idolatry
        - iii. The reasons they must be executed (v. 6-7)
            - aa. The wrath of God (v. 6a)
            - bb. Your new character (v. 6b-7)

b. *Strip away [put off/throw] the things that formerly controlled your attitudes and speech (v. 8-11)*
   i. The command to put off the things that formerly controlled your attitudes and speech (v. 8a)
   ii. The description of what formerly controlled you (v. 8-9a)
      aa. Anger
      bb. Wrath
      cc. Malice
      dd. Slander
      ee. Abusive Speech
      ff. Lying [Stop lying—is parallel grammatically with points *a* and *b* in this outline ("put to death"; "put aside"), but thematically fits into this list of vices] (v. 9a)
   iii. The reasons they must be put off/thrown away (v. 9b-11)
      aa. You laid aside the old self (v. 9a)
      bb. You have put on the new self (v. 10a)
      cc. You are being renewed into the image of Christ (v. 10b)
      dd. You are part of the body, which is Christ's body—and He is supreme (v. 11)

2. Put on the new life [Christlikeness] (3:12-17)

a. *Remember who you are in Christ (v. 12a)*
   i. A new man, part of the body of Christ
   ii. Elect of God
   iii. Holy
   iv. Beloved
b. *Remember your responsibility to pursue Christlikeness (v. 12b)*
c. *Remember the character of those who are chosen of God (v. 12c-14)*
   i. Compassion
   ii. Kindness
   iii. Humility
   iv. Gentleness
   v. Patience
   vi. Bearing with one another
   vii. Forgiving each other
   viii. Love
      aa. The supreme characteristic
      bb. The perfect bond of unity
d. *Remember/Realize how to pursue Christlikeness (v. 15-17)*
   i. Be covered, consoled and constrained by the peace of Christ (v. 15)
      aa. The command concerning peace
      bb. The source of peace

cc. The rule of peace

dd. The unity of peace

ii. Be continually thankful (v. 15c)

iii. Be controlled by the indwelling word of Christ (v. 16; cf. Eph. 5:18-20)

aa. The command

bb. The consequences include teaching

cc. The consequences include admonishing

dd. The consequences include singing

iv. Be consumed with the fame and reputation of Jesus Christ (v. 17)

aa. In the name of the Lord Jesus

bb. In word

cc. In deed

dd. With thankfulness

C. The fruit of your life in specific social relationships: Your relationships should reflect your completeness in Christ (3:18-4:1)

1. Relationships within the family [the family ruled by the peace of Christ (v. 15); controlled by the Word of Christ (v. 16); and doing all in the name of Christ (v. 17)] (3:18-21)

a. Wives—continually submit to your husbands (v. 18)

i. The command—continually rank yourself under your husband's authority

ii. The manner—as is fitting in the Lord

b. Husbands—continually love your wives and do not treat them harshly (v. 19)

i. The 1st command—continually love your wives

ii. The 2nd command—be not embittered against them

c. Children—continually obey your parents (v. 20)

i. The command—continually obey your parents

ii. The scope of obedience—in all things

iii. The reason for obedience—for this is well pleasing to the Lord

d. Fathers—do not exasperate your children (v. 21)

i. The command—do not exasperate your children

ii The reason—so that they will not lose heart

2. Relationships within the work environment [the work environment ruled by the peace of Christ (v. 15); controlled by the Word of Christ (v. 16); and doing all in the name of Christ (v. 17)] (3:22-4:1)
    a. *Slaves/employees—continually obey your earthly masters and work hard for the Lord (v. 22-25)*
        i. The 1st command—continually obey your masters on earth (v. 22)
            aa. The scope of obedience—in all things
            bb. The manner of obedience—with sincerity of heart
            cc. The motive of obedience—reverence for Christ
        ii. The 2nd command—continually work hard (v. 23-25)
            aa. The scope of service—whatever you do (v. 23a)
            bb. The manner of service—heartily (v. 23b)
            cc. The motive of service—as for the Lord (v. 23c)
            dd. The encouragement of service—heavenly reward and service to Christ (v. 24)
            ee. The consequences of poor service (v. 25)
    b. *Masters/employers—continually grant justice and fairness to your slaves (4:1)*
        i. The command—continually grant justice and fairness to your slaves
        ii. The motive—knowing that you too have a Master in heaven

D. The fruit of your life in prayer and evangelism: Your prayer life and witness should reflect your completeness in Christ (4:2-6)

1. Continually occupy yourself with prayer (4:2-4)
    a. *The command—continually devote yourself to prayer (v. 2a)*
    b. *The manner of prayer (v. 2b)*
        i. Keeping alert in it
        ii. With thanksgiving
    c. *The content of prayer (v. 2-4)*
        i. Implied by the preceding and following contexts (v. 2-3; cf. 3:17-4:1, 5-6)
        ii. Explicitly stated—For God's spokesmen and the progress of the gospel (v. 3-4)
2. Continually look for ways to witness for Christ by the way you live and what you say (4:5-6)
    a. *Your life should reveal Christ and His character to non-believers (v. 5)*
        i. The command to reveal Christ's character through your daily conduct—continually walk with wisdom
        ii. The human audience—outsiders
        iii. The urgency

   b. *Your lips should reveal Christ and His character to non-believers (v. 6)*
      i. Your speech should always exhibit grace
      ii. Your speech should be both tasteful, and yet useful as a preservative—seasoned with salt
      iii. Your speech should be sensitive to the need of the moment

VI. Information/Participation: Completeness in Christ brings fellowship, love and concern for the brethren (4:7-18)[3]

A. Paul sent two representatives to both inform and encourage the Colossians because of his fellowship, love and concern for them—and they for him (4:7-9)

1. Tychicus—the trusted missionary and messenger (4:7-8)
   a. *His character (v. 7a)*
      i. Beloved brother
      ii. Faithful servant
      iii. Fellow bond-servant in the Lord
   b. *His mission (v. 7-8)*
      i. Information
      ii. Encouragement
2. Onesimus—the former runaway slave, now faithful brother (4:9)
   a. *His character (v. 9a)*
      i. Faithful and beloved brother
      ii. One of your number
   b. *His mission (v. 9b)*
      i. Information
      ii Reconciliation (cf. Philemon)

B. Paul sent greetings from other believers of note to the Colossians because of their mutual fellowship, love and concern (4:10-14)

1. The Jewish brethren with whom they partnered with for Christ's glory (4:10-11)
   a. *Aristarchus—the selfless missionary from Macedonia [Thessalonica] (v. 10a)*
   b. *Mark—the famous minister (v. 10b)*
      i. He had a famous cousin
      ii. He was famous for his failure
      iii. He would be famous for his service

---

[3] These weren't superficial closing remarks, but were meant to foster fellowship, love and mutual care for those complete in Christ—between both Jewish and Gentile believers.

c. *Jesus called Justus—the man who bore the name of His Savior, and His Savior's character (v. 11a)*

d. *Their collective encouragement (v. 11b)*

2. The gentile brethren with whom they partnered with for Christ's glory (4:12-14)

a. *Epaphras—the passionate pastor and prayer warrior on behalf of the Colossians (v. 12-13)*

i. A Colossian

ii. A bond-slave of Jesus Christ

iii. A fervent intercessor

iv. A concerned brother

b. *Luke—the brilliant writer and beloved physician (v. 14a)*

c. *Demas—the future deserter (v. 14b)*

C. Paul sent his final instructions, and personal greetings to promote mutual fellowship, love and concern (4:15-18)

1. Paul expected that fellowship would take place between different congregations (4:15-16)

a. *Fellowship with, and a desire of blessing for the brethren in Laodicea (v. 15a)*

b. *Fellowship with, and a desire of blessing for Nympha and the church in her house (v. 15b)*

c. *Fellowship in the Scriptures between congregations (v. 16)*

2. Paul sought to encourage Archippus in fulfilling his ministry (4:17)

3. Paul personally cared for those believers he had never personally met, and believed that they cared for him (4:18)

1 Thessalonians

Kress Biblical Resources

Overview Outline of 1 Thessalonians

The Coming of Christ for His Church Calls Us to Excel Still More in Holiness, Hope, and Love

I. Paul's personal introduction (1:1)

A. The author (1:1a)

1. The human author and his associates (1:1a)
2. The divine Author (2 Tim. 3:16-17; 2 Pet. 1:12-21, 3:15-16; cf. Col. 4:16; 1 Thes. 2:13; 5:27; 2 Thes. 3:1-4; cf. 1 Tim. 5:18 in which Paul quotes Luke alongside Deut. 25:4 and calls them "Scripture")

B. The audience (1:1b)

1. The original audience (1:1b; Acts 17:1-13)
2. The current audience (cf. 2 Pet. 3:16)

C. The aim/reasons

1. To express Paul's joy after Timothy's report of the church's steadfastness—in spite of great affliction (1:2-10; 3:1-10)
2. To defend Paul and his associates' ministry and integrity in Thessalonica—against some who were questioning God's work through them there (2:1-20)
   —This reveals a model for pastoral ministry and integrity
3. To instruct the faithful, but fledgling church on how to better live out their new faith in Christ (4:1-5:28; cf. especially 4:1, 9-10; 5:11—excel still more)
4. Summary theme: Encouragement to remaining steadfast in the faith no matter the afflictions we may face, and excel still more in our walk with God (3:1-8; 4:1, 10; 5:11)

D. The Apostolic greeting (1:1c)

II. Paul's prayer-report of thanksgiving—recounting the evidence of genuine conversion (1:2-10)

A. The prayers of thankful pastors (1:2)

B. The picture of transformed lives (1:3)

C. The proclamation of a theological mystery—and the proofs that confirm God's electing love (1:4-10)

1. The doctrine of election declared—God's electing love should be a source of comfort, rather than a source of contention (1:4)
2. The doctrine of election demonstrated—God's electing love results in supernatural evidence— a Spirit-empowered gospel heard; faith, hope, and love lived out (1:5-10)

Alternate outline for 1:5-10

[D. The particulars of a transformed life (1:5-10)

1. <u>A sincere faith</u> in the truth and power of the Gospel (1:5)
2. <u>A supernatural joy</u> in the midst of much tribulation (1:6-7)

3. A solid testimony to the word of the Lord, genuine faith, repentance from sin, and hope in Jesus' deliverance (1:8-10)]

III. Paul's pastoral integrity—recounting the evidence of a God-honoring [sincere] ministry (2:1-3:13)

A. A preaching ministry focused on pleasing God, not men (2:1-6)

1. A preaching ministry characterized by veracity [substance and truth] and conviction (2:1-2)
2. A preaching ministry characterized by purity and devotion—not man pleasing (2:3-4)
3. A preaching ministry characterized by sincerity and humility—not self-promotion (2:5-6)

B. A pastoral ministry focused on shepherding the flock as a family, not a business (2:7-12)

1. A pastoral ministry characterized by motherly love and affection (2:7-8)
2. A pastoral ministry characterized by fatherly leadership and exhortation (2:9-12))

C. A prayer-filled and personally concerned ministry, focused on the sustaining work of God, and perseverance of the saints in faith (2:13-3:13)

1. Persistent thanksgiving for the sovereign work of God in salvation, which sustains believers in the midst of great persecution (2:13-16)
2. Personal concern and prayer for fellowship and the perseverance of the saints (2:17-3:10)

IV. Paul's practical instruction—revealing specific ways to excel still more in holiness, hope, and love (4:1-5:22)

A. Practical instructions concerning living out holiness (4:1-12)

1. Believers must excel still more in obedience to the Lord (4:1-2)
2. Believers must embrace sexual purity as God's will for them personally (4:3-8)
3. Believers must excel still more in love for one another, and work hard as a testimony to unbelievers (4:9-12)

B. Practical instructions concerning living in light of our hope (4:13-5:11)

1. Encourage one another concerning the return of the Lord, the resurrection, and the rapture (4:13-18)
2. Encourage one another concerning the Day of the Lord (5:1-11)

C. Practical instructions concerning living together in harmony (5:12-22)

1. Pursuing peace relationally (5:12-15)
2. Pursuing peace personally, altogether (5:16-22)

V. Paul's prayers in conclusion and closing remarks (5:23-28)

A. The concluding prayer-benediction for holiness (5:23-24)

B. The call for reciprocal prayer (5:25)

C. The call for fellowship around this epistle (5:26-27)

D. The concluding prayer-benediction for grace (5:28)

Introductory Matters

I. The author (1:1a)

A. The human author and his associates (1:1a)

1. Paul[1]
2. Silvanus[2]
3. Timothy[3]

B. The divine Author (2 Tim. 3:16-17; 2 Pet. 1:12-21, 3:15-16; cf. Col. 4:16; 1 Thes. 2:13; 5:27; 2 Thes. 3:1-4; cf. 1 Tim. 5:18 in which Paul quotes Luke alongside Deut. 25:4 and calls them "Scripture")

II. The audience (1:1b)

A. The original audience (1:1b; Acts 17:1-13)

4. The church of the Thessalonians
5. The context in which they lived
6. Their consecrated position

B. The current audience (cf. 2 Pet. 3:15-16)

III. The aim

A. To express Paul's joy after Timothy's report of the church's steadfastness—in spite of great affliction (1:2-10; 3:1-10)

1. This would bring assurance and encouragement to the church (1:2-10; 3:1-10)
2. This would bring comfort in the midst of persecution (cf. 2:14-16)

B. To defend Paul and his associates' ministry and integrity in Thessalonica—against some who were questioning God's work through them there (2:1-20)

—This reveals ***a model for pastoral ministry and integrity***

B. To instruct the faithful, but fledgling church on how to better live out their new faith in Christ (4:1-5:28; cf. especially 4:1, 9-10; 5:11—excel still more)

1. Instruction concerning sexual purity (4:3-8)
2. Instruction concerning laziness (4:11-12)

---

[1] For a biblical biography of the Apostle Paul see Acts 7:58; 8:1; 9:1-30; 11:25-30; 12:25-28:31; 1 Cor. 15:30-32; 2 Cor. 6:4-5; 11:23-30; Gal. 1:13-2:16; Phil. 3:4-14; 2 Thes. 3:8

[2] 2 Cor. 1:19; 1 Pet. 5:12; cf. Acts 15:22-17:15; 18:5

[3] For a biblical biography of Timothy see Acts 16:1; 17:14-15; 18:5; 1 Cor. 4:17; 16:10; Phil. 2:19-23; 1 Thes. 3:2, 6; 1 Tim. 1:2; 5:23; Heb. 13:23

3. Instruction concerning the future and how it relates to life now (4:13-5:11)
4. Instruction concerning church relationships (5:12-27)

C. **Summary theme**: Encouragement to remain steadfast in the faith no matter the afflictions we may face, and excel still more in our walk with God (3:1-8; 4:1, 10; 5:11)

Detailed Outline of 1 Thessalonians

The Coming of Christ for His Church Calls Us to Excel Still More in Holiness, Hope, and Love

I. Introduction (1:1-2)

A. The author (1:1a)

1. The human author and his associates (1:1a)
   a. *Paul*[1]
   b. *Silvanus*[2]
   c. *Timothy*[3]
2. The divine Author (2 Tim. 3:16-17; 2 Pet. 1:12-21, 3:15-16; cf. Col. 4:16; 1 Thes. 2:13; 5:27; 2 Thes. 3:1-4; cf. 1 Tim. 5:18 in which Paul quotes Luke alongside Deut. 25:4 and calls them "Scripture")

B. The audience (1:1b)

1. The original audience (1:1b; Acts 17:1-13)
   a. *The church of the Thessalonians*
   b. *The context in which they lived*
   c. *Their consecrated position*
2. The current audience (cf. 2 Pet. 3:15-16)

C. The Apostolic greeting (1:1c)

1. Grace to you
2. And peace

II. Paul's prayer-report of thanksgiving—recounting the evidence of genuine conversion (1:2-10)

A. The prayers of thankful pastors (1:2)

B. The picture of transformed lives (1:3)

1. Remembering your work of faith
2. Remembering your labor of love
3. Remembering your steadfastness of hope in the Lord Jesus Christ

---

[1] For a biblical biography of the Apostle Paul see Acts 7:58; 8:1; 9:1-30; 11:25-30; 12:25-28:31; 1 Cor. 15:30-32; 2 Cor. 6:4-5; 11:23-30; Gal. 1:13-2:16; Phil. 3:4-14; 2 Thes. 3:8

[2] 2 Cor. 1:19; 1 Pet. 5:12; cf. Acts 15:22-17:15; 18:5

[3] For a biblical biography of Timothy see Acts 16:1; 17:14-15; 18:5; 1 Cor. 4:17; 16:10; Phil. 2:19-23; 1 Thes. 3:2, 6; 1 Tim. 1:2; 5:23; Heb. 13:23

4. Remembering these in prayer before our God and Father

C. The proclamation of a theological mystery—and the proofs that confirm God's electing love (1:4-10)

1. The doctrine of election declared—God's electing love should be a source of comfort, rather than a source of contention (1:4)
    a. *The comfort of God's spiritual family (v. 4a)*
    b. *The comfort of God's steadfast love (v. 4b)*
    c. *The comfort of God's sovereign choice (v. 4c)*
2. The doctrine of election demonstrated—God's electing love results in supernatural evidence— a Spirit-empowered gospel heard; faith, hope, and love lived out (1:5-10)
    a. *The elect have heard a Spirit-empowered gospel (v. 5)*
        i. The message was proclaimed with sincerity and supernatural power (v. 5a)
        ii. The messengers were servants—not those who demand to be served (v. 5b)
    b. *The elect demonstrate a sincere faith, a supernatural joy, and a striking example of the truth and power of the gospel [they are new creatures in Christ] (v. 6-7)*
        i. The gospel produces a sincere faith (v. 6a)
        ii. The gospel produces a sustaining power (v. 6b)
        iii. The gospel produces a supernatural joy (v. 6c)
        iv. The gospel produces a striking example to others (v. 7)
    c. *The elect communicate a sure testimony to others—evangelism and a life of genuine faith, repentance from sin, and hope in Jesus' deliverance (v. 8-10)*
        i. The testimony of love—evangelism/proclamation of the Word of the Lord to others (v. 8)
        ii. The testimony of faith and repentance—evidence of changed devotion (v. 9)
        iii. The testimony of hope—eagerly waiting for Jesus' return (v. 10)

Alternate outline for 1:5-10

[D. The particulars of a transformed life (1:5-10)

1. A sincere faith in the truth and power of the Gospel (1:5)
2. A supernatural joy in the midst of much tribulation (1:6-7)
3. A solid testimony to the word of the Lord, genuine faith, repentance from sin, and hope in Jesus' deliverance (1:8-10)]

III. Paul's pastoral integrity—recounting the evidence of a God-honoring [sincere] ministry (2:1-3:13)

A. A preaching ministry focused on pleasing God, not men (2:1-6)

1. A preaching ministry characterized by veracity [substance and truth] and conviction (2:1-2)
   a. *There is obvious substance and truth—not empty words (v. 1)*
   b. *There is opposition and suffering—but an obvious commitment to the gospel of God (v. 2)*
2. A preaching ministry characterized by purity and devotion—not man pleasing (2:3-4)
   a. *Purity of doctrine (v. 3a)*
   b. *Purity of motive (v. 3b)*
   c. *Pursuing devotion to God—not the approval of men (v. 4)*
3. A preaching ministry characterized by sincerity and humility—not self-promotion (2:5-6)
   a. *Sincerity of speech—without flattery (v. 5a)*
   b. *Sincerity of motive—without greed (v. 5b)*
   c. *Seeking God's approval—rather than glory from men (v. 6)*

B. A pastoral ministry focused on shepherding the flock as a family, not a business (2:7-12)

1. A pastoral ministry characterized by motherly love and affection (2:7-8)
   a. *Motherly love and affection illustrated (v. 7)*
   b. *Motherly love and affection imparted—in soul as well as Scripture (v. 8)*
2. A pastoral ministry characterized by fatherly leadership and exhortation (2:9-12)
   a. *Fatherly love and leadership by example (v. 9-10)*
      i. Pastors should model the reality that the gospel is a calling of love, not a career choice (v. 9)
      ii. Pastors should model the reality that the gospel calls us to obvious integrity, not inordinate influence over other believers (v. 10)
   b. *Fatherly love and leadership by exhortation (v. 11-12)*
      i. A father's methods of instruction (v. 11)
      ii. A father's motive for such instruction (v. 12)

C. A prayer-filled and personally concerned ministry, focused on the sustaining work of God, and perseverance of the saints in faith (2:13-3:13)

1. <u>Persistent thanksgiving</u> for the sovereign work of God in salvation, which sustains believers in the midst of great persecution (2:13-16)
   a. *Thanksgiving for the sovereign work of God in those who come to faith (v. 13)*
      i. The sovereign Person Who constantly deserves thanks for enabling faith in the Word of God (v. 13abc)
      ii. The sovereign power of the Word of God in those who believe (v. 13d)
   b. *Thanksgiving for the sustaining work of God, even in the midst of deadly suffering (v. 13d-16)*
      i. The source of believers' steadfastness (v. 13d)
      ii. The steadfastness that endures severe persecution (v. 14)
      iii. The sins of those who oppose the gospel, and their final reward (v. 15-16)
2. <u>Personal concern and prayer</u> for fellowship and the perseverance of the saints (2:17-3:10)
   a. *A passion for personal fellowship (2:17-20)*
      i. The desire for personal fellowship [possessed and expressed] (v. 17-18a)
      ii. The Devil's opposition to personal fellowship [confirmed] (v. 18b)
      iii. The delight of fellowship at Christ's coming [anticipated] (v. 19)
      iv. The delight of fellowship now [possessed and expressed] (v. 20)
   b. *A passion for the perseverance and encouragement of God's people (3:1-10)*
      i. A genuine concern for those whose faith is tested (v. 1-5)
         aa. A concern that leads to self-sacrificial action (v. 1-2a)
         bb. A concern that seeks to strengthen and encourage those who are being tested (v. 2b-4)
         cc. A concern that seeks the steadfastness/perseverance of those who profess faith (v. 5)
      ii. A genuine joy for those whose faith is triumphant in the midst of such suffering (v. 6-10)
         aa. A joy that comes from truly life-changing news about brothers who are persevering in faith and love (v. 6-8)

            The coming of good news (v. 6)

            The comfort it brings (v. 7)

            The connection between joy and the perseverance of other believers (v. 8) bb. A joy that can't help but thank God for those who persevere in faith—and yet continues to intercede for the fitness of their faith (v. 9-10)

Gratitude to God as the ultimate Source of such good news (v. 9)

Going before God for the furtherance of others' faith (v. 10)

c. *A prayer focus that reflects faith in God's sovereignty in our sanctification (3:11-13)*

i. The Sovereign to whom Paul prayed (v. 11ab)

ii. The supplication for personal fellowship (v. 11c)

iii. The supplication for increased love (v. 12)

iv. The supplication for holiness while waiting in hope (v. 13)

IV. Paul's practical instruction—revealing specific ways to excel still more in holiness, hope, and love (4:1-5:22)

A. Practical instructions concerning living out holiness (4:1-12)

1. Believers must excel still more in obedience to the Lord (4:1-2)

a. *Obedience to the Lord is a family privilege (v. 1a)*

b. *Obedience to the Lord is a blessed obligation (v. 1b)*

c. *Obedience to the Lord can always increase still more (v. 1c)*

d. *Obedience to the Lord cannot be separated from God's Word and the Person of Jesus (v.1-2)*

2. Believers must embrace sexual purity as God's will for them personally (4:3-8)

a. *Purity starts with a real desire to please the Lord and do His will (v. 3)*

b. *Purity demands that you continually keep away from sexual sin (3b)*

c. *Purity continues as you live by the faith-conviction that you can control your body in holiness and honor (v. 4)*

d. *Purity requires cultivating a different passion than unbelievers—the passion to know God (v. 5)*

e. *Purity involves an ongoing choice to love others, rather than take advantage of them (v. 6a)*

f. *Purity must be viewed in light of God's judgment, God's purpose, and God's indwelling Presence (v. 6b-8)*

i. Remember God's judgment (v. 6b)

ii. Remember God's purpose for your life (v. 7)

iii. Remember God's indwelling Presence (v. 8)

3. Believers must excel still more in love for one another, and work hard as a testimony to unbelievers (4:9-12)

a. *Love other believers still more and more (v. 9-10)*

i. Love for other believers is a sovereign gift (v. 9-10a)

ii. Love for other believers is our responsibility, and should be increasing more and more (v. 10b)

b. Lead a quiet life and attend to your own business [as far as it depends on you] (v. 11a)

c. Labor with your own hands and be a good testimony to unbelievers (v. 11b-12)

i. Believers are commanded to work hard (v. 11b)

ii. Believers should be concerned about their testimony even in financial matters (v. 12)

B. Practical instructions concerning living in light of our hope (4:13-5:11)

1. Encourage one another concerning the return of the Lord, the resurrection, and the rapture (4:13-18)

a. The resurrection and return of the Lord bring hope to our grief as believers (v. 13-14)

i. If a believer dies, we ought not grieve as those who have no hope (v. 13)

ii. If we believe in the gospel, we have the promise of resurrection glory with Jesus (v. 14)

b. The return of the Lord, the resurrection, and the rapture guarantee our eternal fellowship with one another and Christ (v. 15-17)

i. The dead in Christ will not miss the return of the Lord (v. 15)

ii. The details of the Lord's return guarantee our glorious reunion and fellowship (v. 16-17)

aa. The return of the Lord (v. 16abc)

bb. The resurrection of the dead in Christ (v. 16d)

cc. The rapture and reunion of the saints (v. 17ab)

dd. The realization of our eternal hope (v. 17c)

c. The reason for biblical eschatology is encouragement—not debate over timing (v. 18)

2. Encourage one another concerning the Day of the Lord (5:1-11)

a. The coming Day of the Lord will be a day of sudden and total destruction for unbelievers (v. 1-5)

i. The chronology of the Day of the Lord (v. 1-2)

aa. It cannot be specifically dated (v. 1-2)

bb. It is sure (v. 2a)

cc. It will come unexpectedly (v. 2b)

ii. The character of the Day of the Lord (v. 3)

aa. For unbelievers, it will be a day of unexpected destruction (v. 3a)

bb. For unbelievers, it will be a day of inescapable destruction (v. 3b)

iii. The comfort for believers concerning the Day of the Lord (v. 4-5)

b. *The coming Day of the Lord exhorts believers to stay spiritually alert and look for salvation of the Lord (v. 6-10)*

i. Keep spiritually alert (v. 6-8)

ii. Keep looking for the rapture [or keep trusting in God's promises of salvation in Christ] (v. 9-10)

c. *The coming Day of the Lord should be a subject of encouragement and edification for believers—not speculation and fear (v. 11)*

C. Practical instructions concerning living together in harmony (5:12-22)

1. Pursuing peace relationally (5:12-15)

a. *We must choose to recognize and respect our shepherds (v. 12-13a)*

i. Recognize their labor, their leadership, and their counsel (v. 12)

ii. Regard them very highly in love (v. 13a)

b. *We must choose to live in peace with one another (v. 13b)*

c. *We must choose to minister to others with wisdom and patience (v. 14)*

i. Admonish those the unruly (v. 14a)

ii. Encourage the fainthearted (v. 14b)

iii. Help the weak (v. 14c)

iv. Be patient with everyone (v. 14d)

d. *We must choose to overlook offenses and seek the good of others (v. 15)*

2. Pursuing peace personally, altogether (5:16-22)

a. *You must choose to rejoice at all times (v. 16)*

b. *You must choose to pray without ceasing (v. 17)*

c. *You must choose to give thanks in everything (v. 18)*

d. *We must choose to be submissive to the ministry of God's Spirit [listen to God's Spirit] (v. 19)*

e. *We must choose to cherish to the ministry of God's Word [love God's Word] (v. 20)*

f. *We must choose to be discerning in all things, holding on to what is good, rejecting every form of evil [learn to live with discernment] (v. 21-22)*

V. Paul's prayers in conclusion and closing remarks (5:23-28)

A. The concluding prayer-benediction for holiness (5:23-24)

1. He prayed in view of God's character as the God of peace (5:23a)
2. He prayed assuming God's sovereignty in sanctification (5:23b)
3. He prayed for our sanctification (5:23c)
4. He prayed for our preservation (5:23d)

5. He prayed for our glorification (5:23e)
6. He pronounced the absolute surety that His prayer will be answered in regard to believers (5:24)

B. The call for reciprocal prayer (5:25)

C. The call for fellowship around this epistle (5:26-27)

1. A public greeting of affection (5:26)
2. A public reading of this epistle (5:27)

D. The concluding prayer-benediction for grace (5:28)

2 Thessalonians

Kress Biblical Resources

Overview Outline of 2 Thessalonians

The Return of Our Lord Jesus Christ in Glory Calls Us to Persevere in the Midst of Persecution

I. Introduction (1:1-2)

A. The author (1:1a)

B. The audience (1:1b)

C. The aim/reasons (see detailed outline)

D. The apostolic greeting (1:2)

II. Comfort and encouragement for those enduring persecution (1:3-12)

A. Know that we praise God for you and proudly tell others about your perseverance and faith (1:3-4)

B. Know that your perseverance in the midst of persecution has a purpose (1:5-10)

C. Know that we're praying for you (1:11-12)

III. Correction and instruction for those exposed to eschatological error (2:1-17)

A. Refrain from believing every teaching that seeks to interpret church age persecution as a sign that the Day of the Lord has come (2:1-2)

B. Remember these fundamental truths concerning the Day of the Lord (2:3-12)

C. Remember these fundamental truths concerning your salvation—and stand firm in the truth of God's Word [Remember God's love for you, God's sovereignty and purpose in salvation, the surety of God's Word, and the prayers of God's people] (2:13-17)

IV. Confrontation and exhortation in regard to the undisciplined, who expected others to support them financially (3:1-15)

A. The humble pastoral introduction (3:1-5)

B. The honest pastoral confrontation (3:6-10)

V. Conclusion (3:16-17)

A. The intercession of peace [The peace of the Lord] (3:16)

B. The identification of truth [The truth of the Lord] (3:17)

C. The invocation of grace [The grace of the Lord] (3:18)

Introductory Matters

I. The author (1:1a)

A. The human author and his associates (1:1a)

1. Paul[1]
2. Silvanus[2]
3. Timothy[3]

B. The divine Author (2 Tim. 3:16-17; 2 Pet. 1:12-21, 3:15-16; cf. Col. 4:16; 1 Thes. 2:13; 5:27; 2 Thes. 3:1-4; cf. 1 Tim. 5:18 in which Paul quotes Luke alongside Deut. 25:4 and calls them "Scripture")

2. The audience (1:1b)

A. The original recipients (1:1b; Acts 17:1-13)

1. The church of the Thessalonians
2. The context in which they lived
3. Their consecrated position

B. The current recipients (cf. 2 Pet. 3:16)

3. The aim

A. To comfort the beloved congregation in the midst of increased persecution—and encourage them to persevere in the faith (1:3-12)

B. To correct false teaching in regard to the Day of the Lord—and encourage them to stand firm in the Apostle's teaching (2:1-17; esp. 2:1-3, 13-16)

C. To confront the unruly among the congregation, who were not working and acting like busybodies—and encourage the faithful to not grow weary of doing good (3:6-15)

D. **Summary theme**: Persevere in faith and love—in spite of fierce persecution, false teaching, and foolish believers.

---

[1] For a biblical biography of the Apostle Paul see Acts 7:58; 8:1; 9:1-30; 11:25-30; 12:25-28:31; 1 Cor. 15:30-32; 2 Cor. 6:4-5; 11:23-30; Gal. 1:13-2:16; Phil. 3:4-14; 2 Thes. 3:8

[2] 2 Cor. 1:19; 1 Pet. 5:12; cf. Acts 15:22-17:15; 18:5

[3] For a biblical biography of Timothy see Acts 16:1; 17:14-15; 18:5; 1 Cor. 4:17; 16:10; Phil. 2:19-23; 1 Thes. 3:2, 6; 1 Tim. 1:2; 5:23; Heb. 13:23

Detailed Outline of 2 Thessalonians

The Return of Our Lord Jesus Christ in Glory Calls Us to Persevere in the Midst of Persecution

I. Introduction (1:1-2)

A. The author (1:1a)

1. The human author and his associates (1:1a)
   - *a. Paul*
   - *b. Silvanus*
   - *c. Timothy*
2. The divine Author (2 Tim. 3:16-17; 2 Pet. 1:12-21, 3:15-16; cf. Col. 4:16; 1 Thes. 2:13; 5:27; 2 Thes. 3:1-4; cf. 1 Tim. 5:18 in which Paul quotes Luke alongside Deut. 25:4 and calls them "Scripture")

B. The audience (1:1b)

1. The original recipients (1:1b)
   - *a. The church of the Thessalonians*
   - *b. The context in which they lived*
   - *c. Their consecrated position*
2. The current recipients (cf. 2 Pet. 3:16)

C. The aim/reasons

1. To comfort the beloved congregation in the midst of increased persecution—and encourage them to persevere in the faith (1:3-12)
2. To correct false teaching in regard to the Day of the Lord—and encourage them to stand firm in the Apostle's teaching (2:1-17; esp. 2:1-3, 13-16)
3. To confront the unruly among the congregation, who were not working and acting like busybodies—and encourage the faithful to not grow weary of doing good (3:6-15)
4. **Summary theme:** Persevere in faith and love—in spite of fierce persecution, false teaching, and foolish believers.

D. The apostolic greeting (1:2)

1. The salutation of grace and peace (1:2a)
2. The Source of grace and peace (1:2b)

II. Comfort and encouragement for those enduring persecution (1:3-12)

A. Know that we praise God for you and proudly tell others about your perseverance and faith (1:3-4)

1. We praise God for you (1:3)
    - *a. The responsibility and rightness of thanking God for believers who are bearing fruit (v. 3a)*
        - i. The responsibility—a moral obligation
        - ii. The reason—a theological implication [God is the Sovereign Source of faith and love]
        - iii. The rightness—an appropriate response to growth
    - *b. The realities of faith and love, which call for constant thanks to God (v. 3b)*
        - i. An enlarged faith
        - ii. An ever-growing love
2. We proudly tell others about your perseverance and faith in the midst of persecution (1:4)
    - *a. The Thessalonian believers were an encouragement to other believers (v. 4a)*
        - i. Their founding pastors
        - ii. Their fellow believers in other churches
    - *b. The Thessalonian believers were exemplifying perseverance and faith in the midst of persecutions and afflictions (v. 4b)*

B. Know that your perseverance in the midst of persecution has a purpose (1:5-10)

1. The perseverance and faith of believers indicate that God's judgment is right (1:5)
2. The punishment of unbelievers and plan of redemption fulfilled for believers will confirm that God's judgment is right (1:6-10)
    - *a. God will repay with affliction those who afflict His people [God's justice will be perfectly just] (v. 6)*
    - *b. God will relieve His people at the revelation of Jesus [God's justice will bring relief to those waiting for the Lord Jesus to return] (v. 7)*
    - *c. God will bring retribution to those who do not obey the gospel [God's justice will result in eternal destruction for those who do not obey the gospel] (v. 8-9)*
        - i. Divine retribution declared (v. 8)
        - ii. Divine retribution described (v. 9)
    - *d. Christ will receive glory and be admired by those who trust His Word [God's justice will result in worship for those who do believe] (v. 10)*

C. Know that we're praying for you (1:11-12)

1. We are praying for you faithfully (1:11a)
2. We are praying for your spiritual fulfillment (1:11b-12)
   a. *That God would favor you with consistency in your walk (v. 11b)*
   b. *That God would fulfill your consecrated desires (v. 11c)*
   c. *That God would fully glorify the name of the Lord Jesus in you, and you in Him, according to His grace (v. 12)*

III. Correction and instruction for those exposed to eschatological error (2:1-17)

A. Refrain from believing every teaching that seeks to interpret church age persecution as a sign that the Day of the Lord has come (2:1-2)

1. Remember that our Lord Jesus Christ is coming and we will be gathered together with Him (2:1)
2. Remain clear-headed about the truth, and realize that false teaching tries to pass itself off as authentic (2:2)

B. Remember these fundamental truths concerning the Day of the Lord (2:3-12)

1. The Day of the Lord will not come until the apostasy [or act of departure] comes and the Antichrist is revealed [therefore you cannot be experiencing the Day of the Lord] (2:3-5)
   a. *The apostasy [or act of departure] and the Antichrist will signal the Day of the Lord (v. 3ab)*
   b. *The attributes and actions of the Antichrist will be unmistakable (v. 3c-4)*
   c. *The Apostle taught these things as part of his initial instruction in the faith (v. 5)*
2. The Antichrist will not be revealed until the restraining influence of the Holy Spirit is removed (2:6-8a)
   a. *The restraint (v. 6-7)*
   b. *The removal of divine restraint (v. 7)*
   c. *The revelation of that lawless one (v. 8a)*
3. The Antichrist is doomed, and will deceive only unbelievers (2:8b-12)
   a. *He will be destroyed at the appearance of our Lord's coming (v. 8b)*
   b. *He will deceive only unbelievers (v. 9-12)*
      i. He will be satanically empowered (v. 9-10a)
      ii. He will deceive only unbelievers (v. 10-12)
         aa. Because they did not receive the love of the truth so as to be saved (v. 10b)

bb. Thus God will send on them a deluding influence so that they believe what is false (v. 11)

cc. This will be their judgment for not believing the truth (v. 12)

C. Remember these fundamental truths concerning your salvation—and stand firm in the truth of God's Word [Remember God's love for you, God's sovereignty and purpose in salvation, the surety of God's Word, and the prayers of God's people] **(2:13-17)**

1. You are beloved by the Lord (2:13a)
2. You are chosen for salvation (2:13b)
3. You are predestined for glory (2:14)
4. You are called to stand firm and hold to the surety of God's Word (2:15)
5. You are in my prayers (2:16-17)
   - *a. I'm praying for you to our Sovereign and our Father (v. 16a)*
   - *b. I'm praying for you in light of His love and gifts of grace (v. 16b)*
   - *c. I'm praying for you to be comforted and strengthened by His enabling power—to live for His glory (v. 17)*

IV. Confrontation and exhortation in regard to the undisciplined, who expected others to support them financially (3:1-15)

A. The humble pastoral introduction (3:1-5)

1. The call for reciprocal prayer (3:1-2)
   - *a. The need for prayer expressed (v. 1a)*
   - *b. The nature of the request (v. 1b-2)*
     - i. The progress of the gospel message—the Word of the Lord (v. 1b)
     - ii. The protection of the gospel messengers—the workers of the Lord (v. 2)
2. The confidence and prayer that precedes confrontation (3:3-5)
   - *a. The steadfastness of the Lord will strengthen and protect you (v. 3)*
   - *b. The sovereignty of the Lord will enable and ennoble you to obey (v. 4)*
   - *c. The supplication to the Lord is that He direct your hearts in God's love and Christ's faithfulness (v. 5)*

B. The honest pastoral confrontation (3:6-15)

1. The command to the church—stay away from every brother who leads an unruly life (3:6-10)
   - *a. The exhortation to disassociate from the unruly in the church—keep away from those who are idle among you (v. 6)*
     - i. The authority of the Lord (v. 6a)
     - ii. The essence of the command (v. 6b)
     - iii. The standard of Word of God (v. 6c)

- *b. The example of a disciplined work ethic—keep following our example (v. 7-9)*
  - i. Paul, Silas, and Timothy set an example of diligence (v. 7-8ab)
  - ii. Paul, Silas, and Timothy were concerned about being a burden to others [an example of love] (v. 8c)
  - iii. Paul, Silas, and Timothy had a God-given right to financial support—but voluntarily set aside that right for the sake of setting the example (v. 9)
- *c. The explicit teaching on a disciplined work ethic—keep in mind, if one is not willing to work then he is not to eat (v. 10)*

2. The command to the unruly—start working and eat your own bread (3:11-12)
   - *a. The report of idleness (v. 11)*
   - *b. The reproof and remedy of idleness (v. 12)*
3. The command to the church in summary—stay faithful in doing good, but stop unrestricted-fellowship with the unruly (3:13-15)
   - *a. Do not grow weary of doing good (v. 13)*
   - *b. Do not affirm the disobedient through unrestricted fellowship (v. 14)*
   - *c. Do not think of him as an enemy, but admonish him as a brother (v. 15)*

V. Conclusion (3:16-17)

A. The intercession of peace [The peace of the Lord] (3:16)

B. The identification of truth [The truth of the Lord] (3:17)

C. The invocation of grace [The grace of the Lord] (3:18)

1 Timothy

Kress Biblical Resources

Overview Outline of 1 Timothy

The Church Must Oppose Error and Uphold the Truth in This World

I. Prologue/Greeting (1:1-2)

A. The writer (1:1)
   1. The human author
   2. The divine Author (2 Tim. 3:16; 2 Pet. 1:21; 3:15-16)

B. The recipient[s] (1:2a)
   1. The original recipient[s]
   2. The current recipients

C. The reasons
   1. Oppose false teaching (1:3ff; 4:1-6)
   2. Order the church so as to uphold the truth (3:14-15)

D. The requisite greeting (1:2b)
   1. The prayer of blessing
   2. The Person[s] behind the blessing

II. Purity in doctrine (1:3-20)

A. Preserve the purity of the gospel (1:2-11)
   1. The pursuit of a faithful shepherd (1:3-5)
   2. The proper use of the Law (1:8-11)

B. Praise Christ and testify of His salvation (1:12-17)
   1. Praise the Lord for the grace of His salvation (1:12-16)
   2. Praise the Lord for the glory of His sovereign Person (1:17)

C. Persevere in the fight (1:18-20)
   1. Persevere in confronting false teaching (1:18a)
   2. Persevere in using your giftedness and calling (1:18b)
   3. Persevere in trusting God and keeping a good conscience (1:19-20)

III. Priorities in church worship and leadership (2:1-3:16)

A. Starting with corporate prayer and proper worship (2:1-15)
   1. The primacy of prayer and male leadership in corporate worship (2:1-7)
   2. The proper conduct of male leadership in corporate worship (2:8)
   3. The proper conduct of women in corporate worship (2:9-15)

B. Sanctified leadership (3:1-16)
   1. The required character of an overseer (3:1-7)
   2. The required character of deacons and their wives (3:8-13)
   3. The reason for this epistle—the church is to uphold the truth (3:14-16)

IV. Pastoral responsibilities (4:1-6:21a)

- A. Concerning godliness and legalistic discipline (4:1-16)
    1. The Spirit's warning against a legalistic approach to godliness (4:1-5)
    2. The shepherd's work in refuting a legalistic approach to godliness (4:6-16)
- B. Concerning godliness and relationships (5:1-6:2)
    1. The pastor, and those he is to encourage/admonish (5:1-2)
    2. The policy of the church towards its widows (5:3-16)
    3. The policy of the church towards its elders (5:17-25)
    4. The practice of believing slaves in relation to their earthly masters (6:1-2)
- C. Concerning godliness and a right view of riches (6:3-19)
    1. The contrast between greed-driven false teachers and true godliness (6:3-10)
    2. The charge to the man of God in the face of such greed-driven opposition (6:11-19)
    3. The charge to guard the faith—that which is truly treasure (6:20-21a)

V. Prayer (6:21b)

Introductory Matters

I. The author (1:1)

A. The human author[1]

1. His name
2. His authority

B. The divine Author (2 Tim. 3:16; 2 Pet. 1:21; 3:15-16)

II. The audience (1:2a)

A. The original recipient[s][2]

1. His name
2. His relationship with Paul
3. The wider audience (6:21b)

B. The current recipients (cf. 2 Pet. 3:15-16)

III. The aim

1. Oppose false teaching and error (1:3ff; 4:1-6)
2. Order the church so as to uphold the truth and exalt the gospel of God in Christ (3:14-15)

---

[1] For a biblical biography of the Apostle Paul see Acts 7:58; 8:1; 9:1-30; 11:25-30; 12:25-28:31; 1 Cor. 15:30-32; 2 Cor. 6:4-5; 11:23-30; Gal. 1:13-2:16; Phil. 3:4-14; 2 Thes. 3:8

[2] For a biblical biography of Timothy see Acts 16:1; 17:14-15; 18:5; 1 Cor. 4:17; 16:10; Phil. 2:19-23; 1 Thes. 3:2, 6; 1 Tim. 1:2; 5:23; Heb. 13:23

Detailed Outline of 1 Timothy

The Church Must Oppose Error and Uphold the Truth in This World

I. Prologue/Greeting (1:1-2)
- **A. The writer (1:1)**
  1. The human author[1]
     - *a. His name*
     - *b. His authority*
  2. The divine Author (2 Tim. 3:16; 2 Pet. 1:21; 3:15-16)
- **B. The recipient[s] (1:2a)**
  1. The original recipient[s][2]
     - *a. His name*
     - *b. His relationship with Paul*
     - *c. The wider audience (6:21b)*
  2. The current recipients (cf. 2 Pet. 3:15-16)
- **C. The requisite greeting (1:2b)**
  1. The prayer of blessing
  2. The Person[s] behind the blessing

II. Purity in doctrine (1:3-20)
- **A. Preserve the purity of the gospel (1:2-11)**
  1. The pursuit of a faithful shepherd (1:3-5)
     - *a. Proclaim the true faith and confront error (v. 3-4)*
       - i. Confront false teaching (v. 3)
       - ii. Curtail speculation that does not further the true faith (v. 4)
     - *b. Promote love through that proclamation (v. 5-7)*
       - i. The end goal of love and its attendant attributes (v. 5)
       - ii. The error of turning aside to fruitless discussions (v. 6)
       - iii. The error of desiring to be a teacher of the Law, but being ignorant of how properly handle the Law (v. 7)
  2. The proper use of the Law (1:8-11)
     - *a. The law is good—if used lawfully (v. 8)*
     - *b. The law is given to incriminate the lawless—not the righteous (v. 9-10)*
     - *c. The law is a governor that points to the glorious gospel (v. 11)*

---

[1] For a biblical biography of the Apostle Paul see Acts 7:58; 8:1; 9:1-30; 11:25-30; 12:25-28:31; 1 Cor. 15:30-32; 2 Cor. 6:4-5; 11:23-30; Gal. 1:13-2:16; Phil. 3:4-14; 2 Thes. 3:8

[2] For a biblical biography of Timothy see Acts 16:1; 17:14-15; 18:5; 1 Cor. 4:17; 16:10; Phil. 2:19-23; 1 Thes. 3:2, 6; 1 Tim. 1:2; 5:23; Heb. 13:23

B. Praise Christ and testify of His salvation (1:12-17)

1. Praise the Lord for the grace of His salvation (1:12-16)
   - *a. The grace of recognizing His thank-worthiness (v. 12a)*
   - *b. The grace of being strengthened for His service (v. 12b)*
   - *c. The grace of receiving His saving mercy (v. 13)*
   - *d. The grace of receiving His abundant grace, with faith and love (v. 14)*
   - *e. The grace of accepting His gospel message as trustworthy (v. 15)*
   - *f. The grace of serving in His gospel ministry (v. 16)*
2. Praise the Lord for the glory of His sovereign Person (1:17)
   - *a. The attributes (v. 17)*
     - i. King of the ages
     - ii. Immortal
     - iii. Invisible
     - iv. Unique
   - *b. The ascription (v. 17)*

C. Persevere in the fight (1:18-20)

1. Persevere in confronting false teaching (1:18a)
2. Persevere in using your giftedness and calling (1:18b)
3. Persevere in trusting God and keeping a good conscience (1:19-20)
   - *a. Fighting the good fight means keeping faith (v. 19a)*
   - *b. Fighting the good fight means keeping a good conscience (v. 19b)*
   - *c. Forsaking the good fight means spiritual shipwreck (v. 19c-20)*
     - i. The truth stated (v. 19c)
     - ii. The two examples named (v. 20a)
     - iii. The training/discipline revealed (v. 20b)

III. Priorities in church worship and leadership (2:1-3:16)

A. Starting with corporate prayer and proper worship (2:1-15)

1. The primacy of prayer and male leadership in corporate worship (2:1-7)
   - *a. The primacy of public prayer (v. 1a)*
   - *b. The particular nuances of public prayer (v. 1b)*
     - i. Entreaties and prayers
     - ii. Petitions and thanksgivings
   - *c. The people we are to pray for in our public prayer (1c-2)*
     - i. On behalf of all men (1c)
     - ii. For kings and all who are in authority (2a)
     - iii. For our own ministry witness (v. 2b

d. *The purpose of public prayer (v. 3-7)*
   i. Our Savior deems it good and acceptable (v. 3)
   ii. Our Savior desires all people to be saved (v. 4-7)
      aa. The simple statement (v. 4)
      bb. The Savior's work as mediator (v. 5)
      cc. The Savior's work of redemption (v. 6)
      dd. The Savior's work through the Apostle to the nations (v. 7)

2. The proper conduct of male leadership in corporate worship (2:8)

a. *Men are to lead in prayer during corporate worship (v. 8a)*
b. *Men are to lead in a spirit of reverence and holiness in corporate worship (v. 8b)*
c. *Men are to lead in a spirit of humility, forgiveness, and peace in corporate worship (v. 8c)*

3. The proper conduct of women in corporate worship (2:9-15)

a. *Women are to adorn themselves modestly and discreetly (2:9)*
b. *Women are to adorn themselves with good works and godliness (2:10)*
c. *Women are to pursue attitudes and actions that reveal submissiveness, humility, and confident faith (2:11-15)*
   i. Teachable, submissive and at rest (v. 11)
   ii. Trusting God's wisdom (v. 12-15)
      aa. Obeying God's command (v. 12)
      bb. Learning from God's Word (v. 13-14)
         - Learning from the deliberate order of creation (v. 13)
         - Learning from the deception of Eve (v. 14)
      cc. Believing God's promise (v. 15)

B. Sanctified leadership (3:1-16)

1. The required character of an overseer (3:1-7)

a. *The desire for the work (v. 1)*
b. *The description of the character (v. 2-7)*
   i. Above reproach—a summary characteristic (v. 2a)
   ii. A one-woman man (v. 2b)
   iii. Self-controlled (v. 2c)
   iv. Sensible (v. 2d)
   v. Respectable (v. 2e)
   vi. A friend of strangers (v. 2f)
   vii. Able to teach (v. 2g)
   viii. Not a drunkard (v. 3a)
   ix. Not a bully (v. 3b)
   x. Gentle (v. 3c)

xi. Peaceable (v. 3d)
xii. Free from the love of money (v. 3e)
xiii. A good manager of his home (v. 4-5)
 aa. His home in summary (v. 4a)
 bb. His parenting (v. 4b)
 cc. The parallel between his house and the house of God (v. 5)
ix. Not a new Christian (v. 6)
x. A good testimony with non-believers (v. 7)

2. The required character of deacons and their wives (3:8-13)

a. The deacon's character (v. 8-10)
 i. Dignified (v. 8a)
 ii. Not double-tongued (v. 8b)
 iii. Not a drunkard (v. 8c)
 iv. Not greedy (v. 8d)
 v. Sincere in the faith (v. 9)
 vi. Faithful and beyond reproach (v. 10)

b. The deacon's wife's character (v. 11)
 i. Dignified (v. 11a)
 ii. Not prone to slander/gossip (v. 11b)
 iii. Self-controlled (v. 11c)
 iv. Faithful (v. 11d)

c. The deacon's character in regard to his home (v. 12)
 i. A one-woman man (v. 12a)
 ii. A good manager of his home (v. 12b)

d. The deacon's comfort (v. 13)

3. The reason for this epistle—the church is to uphold the truth (3:14-16)

a. The purpose of the epistle (v. 14-15)
 i. The potential visit (v. 14)
 ii. The purpose stated (v. 15)
 aa. The purpose of the letter—so one may know how to conduct himself in the church (v. 15a)
 bb. The purpose of the church—to uphold the truth of God in the world (v. 15b)

b. The poetic summary of the gospel (v. 16)
 i. The great mystery which produces reverence for God (v. 16a)
 ii. The incarnation of God (v. 16b)
 iii. The vindication of the Spirit [in the OT Scriptures, at His birth, baptism, temptation, death, resurrection] (v. 16c)

iv. The attention of angels [announcing His coming, at His birth, in the wilderness temptation, in the garden of Gethsemane, at the empty tomb, at the ascencion} (v. 16d)

v. The proclamation of the gospel [by the Apostles, the church, and the Scriptures] (v. 16e)

vi. The reception of the faith (v. 16f)

vii. The ascension in glory [to the right hand of the Father, now interceding for us] (v. 16g)

IV. Pastoral responsibilities (4:1-6:21a)

A. Concerning godliness and legalistic discipline (4:1-16)

1. The Spirit's warning against a legalistic approach to godliness (4:1-5)

a. The Spirit's Word (v. 1a)

b. The Spirit's warning (v. 1b-5)

i. Latter days apostasy (v. 1b)

ii. Lead astray by demonic deceit (v. 1c)

iii. Leaders with seared consciences (v. 2)

iv. Legalism instead of grateful reception of God's gracious gifts (v. 3-5)

aa. Legalism exemplified (v. 3a)

bb. Legalism refuted (v. 3b-5)

- Grateful faith receives God's gifts (v. 3b-4)
- God's Word and prayer sanctify God's gifts to the believer (v. 5)

2. The shepherd's work in refuting a legalistic approach to godliness (4:6-16)

a. Expose the error of legalism and proclaim the true gospel by how you live and what you teach (v. 6-11)

i. Point out the error of legalism (v. 6)

aa. As a good minister of Jesus Christ (v. 6a)

bb. As a man nourished on faith and sound doctrine yourself (v. 6b)

ii. Pass on worldly stories and pursue true training in godliness (v. 7-9)

aa. Turn away from worldly wisdom about godliness (v. 7a)

bb. Train yourself in the reverence of God (v. 7b)

- Physical training is of only limited value (v. 8a)
- Spiritual training in godliness is of eternal value (v. 8b)
- This is a trustworthy statement—training in godliness is infinitely more valuable (v. 9)

iii. Prescribe and teach the true gospel and true godliness (v. 10-11)

aa. The worship of God our Savior [godliness] and the hope of the life to come is our life's work (v. 10)

bb. The work of teaching the true gospel and true godliness is mandated (v. 11)

b. *Example godliness with your life and persevere in the ministry of the Word (v. 12-16)*

i. Model the faith with confidence (v. 12)

aa. Let no one look down on your youthfulness (v. 12a)

bb. Lead by the example of your faith (v. 12b)

ii. Make the public reading, preaching, and applying of the Scriptures a priority (v. 13)

iii. Make sure you are using your giftedness (v. 14-15)

aa. Do not neglect your spiritual giftedness (v. 14)

bb. Be diligent to cultivate and use your giftedness (v. 15)

iv. Make personal godliness and preaching/teaching your focus (v. 16)

aa. The command (v. 16a)

bb. The comfort (v. 16b)

B. Concerning godliness and relationships (5:1-6:2)

1. The pastor, and those he is to encourage/admonish (5:1-2)

a. *His duty—appeal/admonish/encourage (v. 1a)*

b. *His demeanor—a familial approach (v. 1-2)*

i. Encouraging an older man (v. 1a)

ii. Encouraging younger men (v. 1b)

iii. Encouraging older women (v. 2a)

iv. Encouraging younger women (v. 2b)

2. The policy of the church towards its widows (5:3-16)

a. *Properly value and verify widows in need (v. 3-8)*

i. The command (v. 3)

ii. The call to families to care for their widows (v. 4)

iii. The contrast between a godly widow and a worldly widow (v. 5-6)

aa. The faith-filled widow (v. 5)

bb. The frivolous widow (v. 6)

iv. The call to families reinforced (v. 7-8)

aa. The duty of a faithful shepherd (v. 7)

bb. The duty of a faithful family (v. 8)

b. *Properly enroll and permanently assist widows in need (v. 9-16)*

i. Widows who qualify for permanent church assistance (v. 9-10)

aa. Sixty years old (v. 9a)

bb. A one-man woman (v. 9b)

cc. Of good reputation (v. 10a)

dd. A respectable mother (v. 10b)

ee. Shown hospitality to strangers (v. 10c)

ff. Humble service to other believers (v. 10d)

gg. Generous and compassionate (v. 10e)

hh. Devoted to every good work (v. 10f)

ii. Widows who do not qualify for permanent church assistance (v. 11-13)

aa. Those who are younger (v. 11-12)

- For whom marriage is an option
- Who may set aside their convictions in order to be married

bb. Those who are prone to laziness and gossip (v. 13)

iii. Widows who are not yet truly in need of permanent church assistance (v. 14-16)

aa. Those that can get married and/or take care of their own needs (v. 14-15)

bb. Those who have relatives or relationships that can relieve the burden off of the church (v. 16)

3. The policy of the church towards its elders (5:17-25)

a. Remunerating elders (v. 17-18)

i. The standard—respect and remuneration for elders (v. 17)

aa. Double honor for elders who rule well

bb. Double honor especially for elders who are diligent in the work of preaching and teaching

ii. The Scriptural support (v. 18)

aa. Deuteronomy 25:4

bb. Luke 10:7

c. Rebuking elders (v. 19-21)

i. Reject unverifiable accusations against an elder (v. 19)

ii. Rebuke publicly those who continue in sin (v. 20)

iii. Remain steadfast and impartial in these principles (v. 21)

d. Recognizing elders (v. 22-25)

i. Do not appoint elders too quickly (v. 22)

ii. Do not adopt extra-biblical/unbiblical standards in evaluating elders (v. 23-25)

aa. The example of wine and Timothy's ailments (v. 23)

bb. The evidence of men's sins may be hidden at first, but they are eventually revealed (v. 24)

cc. The evidence of men's good deeds will also eventually be exposed (v. 25)

4. The practice of believing slaves in relation to their earthly masters (6:1-2)

   a. *Slaves are to honor their own masters so that the gospel is not slandered (v. 1)*

   b. *Slaves with believing masters are to respect and serve them all the more because they are believers (v. 2)*

C. Concerning godliness and a right view of riches (6:3-19)

1. The contrast between greed-driven false teachers and true godliness (6:3-10)

   a. *The character of greed-driven teachers (v. 3-5)*

      i. They are advocates of unhealthy doctrine (v. 3)

      ii. They are arrogant and attracted to controversy (v. 4-5a)

      iii. They are avaricious/greedy for gain (v. 5b)

   b. *The contentment of true godliness (v. 6-8)*

      i. Godliness with contentment is great gain (v. 6)

      ii. Godliness has eternal ramifications (v. 7-8)

         aa. Temporal possessions are merely temporal (v. 7)

         bb. Temporal needs are quite limited (v. 8)

   c. *The caution concerning the love of money (v. 9-10)*

      i. Desire for riches exposes one to a myriad of destructive temptations (v. 9)

      ii. Devotion to money is a root of all sorts of evil—even apostasy (v. 10)

2. The charge to the man of God in the face of such greed-driven opposition (6:11-19)

   a. *Flee from sin and pursue holiness (v. 11)*

   b. *Fight the good fight of faith (v. 12)*

   c. *Fulfill the ministry of the Word of God in light of the glory of God (v. 13-16)*

      i. Remember that God is the Giver of life (v. 13a)

      ii. Remember that Christ Jesus was faithful even to death (v. 13b)

      iii. Remain faithful to the Word of God until Christ returns (v. 14)

      iv. Remember the sovereign and majesty of the One you serve (v. 15-16)

         aa. He is absolutely sovereign over all things (v. 15)

         bb. He is uniquely and intrinsically worthy of our worship in every way (v. 16)

   d. *Faithfully teach the rich in this present world to fix their hope on God rather than their riches (v. 17-19)*

      i. Instruct the rich to avoid arrogance and not to put confidence in their riches (v. 17ab)

ii. Instruct the rich to put their confidence in God, to do good and to be generous (v. 17c-18)

iii. Instill in the rich a perspective that sees the use of their temporal wealth as a means by which they can store up treasure in heaven (v. 19)

3. The charge to guard the faith—that which is truly treasure (6:20-21a)

a. Actively guard the treasure of the Word of God (v. 20a)

b. Avoid all "knowledge" that opposes the Word of God (v. 20b-21)

i. Reject all "knowledge" that opposes God's Word (v. 20b)

ii. Remember the results of such "knowledge" (v. 21)

V. Prayer (6:21b)

A. The benediction

B. The beneficiaries

2 Timothy

Kress Biblical Resources

Overview Outline of 2 Timothy

Persevere in the Ministry and Do Not Be Ashamed to Suffer for the Gospel

I. Prologue/Introduction (1:1-2)

A. The writer (1:1)

B. The recipient[s] (1:2a)

C. The reasons (see detailed outline)

D. The requisite greeting (1:2b)

II. Persevere in the ministry and be unashamed to suffer for the gospel (1:3-2:13)

A. Be unashamed of the testimony of the Lord and His suffering servants (1:3-18)

1. Remember the roots and relationships that are connected to your faith in Christ (1:3-5)
2. Remember you must intentionally fan the flame of your giftedness in Christ (1:6-7)
3. Regard suffering for the gospel as an opportunity to demonstrate the power of God (1:8-12)
4. Reverence the gospel as treasure to be guarded and preserved (1:13-14)
5. Recognize that suffering for the gospel is scandalous to some and an opportunity to serve for others (1:15-18)

B. Be undeterred [be steadfast] in your service to the Lord and His suffering servants in hope (2:1-13)

1. Be faithful and patient in your ministry (2:1-7)
2. Be mindful of the ultimate motivation for faithful ministry (2:8-13)

III. Proclaim the truth and be unashamed to confront error (2:14-4:8)

A. Focus your life and ministry on the clarity of God's Word in the face theological speculation (2:14-26)

1. Confront error with the careful exposition of God's Word (2:14-18)
2. Cleanse yourself for honorable service to God (2:19-22)
3. Correct with gentleness those who are in opposition (2:23-26)

B. Focus your life and ministry on the sufficiency of God's Word in an age of apostacy (3:1-17)

1. Recognize the peril of apostacy in the latter days (3:1-9)
2. Remember and rely on the power and sufficiency of the Word of God (3:10-17)

C. Finish your life faithfully and fulfill your ministry by proclaiming God's Word whether people want to hear it or not (4:1-8)

1. Faithfully preach the Word (4:1-4)
2. Faithfully persevere in the work of the ministry (4:5-8)

IV. Partner with those who are faithful in the ministry and unashamed to suffer for the gospel (4:9-21)

A. Be ready to partner with those who are faithful to the gospel and those who suffer for the gospel (4:9-15)

B. Be realistic in your expectations of gospel partners (4:16-18)

C. Be relational in your communication and fellowship with others (4:19-21)

V. Prayer/Benediction (4:22)

Introductory Matters

I. The author (1:1)

A. The human author[1]

1. His name
2. His authority
3. His hope

B. The divine Author (2 Tim. 3:16; 2 Pet. 1:21; 3:15-16)

II. The audience[s] (1:2a)

A. The original recipient[s][2]

1. His name
2. His relationship with Paul
3. The wider audience (4:22b)

B. The current recipients (cf. 2 Pet. 3:15-16)

III. The aim

A. To encourage Timothy to persevere in the ministry, even in the face of suffering (1:8, 13-14; 2:1-3; 4:5)

B. To request Timothy's presence with the Apostle in Rome (1:4; 4:9, 12-13, 21)

C. To serve as the final recorded testimony of the Apostle Paul before his death (4:6-7, 16-18)

---

[1] For a biblical biography of the Apostle Paul see Acts 7:58; 8:1; 9:1-30; 11:25-30; 12:25-28:31; 1 Cor. 15:30-32; 2 Cor. 6:4-5; 11:23-30; Gal. 1:13-2:16; Phil. 3:4-14; 2 Thes. 3:8

[2] For a biblical biography of Timothy see Acts 16:1; 17:14-15; 18:5; 1 Cor. 4:17; 16:10; Phil. 2:19-23; 1 Thes. 3:2, 6; 1 Tim. 1:2; 5:23; Heb. 13:23

Detailed Outline of 2 Timothy

Persevere in the Ministry and Do Not Be Ashamed to Suffer for the Gospel

I. Prologue/Introduction (1:1-2)

A. The writer (1:1)

1. The human author[1]
   - a. *His name*
   - b. *His authority*
   - c. *His hope*
2. The divine Author (2 Tim. 3:16; 2 Pet. 1:21; 3:15-16)

B. The recipient[s] (1:2a)

1. The original recipient[s][2]
   - a. *His name*
   - b. *His relationship with Paul*
   - c. *The wider audience (4:22b)*
2. The current recipients (cf. 2 Pet. 3:15-16)

C. The requisite greeting (1:2b)

1. The prayer of blessing
2. The Person[s] behind the blessing

II. Persevere in the ministry and be unashamed to suffer for the gospel (1:3-2:13)

A. Be unashamed of the testimony of the Lord and His suffering servants (1:3-18)

1. Remember the roots and relationships that are connected to your faith in Christ (1:3-5)
   - a. *Remember those who know you and pray for you in the Lord (v. 3-4)*
     - i. Paul's thankfulness for Timothy (v. 3a)
     - ii. Paul's character before the Lord (v. 3b)
     - iii. Paul's prayers for Timothy (v. 3c)
     - iv. Paul's longing for fellowship with Timothy (v. 4)
   - b. Remember those who passed the faith on to you (v. 5)
     - i. The affirmation of his faith (v. 5a)

---

[1] For a biblical biography of the Apostle Paul see Acts 7:58; 8:1; 9:1-30; 11:25-30; 12:25-28:31; 1 Cor. 15:30-32; 2 Cor. 6:4-5; 11:23-30; Gal. 1:13-2:16; Phil. 3:4-14; 2 Thes. 3:8

[2] For a biblical biography of Timothy see Acts 16:1; 17:14-15; 18:5; 1 Cor. 4:17; 16:10; Phil. 2:19-23; 1 Thes. 3:2, 6; 1 Tim. 1:2; 5:23; Heb. 13:23

ii. The ancestry of his faith (v. 5b)

2. Remember you must intentionally fan the flame of your giftedness in Christ (1:6-7)
    a. *You have a stewardship from God (v. 6)*
        i. You are responsible to use your giftedness (v. 6a)
        ii. You are to remember the affirmation of those who recognized your giftedness (v. 6b)
    b. *You have a spirit of power, love and discipline from God (v. 7)*
        i. God's gifting does produce cowardice (v. 7a)
        ii. God's gifting produces power, love and discipline (v. 7b)
3. Regard suffering for the gospel as an opportunity to demonstrate the power of God (1:8-12)
    a. *Do not be embarrassed of the testimony of our Lord (v. 8a)*
    b. *Do not be embarrassed of those suffering for the Lord (v. 8b)*
    c. *Dare to suffer with those who suffer for the Lord (v. 8c)*
    d. *Demonstrate the power of God [the gospel] in your suffering (v. 8d-12)*
        i. The gospel empowers us in suffering (v. 8d)
        ii. The gospel encapsulates our salvation (v. 9-10)
            aa. God saved us and called us to be set apart (v. 9a)
            bb. God saved us by sovereign grace (v. 9b)
            cc. God saved us through the Person and work of Jesus Christ (v. 10)
        iii. The gospel entrusts us with ministry (v. 11)
        iv. The gospel engenders hope in the certainty of our salvation (v. 12)
4. Reverence the gospel as treasure to be guarded and preserved (1:13-14)
    a. *Hold on to the apostolic gospel in faith and love (v. 13)*
    b. *Honor the gospel deposit by guarding it through the power of the Holy Spirit (v. 14)*
5. Recognize that suffering for the gospel is scandalous to some and an opportunity to serve for others (1:15-18)
    a. *Suffering for the gospel will cause some to stumble (v. 15)*
    b. *Suffering for the gospel will compel some to serve (v. 16-18)*
        i. The request for blessing (v. 16a)
        ii. The reason (v. 16b)
        iii. The readiness/eagerness to serve a suffering brother (v. 17)
        iv. The request expanded (v. 18a)
        v. The reputation well-known (v. 18b)

ERRATA

2.b.i. should read "God's gifting does not produce cowardice (v. 7a)"

B. Be undeterred [be steadfast] in your service to the Lord and His suffering servants in hope (2:1-13)

1. Be faithful and patient in your ministry (2:1-7)

- *a. Be strong and train other faithful men in the gospel ministry (v. 1-2)*
  - i. The command—be strong in the grace of Christ (v. 1)
  - ii. The commission—entrust these things to other faithful men (v. 2)
- *b. Be steadfast and suffer hardship in hope of the reward (v. 3-7)*
  - i. The illustrations of endurance and reward (v. 3-6)
    - aa. The reward of a good soldier—commendation by his commanding officer (v. 3-4)
      - The command
      - The commendation
    - bb. The reward of an athlete who finishes the competition—the crown of glory (v. 5)
    - cc. The reward of the hardworking farmer—enjoying the fruit of his labors and finding rest (v. 6)
  - ii. The illumination of God while considering the illustrations (v. 7)
    - aa. Ponder the illustrations
    - bb. Praise God for His illumination of His Word

2. Be mindful of the ultimate motivation for faithful ministry (2:8-13)

- *a. Remember the foundational truths about Christ and the glorious gospel of salvation (v. 8-10)*
  - i. He is the resurrected God-man, King and Messiah (v. 8)
  - ii. Believers endure suffering for the sake of the salvation of the elect and eternal glory to come (v. 9-10)
    - aa. Paul suffered chains for the gospel (v. 9a)
    - bb. But the Word of God is not chained (v. 9b)
    - cc. Paul endured for the sake of eternal salvation of the elect (v. 10)
- *b. Remember the faithfulness of Christ and truth about faith, faithlessness, and unfaithfulness (v. 11-13)*
  - i. The faithful saying (v. 11a)
  - ii. The future of believers (v. 11b-12a)
  - iii. The future of apostates (v. 12b)
  - iv. The faithfulness of Christ [even when believers fail to be faithful] (v. 13)

III. Proclaim the truth and be unashamed to confront error (2:14-4:8)

A. Focus your life and ministry on the clarity of God's Word in the face theological speculation (2:14-26)

1. Confront error with the careful exposition of God's Word (2:14-18)
   a. *Warn people solemnly not to fight over words (v. 14)*
   b. *Work diligently to handle accurately the Word of God (v. 15)*
   c. *Walk away from worldly and empty words (v. 16-18)*
      i. The command (v. 16a)
      ii. The concern (v. 16b-17)
      iii. The case to consider (v. 17c-18)
2. Cleanse yourself for honorable service to God (2:19-22)
   a. *The imperative—personal holiness is the responsibility of those who belong to God (v. 19)*
   b. *The illustration—pitchers can contain prized possessions or waste products (v. 20)*
   c. *The instruction—pursuing holiness will be honored and used by God (v. 21)*
   d. *The imperative—pursue holiness, while fleeing immorality (v. 22)*
3. Correct with gentleness those who are in opposition (2:23-26)
   a. *Walk away from ignorant speculations (v. 23)*
   b. *Work diligently at being patient and kind, while correcting error (v. 24-26)*
      i. The character to pursue (v. 24-25a)
      ii. The correction to be administered (v. 25bc)
      iii. The conviction and/or conversion to the truth (v. 26)

B. Focus your life and ministry on the sufficiency of God's Word in an age of apostacy (3:1-17)

1. Recognize the peril of apostacy in the latter days (3:1-9)
   a. *The character traits of an apostate age (v. 1-5)*
      i. The certainty of difficult times ahead (v. 1)
      ii. The character of men in those times (v. 2-5a)
         aa. Self-consumed (v. 2a)
         bb. Covetous (v. 2b)
         cc. Self-promoting (v. 2c)
         dd. Verbally abusive (v. 2d)
         ee. Contemptuous of parents (v. 2e)
         ff. Ungrateful (v. 2f)
         gg. Irreverent (v. 2g)
         hh. Without natural affection (v. 3a)

ii. Unforgiving (v. 3b)
jj. Accusatory (v. 3c)
kk. Without self-restrained (v. 3d)
ll. Savage (v. 3e)
mm. Cynical/no interest in what is good (v. 3f)
nn. Traitorous (v. 4a)
oo. Daring (v. 4b)
pp. Conceited (v. 4c)
qq. Devoted to pleasure rather than God (v. 4d)
rr. Religious but disavowing God's power (v. 5a)

iii. The caution—avoid such men (v. 5b)

b. *The conduct of apostates (v. 6-9)*

i. They prey on weak-willed, desire-driven people (v. 6)
ii. They prey on learners who never seem to learn the truth (v. 7)
iii. They protest against the truth, which ultimately reveals their folly (v. 8-9)

aa. The opposition of Jannes and Jambres to Moses (v. 8)
bb. The obvious failure of apostates to oppose the truth of God's Word (v. 9)

2. Remember and rely on the power and sufficiency of the Word of God (3:10-17)

a. *Remember Paul's teaching and example in the midst of suffering (v. 10-13)*

i. Paul's ministry testified to both persecution and divine preservation (v. 10-11)

aa. Timothy had witnessed Paul's persecution (v. 10-11a)
bb. Timothy has witnessed Paul's perseverance and the Lord's preservation (v. 11b)

ii. Paul maintained that both persecution and the rise of deception would characterize this age (v. 12-13)

aa. The promise of persecution (v. 12)
bb. The promise of progressive deception (v. 13)

b. *Rely on the wisdom, power and sufficiency of the Scripture (v. 14-17)*

i. The command to continue in the truth (v. 14)
ii. The content of the Scriptures—the wisdom that leads to salvation which is through faith in Christ (v. 15)
iii. The character of the Scriptures (v. 16)

aa. God-breathed
bb. Profitable

- For teaching
- For reproof
- For correction

- For training in righteousness

iv. The complete sufficiency of the Scriptures (v. 17)

C. Finish your life faithfully and fulfill your ministry by proclaiming God's Word whether people want to hear it or not (4:1-8)

1. Faithfully preach the Word (4:1-4)

a. The solemn accountability of preaching the Word (v. 1)

b. The singular responsibility of preaching the Word (v. 2a)

c. The steadfast consistency of preaching the Word (v. 2b)

d. The specific applicability of preaching the Word (v. 2c)

i. Challenge

ii. Censure

iii. Comfort

iv. With great constancy/patience

v. With content driven instruction

e. The sad prophecy about the future of preaching the Word (v. 3-4)

i. The professing church will not endure sound doctrine (v. 3a)

ii. The professing church will enlist those who preach according to their own desires (v. 3b)

iii. The professing church will be eager for stories instead of scriptural truth (v. 4)

2. Faithfully persevere in the work of the ministry (4:5-8)

a. Fulfill the ministry God has given you (v. 5)

i. Focus in all things (v. 5a)

ii. Face hardship with fortitude (v. 5b)

iii. Faithfully proclaim the gospel (v. 5c)

iv. Fulfill your ministry (v. 5d)

b. Follow Paul's example—fight the good fight and keep the faith (v. 6-8)

i. Count all of life and even death as worship (v. 6)

ii. Carry out your ministry with a view to the prize (v. 7-8)

aa. Embrace the struggle (v. 7a)

bb. Endure to the end of the race (v. 7b)

cc. Ensure that the faith has been properly guarded (v. 7c)

dd. Eagerly anticipate the prize (v. 8)

- Crown of righteousness
- Communion with the Lord
- Communion with all who have loved His appearing

IV. Partner with those who are faithful in the ministry and unashamed to suffer for the gospel (4:9-21)

A. Be ready to partner with those who are faithful to the gospel and those who suffer for the gospel (4:9-15)

1. The call for ministry partnership (4:9-13)
   a. *The urgent request (v. 9)*
   b. *The unmistakable need (v. 10-11a)*
      i. Demas' deserted Paul and left for Thessalonica (v. 10a)
      ii. Crescens was away in Galatia (v. 10b)
      iii. Titus was away in Dalmatia (v. 10c)
      iv. Luke alone was with Paul (v. 11a)
   c. *The unlikely partner—Mark (v. 11)*
   d. *The unwavering messenger—Tychicus (v. 12)*
   e. *The unique needs of the situation (v. 13)*
2. The caution concerning ministry opposition (4:14-15)
   a. *Opposition is real and personal (v. 14a)*
   b. *Opposition will be repaid by the Lord (v. 14b)*
   c. *Opposition should be guarded against for the sake of the gospel (v. 15)*

B. Be realistic in your expectations of gospel partners (4:16-18)

1. Realize that men often fail (4:16)
   a. *Friends may fail you (v. 16a)*
   b. *Forgive and pray for those who do (v. 16b)*
2. Recognize that the Lord never fails (4:17)
   a. *Recognize the Lord's presence in your trial (v. 17a)*
   b. *Recognize the Lord's power in your trial (v. 17b)*
   c. *Recognize the Lord's preservation in your trial (v. 17c)*
3. Rely upon the Lord to fulfill His promises (4:18ab)
   a. *He has promised spiritual rescue (v. 18a)*
   b. *He has promised heavenly rule (v. 18b)*
4. Reverence the Lord by proclaiming His eternal glory (v. 18c)

C. Be relational in your communication and fellowship with others (4:19-21)

1. The call to greet ministry partners (4:19)
   a. *Greet Prisca and Aquila (v. 19a)*
   b. *Greet the household of Onesiphorus (v. 19b)*
2. The concern to update ministry partners (4:20)
   a. *The update on Erastus (v. 20a)*
   b. *The update on Trophimus (v. 20b)*

3. The communication of fellowship and affection (v. 21)
    a. *The expression of need (v. 21a)*
    b. *The expressions of affection and fellowship (v. 21b)*
        i. Eubulus
        ii. Pudens
        iii. Linus
        iv. Claudia
        v. All the brethren

V. Prayer/Benediction (4:22)

A. A personal prayer for Timothy (4:22a)

B. A public prayer for the church (4:22b)

Titus

Kress Biblical Resources

Overview Outline of Titus

The Gospel of Grace Calls Us to Adorn the Doctrine of God as Savior

I. Introduction [An introduction to the doctrine of God as Savior] (1:1-4)

A. The writer

B. The recipients (1:4a, 2:5, 12-13, 15; 3:15c)

C. The reasons (see detailed outline)

D. The requisite greeting (1:4b)

II. Church leadership that adorns the doctrine of God as Savior (1:5-16)

A. The charge to Titus recalled (1:5)

B. The character and conduct of an elder revealed (1:6-9)

C. The character and conduct of false teachers rebuked (1:10-16)

III. Christian living that adorns the doctrine of God as Savior (2:1-3:11)

A. The character and conduct of various groups within the church (2:1-15)

1. Sound doctrine and the grace of God practically applied to believers (2:1-10)
2. Sound doctrine and the grace of God powerfully explained to believers [as the motive and power for godly living] (2:11-15)

B. The character and conduct of all toward those outside the church (3:1-11)

1. Salvation practically applied—submission to authority and love toward all men (3:1-2)
2. Salvation powerfully explained—salvation by God's grace as the basis and motive for that submission and love (3:3-7)
3. Salvation and its practical ramifications summarized (3:8-11)

IV. Conclusion [An itinerary and prayer that adorns the doctrine of God as Savior by emphasizing good works based on grace] (3:12-15)

A. The itinerary of good works specifically applied to Titus' context (3:12-14)

B. The issuing of greetings (3:15a)

C. The invocation of grace (3:15b)

Alternate Overview Outline[1]

I. God's people need leadership to live for God's purpose. (1:1-16)
II. God's people need order to live as God's people. (2:1-15)
III. God's people need counsel to live in God's world. (3:1-15)

[1] Kitchen, John A., *The Pastoral Epistles for Pastors*, p. 611, Kress Biblical Resources.

Introductory Matters

I. The author

A. The human author (1:1-3)[1]

1. His name (v. 1a)
2. His calling (v. 1b-3)
    - *a. A slave of God (v. 1b)*
    - *b. A sent one [Apostle] of Jesus Christ (v. 1c)*
    - *c. A saving message to proclaim (v. 1d-3)*
        - i. For the faith of God's elect/chosen (v. 1d)
        - ii. For the knowledge of the truth, which is connected to godliness (v. 1e)
        - iii. Based on the hope/expectation/anticipation of eternal life (v. 2a)
        - iv. Promised by the God who cannot lie (v. 2b)
        - v. Promised before time began (v. 2c)
        - vi. Proclaimed by Paul at the proper time in history, who was entrusted with it by God our Savior (v. 3)

B. The divine Author (2 Tim. 3:16-17; 2 Pet. 1:12-21, 3:15-16; cf. Col. 4:16; 1 Thes. 2:13; 5:27; 2 Thes. 3:1-4; 1 Tim. 5:18 in which Paul quotes Luke alongside Deut. 25:4 and calls them "Scripture")

II. The audience (1:4a, 2:5, 12-13, 15; 3:15c)

A. The original recipients[2]

1. Titus (1:4a)
    - *a. The filial relationship he had with Paul spiritually*
    - *b. The faith that he held in common with Paul*
2. The church in Crete (2:5, 12-13, 15; 3:15c)
    - *c. The culture they lived in (1:10-13)*
    - *d. The kinds of people that made up the church (2:2-9; 3:1-3)*

B. The current recipients (cf. 2 Pet. 3:15-16)

III. The aim

A. To give Titus further instruction on how to "set in order" leadership and relationships within the churches in Crete (1:5ff)

B. To ask Titus to meet Paul in Nicopolis once Artemas or Tychicus arrives in Crete (3:12)

---

[1] For a biblical biography of the Apostle Paul see Acts 7:58; 8:1; 9:1-30; 11:25-30; 12:25-28:31; 1 Cor. 15:30-32; 2 Cor. 6:4-5; 11:23-30; Gal. 1:13-2:16; Phil. 3:4-14; 2 Thes. 3:8

[2] For a biblical biography of Titus see 2 Cor. 2:13; 7:6, 13-14; 8:6, 16. 23; 12:18; Gal. 2:1-3

C. To ask Titus to diligently help Zenas the lawyer and Apollos with provisions for their ministry travels (3:13)

D. To strengthen and encourage Titus, especially in the ministry of countering false teaching (1:4, 10-11; 2:1, 15; 3:9-11, 15)

E. To emphasize that the gospel of God's grace should result in godly living, so that God's glory as Savior is clearly manifest (1:10, 16; 2:5c, 8, 10, 11-14; 3:1-7, 8, 14)

F. Summary theme: Adorning the doctrine of God as Savior (cf. 2:10b-14)

Detailed Outline of Titus

The Gospel of Grace Calls Us to Adorn the Doctrine of God as Savior

I. Introduction [An introduction to the doctrine of God as Savior] (1:1-4)

A. The writer

1. The human author (1:1-3)[1]
   - *a. His name (v. 1a)*
   - *b. His calling (v. 1b-3)*
     - i. A slave of God (v. 1b)
     - ii. A sent one [Apostle] of Jesus Christ (v. 1c)
     - iii. A saving message to proclaim (v. 1d-3)
       - aa. For the faith of God's elect/chosen (v. 1d)
       - bb. For the knowledge of the truth, which is connected to godliness (v. 1e)
       - cc. Based on the hope/expectation/anticipation of eternal life (v. 2a)
       - dd. Promised by the God who cannot lie (v. 2b)
       - ee. Promised before time began (v. 2c)
       - ff. Proclaimed by Paul at the proper time in history, who was entrusted with it by God our Savior (v. 3)
2. The divine Author (2 Tim. 3:16-17; 2 Pet. 1:12-21, 3:15-16; cf. Col. 4:16; 1 Thes. 2:13; 5:27; 2 Thes. 3:1-4; 1 Tim. 5:18 in which Paul quotes Luke alongside Deut. 25:4 and calls them "Scripture")

B. The recipients (1:4a, 2:5, 12-13, 15; 3:15c)

1. The original recipients[2]
   - *a. Titus (1:4a)*
     - i. The filial relationship he had with Paul spiritually
     - ii. The faith that he held in common with Paul
   - *b. The church in Crete (2:5, 12-13, 15; 3:15c)*
     - i. The culture they lived in (1:10-13)
     - ii. The kinds of people that made up the church (2:2-9; 3:1-3)
2. The current recipients (cf. 2 Pet. 3:15-16)

---

[1] For a biblical biography of the Apostle Paul see Acts 7:58; 8:1; 9:1-30; 11:25-30; 12:25-28:31; 1 Cor. 15:30-32; 2 Cor. 6:4-5; 11:23-30; Gal. 1:13-2:16; Phil. 3:4-14; 2 Thes. 3:8

[2] For a biblical biography of Titus see 2 Cor. 2:13; 7:6, 13-14; 8:6, 16. 23; 12:18; Gal. 2:1-3

D. The requisite greeting (v. 4b)

1. The greeting/prayer of grace and peace
2. The Giver of grace and peace

II. Church leadership that adorns the doctrine of God as Savior (1:5-16)

A. The charge to Titus recalled (1:5)

1. He was to serve as an Apostolic representative in Crete
2. He was to set in order what remained concerning the Church
3. He was to select/appoint elders in every city as Paul had directed him

B. The character and conduct of an elder revealed (1:6-9)

1. He must be above reproach concerning his family (1:6)
    a. *An overarching qualification—above reproach*
    b. *A one-woman-man*
    c. *An obvious influence on the faith/faithfulness of his children*
2. He must be above reproach as God's steward/manager (1:7-8)
    a. *The critical qualification repeated—above reproach (v. 7a)*
    b. *The character and conduct he avoids (v. 7b)*
        i. Not self-willed
        ii. Not quick-tempered
        iii. Not addicted to wine
        iv. Not pugnacious
        v. Not fond of sordid gain
    c. *The character and conduct he pursues (v. 8)*
        i. Hospitable
        ii. Loving what is good
        iii. Sensible
        iv. Just
        v. Devout
        vi. Self-controlled
3. He must be actively devoted to God's Word—able to both teach it, and refute those who contradict (1:9)
    a. *The active devotion*
    b. *The ability to exhort in sound doctrine*
    c. *The ability to refute those who contradict*

C. The character and conduct of false teachers rebuked (1:10-16)

1. The description and danger of false teachers (1:10-11)

- *a. The description of false teachers (v. 10)*
  - i. They are many
  - ii. They are independent/insubordinate
  - iii. They are idle talkers
  - iv. They are misleaders/deceivers
  - v. They are many times associated with some form of Jewish legalism
- *b. The danger of false teachers (v. 11)*
  - i. They must be silenced
  - ii. They mislead/overthrow whole families by teaching things they shouldn't
  - iii. They are motivated by the pleasure of shameful gain

2. The description of Cretan society and the demand for severe reproof (1:12-14)

- *a. The description of Cretan society in general that specifically characterized the false teachers (v. 12-13a)*
  - i. A cultural-assessment by one of their own prophets
  - ii. Ever liars
  - iii. Evil beasts
  - iv. Lazy gluttons [literally, "slow bellies"]
  - v. An Apostolic-assessment by Paul
- *b. The demand for severe reproof (v. 13b-14)*
  - i. The powerful reproof demanded
    - aa. The sinful cultural climate
    - bb. The severe rebuke commanded
  - ii. The purpose of the reproof demanded
    - aa. That they may be healthy in the faith
    - bb. That they may not heed error

3. The defilement and denunciation of false teachers (1:15-16)

- *a. They are defiled in character (v. 15)*
  - i. To the pure all things are pure
  - ii. To the perverted [defiled and unbelieving] nothing is pure, but both their mind and conscience are defiled
- *b. They are deniers of God in conduct (v. 16)*
  - i. Their profession
  - ii. Their practice

III. Christian living that adorns the doctrine of God as Savior (2:1-3:11)

A. The character and conduct of various groups within the church (2:1-15)

1. Sound doctrine and the grace of God practically applied to believers (2:1-10)
    a. *The first command to Titus (v. 1)*
        i. The contrast with false teachers
        ii. The command to speak the things that are fitting for sound doctrine
    b. *The fitting character and conduct of older men (v. 2)*
        i. Temperate
        ii. Dignified
        iii. Sensible
        iv. Sound in faith, in love, in perseverance
    c. *The fitting character and conduct of older women (v. 3-4a)*
        i. Reverent in their behavior
        ii. Not malicious gossips
        iii. Nor enslaved to much wine
        iv. Teachers of good
        v. Train the young women in sensibility
    d. *The fitting character and conduct of young women (v. 4b-5)*
        i. Love their husbands
        ii. Love their children
        iii. Sensible
        iv. Pure
        v. Workers at home
        vi. Good/kind
        vii. Subject to their own husbands
    e. *The fitting motivation (v. 5b)*
    f. *The fitting character and conduct of young men and Titus (v. 6-8)*
        i. Sensible in all things (v. 6-7a)
        ii. Titus' example (v. 7b-8)
            aa. An example of good deeds
            bb. Purity in doctrine
            cc. Dignified in teaching
            dd. Sound in speech which is beyond reproach
        iii. The motivation (v. 8b)

g. The fitting character and conduct of bondslaves (v. 9-10)

i. Subject to their own masters in everything

ii. Well-pleasing

iii. Not argumentative

iv. Not pilfering

v. Showing all good faith

vi. The motivation

2. Sound doctrine and the grace of God powerfully explained to believers [as the motive and power for godly living] (2:11-15)

a. God's grace issues in a wonderful salvation (v. 11)

i. The showing/shining of the grace of God to all men [in the life, death and resurrection of Christ]

ii. The saving grace of God

b. God's grace instructs in a practical sanctification (v. 12)

i. What we are instructed to forsake

aa. Forsaking ungodliness

bb. Forsaking worldly desires

ii. What we are instructed to follow after

aa. Living sensibly

bb. Living righteously

cc. Living godly

c. God's grace induces a hopeful anticipation (v. 13)

i. The perspective of our hope

ii. The Person of our hope

d. God's grace includes a purposeful redemption (v. 14)

i. Redeemed by—Christ's Person and work ["who gave Himself for us"]

ii. Redeemed from—every lawless deed

iii. Redeemed for

aa. A personal relationship with the Holy One

bb. A passion for good deeds

e. God's grace (practically applied and theologically defined) necessitates an authoritative proclamation [The second command to Titus to "speak" in chapter two] (v. 15)

B. The character and conduct of all toward those outside the church (3:1-11)

1. Salvation practically applied—submission to authority and love toward all men [Remember how you now are to think and live as a believer] (3:1-2)
    a. *A life characterized by submission to God's Word*
    b. *A life characterized by submission and obedience to societal authorities*
    c. *A life characterized by readiness for good deeds*
    d. *A life characterized by edifying speech towards others*
    e. *A life characterized by non-contentiousness*
    f. *A life characterized by gentleness/kindness*
    g. *A life characterized by humility toward all men*
2. Salvation powerfully explained—salvation by God's grace as the basis and motive for that submission and love [Remember how you used to think and live as an unbeliever, and how you were saved by grace through no merit of your own] (3:3-7)
    a. *Remember the grim reality of who we were apart from Christ (v. 3)*
        i. Foolish
        ii. Disobedient
        iii. Deceived
        iv. Enslaved to various lusts and pleasures
        v. Spending our life in malice and envy
        vi. Hateful, hating one another
    b. *Remember the glorious reality of what God has done for us through Christ (v. 4-7)*
        i. He saved us out of kindness and love, through Christ (v. 4-5a)
        ii. He saved us not on the basis of good works, but because of His mercy (v. 5b)
        iii. He saved us by causing us to be born again by the Holy Spirit, through the Person and work of Christ (v. 5c-6)
            aa. The washing of rebirth and the renewing of the Holy Spirit (v. 5b)
            bb. The wondrous Person and work of Jesus Christ our Savior (v. 6)
        iv. He saved us by grace so that we would inherit eternal life (v. 7)
            aa. Our position—being made righteous by grace
            bb. Our possession—heirs of eternal life according to hope

3. Salvation and its practical ramifications summarized [Remember how God reckons what is profitable and what is worthless] (3:8-11)
    a. *The surety of both the explanation and application of salvation (v. 8a)*
    b. *The solemn responsibility of believers to practically live out their gracious salvation in good deeds (v. 8b)*
    c. *The shunning of unprofitable discussions (v. 9)*
    d. *The sending away of a factious man (v. 10-11)*
        i. The discipline process—after a first and second warning
        ii. The description of a factious man—perverted, sinning, self-condemned

IV. Conclusion [An itinerary and prayer that adorns the doctrine of God as Savior by emphasizing good works based on grace (3:12-15)

A. The itinerary of good works specifically applied to Titus' context (3:12-14)

1. A personal ministry to Paul (3:12)
    a. *After Artemas or Tychicus arrive*
    b. *At Nicopolis*
2. A proper provision for Zenas and Apollos (3:13)
    a. *The persons involved*
    b. *The proper provision*
3. A pursuit of congregational fruitfulness in meeting pressing needs (3:14)

B. The issuing of greetings (3:15a)

1. To Titus
2. To the believers in Crete

C. The invocation of grace (3:15b)

Philemon

Kress Biblical Resources

Overview Outline of Philemon

Forgiveness and Reconciliation Flow from a Transformed Life of Love, Faith and Obedience

I. Personal introduction: An epistle seeking true forgiveness and restoration between individuals (1:1-3)

A. The writer (1:1a)

B. The recipients (1:1b- 2)

C. The reasons (see detailed outline)

D. The requisite greeting (1:3)

II. Praise, prayer and encouragement for one who could be counted on to forgive and restore another (1:4-7)

A. Paul thanked God for Philemon's transformed character (1:4-5)

B. Paul prayed for Philemon's further growth in Christ (1: 6)

C. Paul testified that Philemon's active love for the saints had been a joy and comfort to him (1:7)

III. Principles gleaned from Paul's appeal to forgive and restore (1:8-21)

A. Forgiveness and restoration should be seen as an issue of obedience, yet freely given (1:8-14)

B. Forgiveness and restoration should be seen in the light of the sovereignty of God (1:15-16)

C. Forgiveness and restoration should take into account the benefit to the work of the ministry and the glory of Christ (1:17, 20)

D. Forgiveness and restoration should be seen in the light of the greater debt God has forgiven (1:18-19)

E. Forgiveness and restoration should go beyond the minimum requirement, and overflow in abundance (1:17, 20-21)

IV. Preparations and personal greetings (1:22-25)

A. Preparation and prayer requested (1:22)

B. Personal greetings (1:23-24)

C. Prayer for all involved (1:25)

Introductory Matters

I. The author (1:1a)

A. The human author

1. Paul[1]
2. In association with Timothy[2]

B. The Divine author (1 Tim. 3:16; 2 Pet. 3:15-16)

II. The audience (1:1b- 2)

A. The original recipients

1. Philemon
   a. *Beloved*
   b. *Fellow worker*
2. Apphia (possibly Philemon's wife)
3. Archippus (possibly Philemon's pastor or son; cf. Col. 4:17)
4. The church in Philemon's house

B. The current recipients (cf. 2 Pet. 3:15-16)

III. The aim

A. To encourage Philemon and foster fellowship between believers (1:1-3, 4-7, 23-25)

B. To seek Philemon's restoration and forgiveness of Onesimus (v. 8-21; Col. 4:9)

C. To seek preparation and prayer for a desired visit from Paul (1:22)

---

[1] For a biblical biography of the Apostle Paul see Acts 7:58; 8:1; 9:1-30; 11:25-30; 12:25-28:31; 1 Cor. 15:30-32; 2 Cor. 6:4-5; 11:23-30; Gal. 1:13-2:16; Phil. 3:4-14; 2 Thes. 3:8

[2] For a biblical biography of Timothy see Acts 16:1; 17:14-15; 18:5; 1 Cor. 4:17; 16:10; Phil. 2:19-23; 1 Thes. 3:2, 6; 1 Tim. 1:2; 5:23; Heb. 13:23

Detailed Outline of Philemon

Forgiveness and Reconciliation Flow from a Transformed Life of Love, Faith and Obedience

I. Personal introduction: An epistle seeking true forgiveness and restoration between individuals (1:1-3) [Do you seek to be a peacemaker?]

A. The writer (1:1a)

1. The human author
   - *a. Paul*[1]
   - *b. In association with Timothy*[2]
2. The Divine author (1 Tim. 3:16; 2 Pet. 3:15-16)

B. The recipients (1:1b- 2)

1. The original recipients
   - *a. Philemon*
     - i. Beloved
     - ii. Fellow worker
   - *b. Apphia (possibly Philemon's wife)*
   - *c. Archippus (possibly Philemon's pastor or son; cf. Col. 4:17)*
   - *d. The church in Philemon's house*
2. The current recipients (cf. 2 Pet. 3:15-16)

C. The requisite greeting (1:3)

1. The salutation of grace and peace
2. The Source of grace and peace

II. Praise, prayer and encouragement for one who could be counted on to forgive and restore another (1:4-7) [Do you exhibit a transformed character, that can be counted on to forgive and restore others?]

A. Paul thanked God for Philemon's transformed character (1:4-5) [Do others thank God for your transformed character?]

1. The record of Paul's thankfulness for Philemon (v. 4)
   - *a. It was Godward*
   - *b. It was consistent*
   - *c. It was in the midst of his intercession*

---

[1] For a biblical biography of the Apostle Paul see Acts 7:58; 8:1; 9:1-30; 11:25-30; 12:25-28:31; 1 Cor. 15:30-32; 2 Cor. 6:4-5; 11:23-30; Gal. 1:13-2:16; Phil. 3:4-14; 2 Thes. 3:8

[2] For a biblical biography of Timothy see Acts 16:1; 17:14-15; 18:5; 1 Cor. 4:17; 16:10; Phil. 2:19-23; 1 Thes. 3:2, 6; 1 Tim. 1:2; 5:23; Heb. 13:23

2. The reasons for Paul's thankfulness for Philemon (v. 5)
    a. *The reports of Philemon's love*
    b. *The reports of Philemon's faith*

B. Paul prayed for Philemon's further growth in Christ (1:6) [Do others pray for your even further growth in Christ?]

1. The powerful partnership of faith
2. The power that comes through true knowledge of Christ's character lived out in you

C. Paul testified that Philemon's active love for the saints had been a joy and comfort to him (1:7) [Do others see and hear of your active love for other believers?]

1. The record of Paul's joy and comfort in Philemon's love
2. The reason for Paul's joy and comfort in Philemon's love

III. Principles gleaned from Paul's appeal to forgive and restore (1:8-21) [Is your life marked by obedience to God's mandate to forgive and restore others, because you're motivated by love, faith and a passion for the work of the ministry?]

A. Forgiveness and restoration should be seen as an issue of obedience, yet freely given (1:8-14)

1. It is a matter of duty and propriety (v. 8)
    a. *Duty*
    b. *Propriety*
2. It is a matter of love (v. 9-13)
    a. *For the sake of love (v. 9a)*
    b. *For the sake of a beloved brother (9b-13)*
        i. Paul's situation (v. 9b)
        ii. Paul's spiritual son (v. 10)
        iii. Paul's helper (v. 11)
        iv. Paul's heart (v. 12)
        vi. Paul's wish (v. 13)
3. It is a matter of reconciliation (v. 11-12)
    a. *The rift recalled (v. 11)*
    b. *The reconciliation desired (v. 12)*
4. It is a matter of choice (v. 13-14)
    a. *Paul chose to send Onesimus back though he didn't feel like parting with him (v. 13)*
    b. *Philemon's goodness in the matter was not to be by compulsion, but of his own free will (v. 14)*

B. Forgiveness and restoration should be seen in the light of the sovereignty of God (1:15-16)

1. The temporary separation was within the scope of God's sovereignty (v. 15a)
2. The timeless blessings were wrought by God's sovereign love (v. 15b-16)

C. Forgiveness and restoration should take into account the benefit to the work of the ministry and the glory of Christ (1:17, 20)

1. It strengthens the partnership that believers have in the ministry (v. 17)
2. It stimulates and refreshes others who are partners in the ministry (v. 20)

D. Forgiveness and restoration should be seen in the light of the greater debt God has forgiven (1:18-19)

1. The pledge of payment—an implicit reminder of Christ's substitutionary sacrifice (v. 18)
2. The personal relationship—an explicit reminder of the proper perspective on debt and forgiveness (v. 19)

E. Forgiveness and restoration should go beyond the minimum requirement, and overflow in abundance (1:17, 20-21)

1. It should be as if he were accepting the Apostle Himself (v. 17)
2. It should bring refreshment to others, not suspicions as to the whether you've fully forgiven or not (v. 20b)
3. It should overflow well beyond minimum obedience (v. 21)

IV. Preparations and personal greetings [Paul's closing remarks clearly reveal how important unhindered fellowship is to the body of Christ] **(1:22-25)**

A. Preparation and prayer requested (1:22)

B. Personal greetings (1:23-24)

1. Epaphras—The pastor, prayer warrior and prisoner (v. 23)
2. Mark—The famous failure, who himself had been forgiven and restored (v. 24a)
3. Aristarchus—The selfless missionary from Macedonia (v. 24b)
4. Demas—The future deserter (v. 24c)
5. Luke—The brilliant writer, the beloved physician and servant of Paul (v. 24d)

6. Summary concerning all of them (v. 24e)

C. Prayer for all involved (1:25)

1. The supplication for grace
2. The Sovereign Source of all grace
3. The spiritual fellowship of grace